Religious Freedom
Under Scrutiny

PENNSYLVANIA STUDIES IN HUMAN RIGHTS

Bert B. Lockwood, Series Editor

A complete list of books in the series
is available from the publisher.

RELIGIOUS FREEDOM UNDER SCRUTINY

Heiner Bielefeldt

and

Michael Wiener

PENN

UNIVERSITY OF PENNSYLVANIA PRESS

PHILADELPHIA

Published by
University of Pennsylvania Press
Philadelphia, Pennsylvania 19104-4112
www.upenn.edu/pennpress

Printed in the United States of America on acid-free paper
1 3 5 7 9 10 8 6 4 2

A Cataloging-in-Publication record is available from the Library of Congress
ISBN 978-0-8122-5180-7

In memory of Asma Jahangir (1952–2018)

CONTENTS

Religious Freedom
Under Scrutiny

INTRODUCTION

1. A Right Both Classical and Provocative

Freedom of religion or belief radiates the aura of a well-established human right, deeply entrenched in international human rights conventions and constitutional traditions across the continents.[1] At the United Nations (UN) level, the most important guarantees are Article 18 of the 1948 Universal Declaration of Human Rights (UDHR) and Article 18 of the International Covenant on Civil and Political Rights (ICCPR), which the UN General Assembly adopted in 1966. Based on Article 9 of the European Convention on Human Rights (ECHR), an instrument of the Council of Europe adopted in 1950, a rich regional jurisprudence on freedom of religion or belief has developed. Similar regional guarantees exist in the framework of the Organization of American States as well as within the African Union. Freedom of religion or belief has furthermore found recognition in numerous national constitutions. Some governments show a particularly strong commitment to the international promotion of this right. Parliamentarians from across the globe have established networks to support each other in the defense of freedom of religion or belief in their home countries;[2] and civil society organizations, both faith-based and secular, have established cooperation for a worldwide implementation of this human right.[3] Moreover, while historians have debated the precise contribution of freedom of religion or belief (shorthand: "religious freedom") for the genesis of human rights in early modernity,[4] no one seriously doubts that its role was highly significant. Commentators appreciate its historical and contemporary function as a door opener for other human rights, in particular freedom of expression, freedom of peaceful assembly, and freedom of association. In short, freedom of religion or belief enjoys the reputation of a "classical" human right.

The adjective "classical" suggests that something has an elevated status beyond dispute and contestation. Appreciating freedom of religion or belief as a "classical" human right may thus convey the impression that there is no need for making serious intellectual investments in its support. However, this conclusion would be premature. As Manfred Nowak has observed, freedom of religion or belief is "a particularly controversial right."[5] Many governments show ambivalence when it comes to realizing the practical consequences of their formal recognition of religious freedom. Whereas some states reserve the enjoyment of this right to the followers of "real" religions (whatever that may mean), others narrowly limit religious practices, which are supposed to remain within the confines of a state-defined "normalcy." In both cases, the state claims broad discretion in either permitting or prohibiting religious manifestations. Nationalist identity politics confines freedom of religion or belief to those religious communities that fit into the dominant national narrative, often at the expense of "foreign sects" or new religious movements. Governments that stage themselves as custodians of religious truth dilute the liberating thrust of freedom of religion or belief by mixing human rights language with a vague rhetoric of limited religious tolerance. Some progressive politicians in turn may invoke secularism, a concept that can carry very different meanings, in order to push religious manifestations back into a merely private sphere. Furthermore, some states have attempted in United Nations fora to twist freedom of religion or belief into an anti-liberal barrier against human rights advancements in the areas of intellectual freedom or gender emancipation.[6]

Freedom of religion or belief furthermore continues to spark political, legal, theological, and philosophical controversies, even heated ones. For critics from different political, ideological, and religious camps, this human right has disturbing features. The reasons for mixed feelings and ambivalent attitudes differ widely. While religious traditionalists may fear that guarantees of individual freedom could dissolve religious bonds and loyalties, secular-minded liberals in turn may wonder whether freedom of religion or belief would not function as a "Trojan horse" by readmitting religious obscurantism to public political culture. Some accuse the right to religious freedom of trivializing religion by turning it into a commodity and a matter of individual tastes and preferences. By contrast, others see the danger that freedom of religion or belief could undermine dearly won achievements of modern enlightenment. In short, it may well be true that freedom of religion or belief is a classical human right. Yet it is equally true that it harbors enormous provocative potential.

2. Ambiguous Reactions

Freedom of religion or belief is not the only example of a classical human right with obvious provocative potential. We could say the same about freedom of expression or freedom of peaceful assembly, which likewise enjoy the reputation of old established rights and nonetheless continue to provoke and disturb. It is a general feature of human rights to challenge existing hegemonies by demanding equal rights of freedom for everyone. No wonder if human rights, in spite of their broad formal endorsement, trigger ambivalent reactions. However, in the case of freedom of religion or belief an additional source of provocation comes to the fore: religion. Within the human rights framework, freedom of religion or belief opens the space for the articulation of religious convictions, religious values, religious interests, religious identities, and religious needs. In other words, freedom of religion or belief functions as the entry-point for religion as a human rights issue.[7]

Religion both fascinates and polarizes. On the one hand, religious traditions contain an inexhaustible wealth of prophecies, promises, admonishments, narrations, parables, and metaphors. They shape personal identities and collective moralities, create profound bonds of loyalty, and have a lasting impact upon the cultural and historical makeup of countries and wider regions. On the other hand, religions can spark conflicts and divide societies. In past and present, they have justified discrimination, oppression, and violence.[8] Ambivalent reactions to religion may also cast a shadow on the human right to freedom of religion or belief. In spite of its reputation as part of the established canon of "liberal" rights,[9] freedom of religion or belief paradoxically does not receive unanimous applause among all liberals. Even within the human rights movement, practical commitment and skeptical reluctance frequently overlap.

Much of the existing reluctance seems to rest on the assumption that religions historically often stood in the way of modern emancipation. Whether and to which degree this assumption is fully justified requires further analysis. At any rate, the perception exists. In fact, even today religiously motivated opposition is one of the main obstacles to the realization of certain human rights claims, especially in the area of gender equality and sexual orientation, to mention the most obvious examples. Is this a mere coincidence, or do we have to assume a general antagonism between human rights and religions?[10] If so, would this not undermine the legitimacy of freedom of religion or belief within the framework of human rights? Is freedom of religion or belief a human right that factually hinders the advancement of secular human rights agendas? This is not the only disquieting question in this context. Take the issue of universalism. Human rights epitomize a universalistic normative aspiration based on the acknowledgement of the equal dignity and equal rights of all human beings.[11] Can freedom of religion or belief be universalistic in this understanding? Does the title of this right not indicate a policy of privileging believers over nonbelievers? Moreover, human rights empower people by guaranteeing their freedom in various spheres of society, from family life to employment to the political arena. This empowerment function is essential to the understanding of human rights; it defines their raison d'être.[12] Rather than empowering individuals, however, religions have subjected people to divine authorities, thus ultimately disempowering them—or this may be the perception of many critics. Against this background, would a human right to religious freedom not come close to a contradiction in terms? Would it not be more plausible to associate "human rights" with "humanism" and the values of humanist enlightenment, for which people had to fight over generations, often against massive resistance from religious authorities? Maybe some of these questions rest on problematic historical and political assumptions. We therefore should be cautious and not jump to conclusions. What is prima facie clear, at any rate, is that freedom of religion or belief raises complicated questions, some of which even affect its very legitimacy as part of the canon of human rights.

What we can currently witness is that freedom of religion or belief has come under attack from different sides. The main obstacles to its full recognition and consistent implementation stem from political, cultural, and religious authoritarianism.[13] In this regard, freedom of religion or belief is exactly on the same page as freedom of expression, freedom of peaceful assembly, and other human rights. It is important to bear this in mind. While some authoritarian governments stage themselves as custodians of religious truth claims, others defend religious hegemonies as part of a nationalistic narrative. Yet others fear that religious communities could become meeting points for dissidents; the governments' usual response is tight control, intimidation, and infiltration. In addition to the ongoing problem of political and religious authoritarianism, however, freedom of religion or belief at times faces reluctance also from within the midst of liberal societies and liberal milieus. This is a very special experience in human rights work. Freedom of religion or belief is probably the only "liberal right" (if we may use this terminology here) that currently evokes mixed feelings among many (albeit certainly not all) liberals. Even within the human rights movement, people wonder what exactly the purpose of freedom of religion or belief should be. Is freedom of religion or belief an entitlement, which for whatever reasons made it into the historical canon of human rights, without fully matching the normative profile of universal rights to freedom and equality? This question is not merely of academic interest, because existing insecurity about the nature and content of freedom of religion or belief may hamper people's commitment in this area. With a grain of salt, Mary Ann Glendon observes that "the greatest challenge facing defenders of religious freedom today may well be the task of convincing people in a secular age that religious freedom is an important human right worth defending at home and abroad."[14]

3. Moses Mendelssohn and the Dialectic of Enlightenment

The complicated discursive configuration just sketched out is not entirely new. More than two centuries ago, Moses Mendelssohn (1729–1785), the father of the Jewish Enlightenment, faced resistance from different camps when striving for the liberation of the Jewish minority in Prussia and elsewhere. On the one hand, he had to tackle anti-Jewish prejudices, which throughout the centuries had prevented the Jews from getting access to many important societal positions. When fighting against hostility, discriminatory practices, and derogatory stereotypes, Mendelssohn saw himself in the same camp with many other philosophers of the Enlightenment, in particular his lifelong friend Gotthold Ephraim Lessing.[15] On the other hand, Mendelssohn's writings betray a concern that the Enlightenment itself could become the breeding ground for new forms of cultural hegemony. Many intellectuals of his day promoted the establishment of *one* "natural religion" or "reasonable religion," which they hoped would in the long run replace the confusing variety of historical religions. This is what causes Mendelssohn's concerns, because it would be the end of genuine diversity. "I am afraid," he writes in a letter addressed to Immanuel Kant, "that philosophy, too, has its fanatics who as aggressively persecute and even more purposefully proselytize than the fanatics of positive religion."[16]

Time and again, Mendelssohn uncovers problematic tendencies of homogenization within the Enlightenment, for example, a propensity among rationalistic intellectuals "to extinguish all other lights in order to let full enlightenment undividedly stream from the light of reason."[17] In his book *Jerusalem* (published in 1783) he critically addresses policies of cultural assimilation, against which he calls for an appreciation of the existing religious diversity: "Brothers, if you care for true piety, let us not feign agreement where diversity is evidently the plan and purpose of Providence. None of us thinks and feels exactly like his fellow man; why then do we wish to deceive each other with delusive words? . . . Why should we make ourselves unrecognizable to each other in the most important concerns of our life by masquerading, since God has stamped everyone, not without reason, with his own facial features?"[18]

Mendelssohn is one of the first philosophers to discover what later would be termed the "dialectic of enlightenment."[19] It is the danger that the liberating thrust of the Enlightenment could collapse into a force of assimilation, to the detriment of religious freedom and diversity. As a member of a religiously discriminated minority, Mendelssohn knows that this danger is not merely hypothetical. The Jews of his day suffer ongoing contempt not only from the side of traditional Christianity; some Enlightenment philosophers, too, equate Judaism to narrowmindedness, empty legalism, and anxious ritualism.[20] The charge of impenitence, an old anti-Jewish prejudice, finds an echo in David Hume's spiteful remarks on the "implacable narrow spirit of the Jews."[21] Benedict de Spinoza blames the Jewish victims for their societal victimization when conjecturing that by cherishing their own religious rituals "they brought the resentment of all men upon themselves."[22] Even Kant is not free from anti-Jewish sentiments. In his "Religion Within the Boundaries of Mere Reason," Judaism represents the very opposite of the intellectually refined religiosity which Kant himself promotes; it stands for obscurantism and empty rituals. Kant's criticism culminates in the verdict that "Judaism as such, taken in its purity, entails absolutely no religious faith."[23]

From the experience of a vulnerable and disdained minority, Mendelssohn formulates his strong plea for religious freedom. In particular, he calls for complete freedom from any coercion in matters of personal conviction: "Hence, neither church nor state has a right to subject men's principles and convictions to any coercion whatsoever. Neither church nor state is authorized to connect privileges and rights, claims on persons and title to things, with principles and convictions, and to weaken through outside interference the influence of the power of truth upon the cognitive faculty. Not even the social contract could grant such a right to either state or church. For a contract concerning things which, by their very nature, are *inalienable*, is intrinsically invalid, and cancels itself."[24] Apart from ongoing political repression—for example, denials of residence permits, marriage restrictions, humiliating special taxes, and so forth—Mendelssohn also addresses possible new risks originating from some currents of Enlightenment philosophy. In particular, he warns against the aspiration that the *one* reasonable "natural religion," which enlightened philosophers wish to promote, should provide the future bond of unity in society. "At bottom, a union of faiths, should it ever come about, could have but the most unfortunate consequences for reason and liberty of conscience. . . . What would thereby be accomplished? Shall we say that all of you would think just alike concerning religious truths? Whoever has but the slightest conception of the nature of the human mind cannot allow himself to be persuaded of this."[25]

More than two centuries after Moses Mendelssohn's death, there are still good reasons for unpacking hidden or forgotten aspects of the "dialectic of enlightenment," as manifested inter alia in ambiguous attitudes toward religious diversity in modern liberal society. While in theory diversity finds almost unanimous endorsement, attitudes can change quickly once religious positions and practices exceed what is considered "normal" in liberal circles. People with pronounced religious convictions often feel exposed to suspicion, since their way of life allegedly stands in conflict with certain liberal values or liberal lifestyles. Proposals to purge the public sphere of any visible signs and symbols of religiosity can count on certain popularity in larger parts of modern societies. This raises far-reaching questions about the self-understanding of liberalism. How accommodating is political liberalism? What is the relationship between the "enlightened" values of political liberalism and traditional religious values and convictions? What is the role of the state in this field? Does the state have a mandate to "liberate" religious communities internally, for instance, by enforcing standards of nondiscrimination within religious institutions, or should the state remain entirely neutral with regard to the existing religious diversity? The last question brings us to the issue of political secularism, which is another contentious theme. Can religious manifestations in the public sphere undermine the secular nature of the state, thus endangering an important achievement of the Enlightenment? Or can religious motives positively contribute to the understanding of an open, inclusive secularity of the state? Other questions concern the specific normative authority that human rights claim in managing diversity. Assuming that human rights provide the binding normative framework for fair coexistence under the conditions of diversity, do human rights seek to replace the normative authority traditionally ascribed to religion? Do they form a global "civil religion," which supersedes the normative ethos of religious traditions, in parts or even in toto? If so, have human rights meanwhile become the object of new forms of "idolatry," as Michael Ignatieff critically puts it?[26]

4. The Indispensability of Religious Freedom

In spite of its reputation as a "classical" human right, freedom of religion or belief continues to evoke political controversies and ambivalent reactions, ranging from enthusiastic support to a certain unease or even open opposition. Obviously, the struggle for religious freedom is far from over. There is not only the challenge of its effective implementation, but its content, significance, meaning, and justification also deserve critical scrutiny. The purpose of the present book is to contribute to more conceptual clarity in this ongoing struggle. We can summarize our position in two closely interrelated hypotheses. Our first hypothesis is that *freedom of religion or belief is a human right, which displays exactly the same normative structure that defines the human rights approach in general.* The first sentence of Article 1 of the Universal Declaration of Human Rights puts it in a nutshell when proclaiming: "All human beings are born free and equal in dignity and rights." Like any other human right, freedom of religion or belief, too, relates to "all human beings," which means it epitomizes the aspirations of normative universalism. It furthermore aims to empower human beings in keeping with the normative principles of freedom and equality. By highlighting that freedom of religion or belief is fully in line with the inherent logic of the human rights approach we embark on a countercriticism to those objections which explicitly or implicitly deny the human rights nature of religious freedom. With our second hypothesis, we go a step further by claiming that *freedom of religion or belief has an indispensable role to play within the framework of human rights.* We argue that by ignoring or marginalizing freedom of religion or belief we would not just end up with a specific gap; such marginalization would ultimately weaken the plausibility, attractiveness, and legitimacy of the entire system of human rights. Without taking freedom of religion or belief seriously, human rights would not be able to do justice to the complex needs, yearnings, and vulnerabilities of human beings. Indeed, without freedom of religion or belief, human rights would cease to be fully humane.

The defining characteristics of human rights—universalism, freedom, and equality—guide Chapters 1 to 3. To be able to make sense of freedom of religion or belief as a *universal right*, we have first to clarify in Chapter 1 that right holders are human beings, not religions or beliefs in themselves. Much of the criticism leveled against freedom of religion or belief misses the point by ignoring this important feature. Like other human rights, religious freedom empowers human beings. Consequently, it is only through the lens of human beings that religious issues come into the focus of human rights. Chapter 2 explores various philosophical, political, and legal aspects of human freedom. Pointing out that freedom of religion or belief is a human right to *freedom* may at first glance sound like a truism. Against the background of positions that wrongly ascribe anti-liberal features to freedom of religion or belief, however, the principle of freedom warrants systematic attention and clarification. In this context, we inter alia emphasize that freedom of religion or belief naturally also includes the freedom *from* religion. The subsequent Chapter 3 is dedicated to the principle of *equality*. We highlight that there is no general antagonism between equality and diversity, because in the context of human rights, equality itself can only make sense as a "diversity-friendly" principle. Measures designed to accommodate the special needs of certain religious minorities, for example, exemptions from generally applicable rules, require justification in the light of egalitarian principles.

After clarifying the nature of freedom of religion or belief as a human right, we tackle its relationship vis-à-vis other human rights as well as the relationship between religious freedom and the state. In Chapter 4, we explore *possible tensions between freedom of religion or belief and other human rights*. As two prominent test cases, we have selected freedom of expression, on the one hand, and gender-related liberation, on the other. Without ignoring complicated conflicts in these areas, we argue for a holistic understanding such that the various human rights norms can mutually complement and reinforce each other. Chapter 5 deals with different *concepts of secularism* and their impact on shaping the relationship between state and religions. From the specific standpoint of freedom of religion or belief, we conceptualize a nondoctrinal and inclusive understanding of state secularism. The guiding idea is that the secular state should provide an open space for the unfolding of religious (and nonreligious) diversity without discrimination.

While the main purpose of this book is to provide clarity and normative orientation in the face of conceptual controversies over freedom of religion or belief, two of its chapters are rather descriptive in nature. In Chapter 6, we provide a *typological overview of violations* of freedom of religion or belief, as they occur in different regions and under most different political, ideological, or religious auspices. Although that chapter is more empirical than the rest of the book, we have decided to insert it in the face of a tendency, often experienced in discussions on religious freedom, to mainly extrapolate from atrocities committed in the Middle East. However, human rights violations do not only relate to one region or one religion. It is our intention to sensitize readers to the multiplicity and complexity of violations of religious freedom, many of which remain under the radar of public attention. Chapter 7 briefly juxtaposes *relevant juridical decisions* taken at the international and regional levels on freedom of religion or belief. The focus is on the UN Human Rights Committee, which is the expert body in charge of monitoring the implementation of the International Covenant on Civil and Political Rights, and comparing its jurisprudence on religious symbols in public life, religious education, and conscientious objection to military service with the case law of the European Court of Human Rights. While the Strasbourg Court's jurisprudence has evoked many political and academic comments, the case law of the Geneva expert bodies has attracted less attention. This has motivated us to give a succinct overview of the UN Human Rights Committee's approach to handling individual cases of religious freedom, which in some important aspects goes further than the European Court of Human Rights.

The two final chapters resume the conceptual discussion—albeit from new angles. The thorny issue of *violence perpetrated in the name of religion* is the subject of Chapter 8. Our main interest in this context is to explore the role that freedom of religion or belief (as well as religious leaders and other faith-based actors) could play to help overcome the scourge of violent acts with religious underpinnings. One important contribution is the emphasis on human agency and thus human responsibility, by which freedom of religion or belief challenges various essentialist misrepresentations of the relationship between religion and violence. In the concluding Chapter 9, we come back to the question, raised already in the above introductory remarks, of how to understand the *dynamic interplay between human rights and religious traditions*. Our point is that by keeping the human rights framework open for the articulation of religious convictions, interests, yearnings, needs, and vulnerabilities, freedom of religion or belief serves as a reminder that human rights themselves do not constitute a religious or quasi-religious authority. It is not least by taking this critical role, that freedom of religion or belief serves as an indispensable component of human rights.

5. Background of the Two Authors

Toward the end of this introduction, we would like to add a few words about ourselves. We understand ourselves as human rights practitioners with a special, albeit not an exclusive, interest in freedom of religion or belief. One of us (Michael Wiener) has been working within the Office of the United Nations High Commissioner for Human Rights since 2006.[27] In this function, he supported the mandate of the UN Special Rapporteur on freedom of religion or belief for more than five years, after having written his doctoral thesis on legal issues of that very mandate.[28] The other author (Heiner Bielefeldt) served as UN Special Rapporteur from 2010 to 2016 and he has been a member of the Panel of Experts of the Organization for Security and Co-operation in Europe (OSCE) Office for Democratic Institutions and Human Rights (ODIHR) on Freedom of Religion or Belief since 2016. The experiences we gained—partially together—in the support of freedom of religion or belief have shaped our outlook on this right, which we always locate within the holistic understanding of human rights. Our activities were not limited to writing reports and participating in discussions within the relevant international and regional fora; we also undertook fact-finding missions in different parts of the world, many of which were eye-opening experiences of great intensity. Incidentally, we should not hide the fact that we both happen to come from Germany, which explains occasional references to German concepts and cases. While we have been working across different academic areas, our main disciplines are philosophy (Heiner Bielefeldt) and law (Michael Wiener).

In our work within the United Nations context, we met with human rights defenders from different parts of the world, from diverse religious or nonreligious backgrounds, and from different societal and educational milieus. Not all of them had an academic training. While this book is obviously an academic project, we are convinced that human rights work does not presuppose an academic education. Human rights flourish owing to their inherent persuasiveness—or they are doomed to collapse. Their fundamental principles—human dignity, freedom, and equality—have a compelling persuasiveness and are easy to understand. This is also true for freedom of religion or belief, which for many people, albeit not for everyone, enjoys an intuitive plausibility. Like many other important issues in human life, however, complications arise once we aspire to a more precise understanding and to a consistent articulation of contents, conditions, and limitations.

We have decided to dedicate this book to the memory of Asma Jahangir (1952–2018) and to donate our royalties to the Asma Jahangir Foundation[29] for its work on legal aid in Pakistan. One of the coauthors worked with Asma Jahangir for four years during her mandate and the other coauthor was her immediate successor as Special Rapporteur on freedom of religion or belief. Throughout her life, Asma Jahangir struggled for religious freedom, both at the international and national levels. She consistently advocated for a holistic understanding of human rights, always taking into account the rights of members belonging to minorities, women's rights, and freedom of expression. With her vision and principled approach, she clarified concepts of religious freedom and managed to defuse related controversies, for example in the context of religious symbols and the debate on "defamation of religions." She stressed the importance of perseverance by stating: "There is always hope in the fight for human rights. There are always possibilities to gain terrain in the protection of victims. There is always ground to turn a negative situation into a positive one."[30]

CHAPTER 1

Universalism Tainted with Particularisms

1. A Controversial Claim

In the twenty-first century, human rights can no longer base their authority on "self-evident truths" or transhistorically imagined "natural rights." Historicity, contextuality, and critical hermeneutics have become keywords in the unfinished business of "deconstructing" previously unquestioned validity claims in morality and law, including in the field of human rights. One idea has been in the center of much criticism: the claim to universal validity, across political, cultural, religious, and other boundaries. This is a very high aspiration, indeed. In the eyes of critics, the claim to universality may actually aim too high to be sustainable even in theory, let alone in practice. However, it is exactly this aspiration that defines the human rights approach in general, as summed up in the 1948 Universal Declaration of Human Rights (UDHR), which in its first article famously proclaims that "All human beings are born free and equal in dignity and rights." Likewise, the preamble of the UDHR professes "recognition of the inherent dignity and of the equal and inalienable rights of all members of the human family." Most of the following articles start with the word "everyone" thus corroborating the claim of universal applicability. In the case of prohibitions (of torture, slavery, etc.) the language of "everyone" shifts to a no less universalistic "no one."

A year before the adoption of the UDHR, the American Anthropological Association published a statement in which the authors expressed concerns that the proclamation of a universal normative standard would impoverish cultural diversity.[1] In a study for UNESCO, anthropologist Claude Lévi-Strauss pointed to the particular cultural and historical contexts that shaped the idea of human rights.[2] Assuming that these rights first emerged in the West, he doubted the usefulness of promoting standards deemed to be applicable to all of humanity, across cultural and historical divides. Those early documents of human rights criticism have meanwhile assumed an iconic status. Among the many critics are Adamantia Pollis and Peter Schwab who entitled one of their articles "Human Rights: A Western Construct with Limited Applicability."[3] Criticism of human rights comes from different political corners, from the right as well as the left, but it can also remain more or less apolitical. Conservative skeptics have objected that by glossing over irredeemable cultural divides, the promotion of universal rights might inadvertently increase the risks of a "clash of civilizations."[4] Left-wing scholars engaged in postcolonial studies have pointed to suspicious continuities between contemporary human rights promotion and earlier forms of a European *mission civilisatrice*.[5] Others base their skepticism on the irrefutable observation that universalistic standards did not emerge in a cultural vacuum. Human rights always presuppose articulation in particular languages and reference to particular historical experiences. They took shape through contingent and contextual trajectories—what else would one expect. The motives underneath the various "deconstructions" of universalism can likewise be manifold. Some critics aggressively discredit the idea of universal rights as a mere cover for political and cultural hegemonies, somehow in line with Carl Schmitt's vitriolic remark that "Whoever invokes humanity just wants to cheat."[6] Others plead for more caution and modesty when designing workable cross-cultural human rights agendas.

Unsurprisingly, the critique of universalism also targets freedom of religion or belief, a right enshrined inter alia in Article 18 of the UDHR. It is no coincidence that the article starts with the word "everyone," which encapsulates the universalistic aspiration underpinning the human rights approach in general. This is the formulation: "Everyone has the right to freedom of thought, conscience and religion; this right includes freedom to change his religion or belief, and freedom, either alone or in community with others and in public or private, to manifest his religion or belief in teaching, practice, worship and observance." During the drafting process, no part of the UDHR evoked more political controversies than Article 18. Above all, the term "change" triggered lasting conflicts among delegates. The representative of Saudi Arabia went so far as to conjure up memories of the crusades and the era of European colonialism when asking notably the United Kingdom, Belgium, and the Netherlands "whether they were not afraid of offending the religious beliefs of their Moslem subjects"[7] by imposing Article 18 on them. To the present day, the right to change one's religion—as well as its counterpart, that is, the right to invite others to change their faith—is in the center of fierce political and legal contestation. Some Islamic states criminalize any attempt to shake a Muslim in his or her faith. Hindu nationalists in India reject the right to conversion, in which they see an attack on the integrity of the Hindu nation. Conservative representatives of the Russian Orthodox Church have questioned the legitimacy of Protestant missionaries accessing Russian soil, which in their view amounts to an illegitimate invasion of "foreign sects."

Conflicts over the right to change one's religion are only one example illustrating the enormous provocative potential inherent in freedom of religion or belief. Indeed, this right can cause far-reaching anxieties by challenging old established customs, cutting through people's religious lifeworlds and shaking traditional cultural and religious collective narratives. Are such challenges legitimate? Doubts come not only from the "usual suspects," namely, religious traditionalists or conservative proponents of national identity politics who wish to preserve existing religious and cultural hegemonies. Critics can be found also within the political left or in liberal circles. Academics from different disciplines have questioned whether freedom of religion or belief might represent a morally problematic hegemonic aspiration. Does this right not necessarily presuppose a differentiation between "good religion" and "bad religion," that is, between religions that are compatible with modern human rights versus those that are not? If so, does the universalistic language of human rights not provide the pretext for concealed forms of religious predominance at a global scale? Could the ultimate purpose be the worldwide promotion of a "Protestant" paradigm of religion, which focuses on the internal faith of the individual while downplaying collective ceremonial and ritual practices? Does freedom of religion or belief amount to a new version of cultural and political imperialism based on a combination of the "Western" concept of human rights and a "Western-Protestant" understanding of religion?

Criticism of freedom of religion or belief has gained more traction in recent years. One example is *Politics of Religious Freedom*, edited by Winnifred Fallers Sullivan, Elizabeth Shakman Hurd, Saba Mahmood, and Peter G. Danchin.[8] The authors come from religious studies, political science, anthropology, and law. What unites most of them is a somewhat skeptical attitude toward freedom of religion or belief. One author conjectures that under the cloak of religious neutrality a "religious freedom crusade" takes place.[9] Others voice careful criticism based on a detailed analysis of relevant court cases or the findings of religious anthropologists. One motif occurring repeatedly is the suspicion that freedom of religion or belief fosters a global unification of the religious landscape, that is, the propagation of a Western-style "Protestant" paradigm of religion, according to which individual believing counts more than community-based ceremonial and ethical practice.[10] Some authors fear that the politics of religious freedom might pave the way for the global hegemony of a neoliberal market of religions largely crafted after the US model. Does the universalistic validity claimed for religious freedom serve the purposes of religious entrepreneurs who, hand in hand with capitalist charity foundations, want to shape the world according to their interests and ideology? Could this lead to new power imbalances, roughly analogous to capitalist hegemony under the auspices of economic neoliberalism? Could freedom of religion or belief produce its own victims? Michael Lambek is one of those who express such fears: "Freedom here too readily comes to mean freedom for the powerful to exercise their power against the vulnerable (as in the free market)."[11]

In the face of such critical questions, we nevertheless propose to make sense of freedom of religion or belief as a universal human right. This is the topic of the present chapter. By universal rights, we understand those *fundamental rights that belong to human beings simply because of their humanness* and thus to all human beings equally. In this sense, universal rights are more than international rights. As stressed by René Cassin in October 1948, the UDHR is an "expression of the rights of all the peoples of the world and not only of the fifty-eight nations then constituting the United Nations."[12] In a more recent formulation proposed by James Griffin, a human right is "a right that we have simply in virtue of being human."[13] The opposite would be entitlements that remain reserved to those holding particular status positions, having particular qualifications or fulfilling particular membership criteria. In the framework of universal rights, the only membership that counts is membership in "the human family," to quote again from the preamble of the 1948 UDHR. The idea of human rights is inextricably linked to normative universalism.[14]

However, after having been exposed to criticism from different angles, universalistic validity claims can no longer be taken for granted. As critics have argued, human rights are not above history and contextuality. Even worse, they may reinforce biases and existing hegemonies. In any case, our attempt to make sense of human rights in general and the right to freedom of religion or belief in particular has to take into consideration the various questions, criticisms, and "deconstructions" to which basic conceptual assumptions underlying human rights have been, and continue to be, subjected. That is why we first sketch out a postdeconstructivist concept, which sees human rights as part of an ongoing learning process based on a willingness to undertake self-criticism, adaptations, and reforms, while at the same time appreciating human dignity as the indispensable core insight (Section 2). We subsequently apply this critical and historically fluid understanding of human rights to freedom of religion or belief. The most important conceptual point, which we have to make in the face of serious misunderstandings, is that freedom of religion or belief, in keeping with the broader human rights approach, protects human beings, not religions or beliefs in themselves (Section 3). In Sections 4 and 5, we take issue with two specific objections, namely, that freedom of religion or belief follows a "Protestant" paradigm in the conceptualization of religion and that it opens the religious landscape worldwide to the influence of a neoliberal market model of religious and spiritual commodities. Section 6 summarizes some of the challenges that need to be unpacked in order to improve the plausibility of freedom of religion or belief as a universal human right.

2. Universalism as Work in Progress

Let us be clear: attempts to uncover "suspicious" motives lurking underneath universal norms and standards will frequently be successful. Universalism pure and simple may exist in mathematics;[15] it certainly does not exist in politics and law. Human rights politics does not take place in a power vacuum. This is nowhere more obvious than in the UN Human Rights Council, where governments invoke old and forge new coalitions, support each other within groups of "likeminded" states and negotiate precarious compromises, which in most cases do not fully satisfy anyone. Whoever looks out for elements of realpolitik cloaked in human rights rhetoric, can be sure to get results. This is also evident with regard to freedom of religion or belief. Whenever this theme is up for discussion in UN fora, some governments will focus on the persecution of Christians in the Middle East, while others may dwell on incidents of Islamophobia in

Europe. Charges of "double standards" are ubiquitous, go in all directions, and often seem justified to a certain degree.

Power-related particular interests are not only part of human rights politics; even worse, particularism permeates the very concept of human rights. In hindsight, we clearly see that the imagined rights holder—"the human being as such"—typically displayed quite specific features. In the eighteenth century, the supposedly universal subject of human rights was usually imagined as having a particular sex (male), a particular skin color (white), and a particular social status (property owner).[16] The wording employed in various declarations of "the rights of man" (*droits de l'homme*) betrays an unconcealed androcentric bias, which most people apparently took for granted. Unquestioned assumptions concerning ethnicity, class, and education likewise made it into the classic human rights documents. Until a few decades ago, experiences of persons with disabilities largely remained outside human rights debates, and the imagined subject of human rights would certainly not be lesbian, gay, bisexual, transgender, or intersex. The antidiscrimination clauses of the 1948 UDHR and the 1966 international covenants remain silent on issues like disability, age, sexual orientation, or gender identity. It is only in retrospect that we see the exclusions stemming from such biases and ignorance.

In addition, many accounts of the intellectual history or prehistory of human rights look hopelessly Eurocentric.[17] Even today, numerous textbooks unquestioningly presuppose that human rights exclusively originated from particular Western sources, such as the Stoic natural law idea, the English Magna Carta and various European Enlightenment philosophies.[18] Largely ignoring profound political conflicts, normative contradictions, and paradoxical learning curves, the still dominant narrative of the genesis of human rights continues to presuppose a mainly European intellectual ownership; it sometimes even assumes a flavor of "white man's burden." Within that hegemonic genealogy, the Protestant Reformation traditionally figured as a decisive turning point toward modern freedom. Hegel praised Martin Luther and other Protestant reformers for paving the way to modern liberalism and rights-based constitutionalism, since they waved the "flag of the *free spirit.*"[19] Drawing on that idea, Georg Jellinek, an influential German lawyer and historian, annoyed his French colleagues when claiming, in a study first published in 1895, that the origins of human rights lie in Wittenberg rather than in Paris.[20] Unsurprisingly, French intellectuals reacted quickly and harshly. What both sides of the bitter "Jellinek controversy" simply took for granted, however, was that human rights have their roots somewhere in the West.

What follows from these critical observations? One possible consequence is to give up the universalistic aspirations of human rights and discard the idea of human rights for all as an irredeemably naïve and hopelessly hypocritical project. In the face of historical path dependencies and inescapably contextual trajectories, one might conclude that human rights can be nothing but "a Western construct with limited applicability," to cite again the abovementioned article by Pollis and Schwab. The assumed lack of normative plausibility and legitimacy may also lead us to question the claims inherent in freedom of religion or belief. Winnifred Fallers Sullivan doubts that freedom of religion can ever be a universal right, as illustrated in the title of her monograph *The Impossibility of Religious Freedom*. In Sullivan's view, freedom of religion necessarily presupposes a prior decision about which type of religion should be recognized and protected: "The right kind of religion, the approved religion, is always that which is protected, while the wrong kind, whether popular or unpopular, is always restricted or even prohibited."[21] According to Sullivan, religious freedom in fairness to all is not only difficult to achieve; it actually comes close to an outright contradiction in terms, since a particularistic bias seems to define the very essence of freedom of religion. What are the practical consequences? Do we have to move "beyond religious freedom," as Elizabeth Shakman Hurd suggests in the title of her book?[22] If so, what would that mean, and which alternatives would be available and viable?

If normative universalism were nothing but a hypocritical illusion, which we should better discard in toto, the disparities of particularistic positions, worldviews, and interests would be the ultimate and insuperable political reality. Consequently, there would be no possibility to appeal to any other norms than the positive standards that happen to exist within the various particular political entities. This exactly was Carl Schmitt's point. His attacks on universalistic normative ideas paved the way for an understanding of politics as a battlefield where political and ideological opponents confront each other in an undisguised and unmitigated conflict instead of resorting to what he thought was "the big lie of humanity."[23] As he phrased it, the international arena is a "*pluriversum* rather than a *universum*."[24] At the end of the day, Schmitt contended, we can do no more than admit our lack of mutual understanding and resign ourselves to our inescapable particularistic ideological orientations or identities. This he thought was the ultimate wisdom of honest politics. In a similarly skeptical vein, Max Weber invoked an irrational battle between conflicting value systems—in his words, between "the Gods underneath the various orders and values"[25]—which he thought was as unavoidable as it was nondecidable from any superior point of view. Those who today call for radically deconstructing the claims of normative universalism may have to face similarly harsh consequences—unless they come up with viable alternatives.

To be sure, human beings inevitably remain influenced by their various particularistic viewpoints, usually without being fully aware of that fact and its implications. No one can claim an untainted, "objective" overview of the various cultural, religious, and other contextual factors that shape their outlook on things. After all, human beings are not fully transparent to themselves; they can never simply position themselves "above" history, contextuality, and other contingencies.[26] To admit that at the end of the day everyone will somehow remain stuck in particularistic biases, which they will never be able to overcome completely, sounds just realistic; it furthermore has the advantage of epistemological and normative modesty. However, what follows for the practice of organizing political coexistence? Should we satisfy ourselves with just remaining imprisoned in our hopelessly particularistic worldviews, contexts, and interests? Can we do no more than admit the ultimate futility of any attempts to open horizons, overcome biases, discover blind spots, and improve the chances for a normative consensus by communicating with one another? Can we actually afford to eschew any serious normative interaction across the political trenches that currently demarcate our conflicting value systems?

In the twenty-first century, Carl Schmitt's *pluriversum* of diverse religions, beliefs, and ideologies has become a reality in the midst of countries, neighborhoods, companies, institutions, and even families. Close coexistence of many people within, across, and beyond boundaries is as irreversible as is deep diversity, with all the concomitant problems and opportunities.[27] Given this reality, how "realistic" is a position that gives up any attempt to work for a normative consensus across cultural, religious, and other boundaries? Admitting to each other our various biases and inescapable particularities may be an honest and indeed modest starting point for a discussion. Yet to conclude the discussion by declaring that the parties involved can do no more than merely "agree to disagree" usually indicates a diplomatic disaster.

A starting point out of the predicament is the insight that the diversity of worldviews, differences of interests, and discrepancies of orientations should at least be *communicatively articulated*, with the intention to avoid serious misunderstanding and potentially fatal consequences that may arise following a lack of exchange. While overcoming all diversities, differences, and discrepancies may ultimately prove impossible, perhaps not even desirable, what we can and should at least ensure is that such differences do not just remain "mute." They should be articulated and communicated. Given the complexities of modern life, especially in the midst of our religiously and ideologically diverse societies, we have strong practical reasons to persist in communicative efforts that aim to reach at least partial understandings and to work for a gradually developing consensus—perhaps a limited and provisional consensus—across political, cultural, religious, and other divides. Surely, such efforts can always fail; there is no guarantee of success. Yet the experience of deep diversities spreading between as well as within our increasingly multicultural and multireligious societies can itself become a powerful and indeed "realistic" incentive for taking that bumpy route and embarking on ever-new interactive endeavors. Human rights have a crucial part to play in this endeavor. As Jürgen Habermas points out, "Since it is no longer realistic to follow Carl Schmitt in entirely rejecting the program of human rights, whose subversive force has in the meantime permeated the pores of *all regions* across the world, today 'realism' assumes a different form."[28]

What precisely can human rights offer in this regard? To begin with, they can improve the conditions for communication across boundaries by providing the "lingua franca of global normative thought," as Michael Ignatieff has put it.[29] Having a common normative language through which to negotiate remaining differences in positions, interests, values, and assessments can certainly be helpful. However, human rights exceed their function as an established medium for communication on normative questions, since they themselves also embody a basic normative insight. Beyond facilitating communicative exchanges across boundaries, human rights aim to secure the unconditioned preconditions of any meaningful normative interaction whatsoever by institutionalizing respect for all human beings in their potential of responsible agency. This brings us to the very nucleus of the human rights project.

Respect for all people's potential of responsible agency is not just one normative principle alongside other principles or one specific value within a broader set of values or even placed on top of a pyramid of values. It is something qualitatively different from that. Such respect lies at the ground of whatever normative principles and values one may imagine, because it refers to the conditio sine qua non of any meaningful normative interaction, be it in the area of morals or in the area of law. Binding personal promises, legal contracts, normative standards, or normative institutions from the local to the global level rest on the assumption, at least implicitly, that human beings have the potential of responsible agency, for which they—indeed all of them—deserve a basic respect. The insight into the significance of responsible agency can thus become the entry-point for conceptualizing a modern, secular concept of human dignity. By insisting that what counts is the mere *potential* of responsible agency, we want to avoid the danger of meritocratic readings, which could even lead to an antiegalitarian conceptualization of dignity. Indeed, human dignity goes deeper than the appreciation of any actions, merits, or performances of this or that individual. It precedes all concrete normative activities, efforts, merits, or accomplishments, to which it relates as their implicit precondition. Given its fundamental status as the precondition of meaningful normative interaction of any kind, the ascription of responsible agency—and thus human dignity—must be inclusive and egalitarian or it fails to make any sense. In Chapter 9 (Section 4), we will elaborate this issue further and add some qualifications and clarifications.

The foundational significance of human dignity comes out clearly in the first words of the preamble of the UDHR. It begins by stressing that the "recognition of the inherent dignity and of the equal and inalienable rights of all members of the human family is the foundation of freedom, justice and peace in the world." The term "recognition" thus literally constitutes the first word of international human rights law, and it addresses all human beings equally as holders of an inherent dignity. The various rights, as listed in the thirty articles of the UDHR, serve the purpose of spelling out the practical consequences by enshrining the due respect for everyone's human dignity in different spheres of society. This happens through human rights, which therefore claim a specific authority as "inalienable rights" within the order of legal norms, as the preamble of the UDHR professes. Based on equal dignity of all, human rights likewise are due to all human beings equally. To say it again in the words of Article 1 of the UDHR: "All human beings are born free and equal in dignity and rights. They are endowed with reason and conscience and should act towards one another in a spirit of brotherhood."[30] This most famous article of the UDHR sums up the normative profile of human rights.[31]

The short reflection just undertaken may not suffice to refute all skepti-cal objections leveled against universal human rights. Although the idea of egalitarian rights of all human beings can be demonstrated in its inherent attractiveness and plausibility, such demonstration does not amount to a quasi-mathematical theoretical "validity proof," by which all possible objec-tions would be refuted once and for all. Epistemologically, such demonstra-tion has the status of a reasonable appeal, not of an irrefutable rational certainty. One can always try to convince those who do not subscribe to human rights, by putting empirical and normative arguments on the table and unfolding the compelling force of human rights as an antidote to repression, exclusion, and discrimination; but people may still disagree. Moreover, it remains true that normative universalism, whatever concep-tual shape it may take, can never exist in a "pure and simple" format. Any formulation of universal validity claims will always carry indexes of time, space, context, and various contingencies. Universalistic concepts like human dignity, freedom, or equality will never be free from particular his-torical legacies. The legal and political techniques of international standard setting likewise have their particular path dependencies. How could it be otherwise? Hence, whenever we try to spell out guiding ideas of normative universalism and turn them into specific philosophical concepts, political declarations, or legally binding norms, they will somehow remain tainted with various "particularisms," and it is good to be self-critically aware of that reality. In this sense, we have in fact to overcome a naïve universalism, which simply takes a given set of norms for granted as supposedly applica-ble to everyone, everywhere, and at any time. Criticism of human rights can serve as an antidote to such naivety, which confuses universalism with "naturalness" and "trans-historicity," as Makau Mutua has put it.[32] The critique of naïve universalism can support the human rights project by constantly reminding those involved how demanding and complicated the task is that they have undertaken and that this task can never be completed. It will remain unfinished business, not only in practice but also at the con-ceptual level. Yet embarking on the never-ending journey of discovering biases, crossing boundaries, and appealing to our common humanity remains a meaningful project.

We have pointed out earlier that in retrospect it is easy to see the deep-seated biases that have permeated historical human rights documents, start-ing from the 1776 Virginia Bill of Rights and the 1789 Déclaration des droits de l'homme et du citoyen to the 1948 UDHR and more recent UN

instruments. It seems plausible to expect that future generations will likewise discover biases that lie underneath our contemporary human rights
formulations, biases of which we are currently not aware. However, on a
more positive note we can also say that the history of human rights has
been an ongoing and at least partially successful project of uncovering and
tackling biases. Women's rights activists have succeeded in broadening the
human rights discourse by exposing numerous violations occurring in the
private sphere, which in a traditional understanding remained largely outside of human rights politics. Persons with disabilities have articulated their
horrific experiences of exclusion and established an international human
rights convention, which specifies the aspirations of a future barrier-free
and inclusive society. More recent nondiscrimination clauses include sexual
orientation and gender identity within the lists of prohibited grounds of
unequal treatment. Moreover, historians have begun to reconsider the
genealogy of human rights by challenging exclusively Eurocentric ownership claims. Civil society organizations regularly criticize governments for
the ambiguities of their human rights rhetoric, with the purpose of ensuring
consistent human rights politics. To put it in more general terms: while
human rights are not above contextuality and historicity, they can still contribute to opening up spaces, broadening horizons, and breaking through
previously hermetic boundaries, in never-ending attempts to promote
respect for human dignity and enlarge the scope of human freedom and
equality.

Normative universalism can only be plausible as "work in progress,"
and criticism of human rights can be in the service of such gradual progress.
Serious human rights commitment requires constant self-criticism as well
as the readiness to also listen to criticism voiced from "outside" the human
rights community. The project of realizing universal human rights can only
flourish in a "listening mode." Progress in that area requires willingness to
reconsider and adapt the standards currently deemed universal, as well as
their underlying concepts, with a view to better accommodate the needs of
people whose experiences of injustice have not yet found adequate recognition and inclusion. Instead of delegitimizing and discarding the idea of
universal rights—along the lines of Carl Schmitt's conspiracy projections—
criticism of human rights may well help to bring about a refined, more
cautious, more modest, and more realistic understanding of universalism,
which is needed in order to keep the human rights project open for ever-
new insights, discoveries, reforms, and adaptations. What is true for human

rights in general, also applies to the right to freedom of religion or belief. Rather than speculating about an alleged "impossibility" of religious freedom, a critical analysis of existing tensions, gaps, blind spots, and unquestioned presuppositions can help to make the right to freedom of religion or belief more plausible, more inclusive, and more realistic.

3. The Human Rights Approach to Religious Diversity

Freedom of religion or belief played a prominent part in the historical genesis of universal rights. As long as the political and legal order was imagined as deriving immediately from the tenets of one particular religion, those professing a different religion (or no religion at all) could hardly find recognition on an equal footing.[33] There was obviously no common understanding, for example, between Roman Catholics, who based their moral rules of conduct on "natural laws" corroborated by the pope, and Protestants, who stigmatized the pope as the "Antichrist." Without a common understanding, however, domestic peace was in constant peril. Hence, religious dissidents or members of confessional minorities faced discrimination, exclusion, deportation, and other forms of persecution. In particular, during the era of the European confessional wars, imprisonment, deportation of minorities, and forced conversion or reconversion took place on a large scale. Religious minorities and dissidents could at best hope for a precarious "tolerance," which even in its more generous versions fell far short of full recognition on an equal footing. In the face of ever-new hostilities, violent conflicts, and concomitant atrocities, people gradually learned that they had to cope with confessional pluralism as an irreversible political reality, which it would be necessary to come to terms with.[34]

Freedom of religion or belief is a human-rights-based response to experiences of grave injustice accumulated over centuries of religious discrimination and persecution in different parts of the world.[35] The human rights approach facilitates recognition of pluralism, which goes well beyond a grudgingly conceded "tolerance." Such recognition rests on the understanding that we can after all identify one common denominator that runs through the conflicting confessional positions, namely the fact that they are always held by human beings. It is human beings who profess, cherish, develop, or change their various beliefs; and it is human beings who may shape their lives in line with the tenets of their different religious (or nonreligious) convictions. Whereas from this angle, existing differences will neither disappear nor become irrelevant, it is nonetheless conceivable to appreciate diversity positively as a manifestation of human dignity. As previously explained, the due respect for everyone's human dignity—that is, their potential of responsible agency—defines the nucleus of human rights in general. It also lies at the heart of the right to freedom of religion or belief.

The recognition facilitated by freedom of religion or belief, strictly speaking, is not due to the various religions, confessions, beliefs, or faith manifestations in themselves. Instead, it relates to human beings, who are the relevant right holders. This clarification has far-reaching implications. Rather than directly dealing with religions in themselves, the right to freedom of religion or belief actually empowers human beings in the broad area of conscientious positions, religious convictions, faith manifestations, and so forth. In other words, it is only through the lens of human beings that religions and beliefs—that is, their dogmas, sacred scriptures, normative rules, rituals, ceremonies, organizational structures, and so forth—come into the focus of human rights.[36] To use a shorthand formula: freedom of religion or belief "protects believers rather than beliefs." One might well object that both aspects, believers and beliefs, are necessarily intertwined. Yet the decisive point is that human rights tackle that interrelatedness between believers and beliefs consistently *from the angle of the human being.*

Human rights only indirectly relate to religions or beliefs, that is to say, by approaching them through the lens of human beings. That peculiar indirectness has far-reaching implications for an adequate understanding of freedom of religion or belief. It means that human beings always have to step in and define what matters to them in the vast area of religious orientations and practices. They are both the decisive right holders and the ones who hold, cherish, and develop their various religious and belief-related identities. By contrast, let us hypothetically assume someone wanted to provide direct legal protection to religion itself. In that case one would first have to answer the question which religions should be worthy of such protection. Given the plurality of existing religious (and nonreligious) orientations and practices, it would be difficult and ultimately impossible to find a plausible answer to that question. The names of God are manifold, and there are even traditions that do not refer to any divine authority; different religions disagree over the ranks of various prophets, while some religions do not subscribe to prophecy at all; and what is sacred to one community may appear blasphemous or simply irrelevant from the standpoint of another community. How can law cope with such irredeemably different positions? Sullivan's verdict is: not at all. She assumes that "legal protection for 'religion' anywhere demands a definition of religion."[37] Any definition, however, will inevitably be partisan, which is the reason why religious freedom will ultimately collapse as a meaningful concept. At least it can never become a universal right—or that is her assumption.

Sullivan would be right, if religious freedom were to aim at the protection of religion. However, this is not the case. Her criticism ignores the human rights nature of freedom of religion or belief. Instead of defining from outside those religions that are "worthy" of protection, freedom of religion or belief leaves the competence of definition to human beings, who are the relevant right holders in that field. Conceptualizing freedom of religion or belief as a universal human right means, above all, to *respect the self-understanding of human beings*. It falls upon them to declare who they are, how they want to be treated, which practices they wish to see respected and which support measures, if any, they may need from the state or from society. It is not to be expected that all their claims will always succeed, and there may be reasons sometimes to question the self-description of certain individuals or groups (we will shortly come back to this point). Yet respecting the self-understanding of human beings—ultimately of all of them—must remain the starting point and the overarching guiding principle for any universalistic conceptualization of freedom of religion or belief. (Having said that, we would like to add in passing that we are not ignorant of the problem that the approach through self-understanding and self-articulation may have unintended side effects, in particular for people who, due to their life circumstances and habits, are less used to articulate themselves. An adequate conceptualization of human rights has to take into account such possible side effects.)

If the self-definition of human beings marks the point of departure for making sense of freedom of religion or belief, it furthermore follows that the scope of this right must be wide. Freedom of religion or belief cannot be conceived as a mere extension of the traditional politics of tolerance, which for example in the Augsburg Peace Treaty of 1555 only covered Catholics and Lutherans before it was cautiously broadened in the Westphalian Peace Treaty of 1648 to also include Calvinists. Even today, some states merely recognize the followers of a predefined list of legitimate religions, a practice often erroneously confused with "freedom of religion."[38] Against that misunderstanding, one cannot emphasize enough that the human rights approach in the area of religion and belief differs fundamentally from the politics of limited tolerance. Rather than having the scope of permissible religious beliefs and practices predefined by the state, the scope of freedom of religion or belief results from what *human beings themselves define as being important to them.* Even though one has to add a few qualifications and caveats, the defining authority of human beings remains crucial for any conceptualization of freedom of religion or belief as a universal right. Consequently, the scope of this right must go far beyond any lists of permissible options as they used to exist—and partially continue to exist—within the traditional tolerance paradigm. In this context, we should remind ourselves that the full title of the human right under discussion is "freedom of thought, conscience, religion or belief."[39] In the international discourse, in particular in the UN context, it has become the standard to use "freedom of religion or belief" as a shorthand formula for that long title. (For ease of language, we will sometimes use the even shorter form of "religious freedom," but mostly use the wording of "freedom of religion or belief.")

The broad understanding of freedom of religion or belief has been corroborated by the UN Human Rights Committee, that is, the expert body in charge of monitoring the implementation of the International Covenant on Civil and Political Rights (ICCPR). In its General Comment No. 22 on freedom of religion or belief (Article 18 of the ICCPR), issued in 1993, the committee points out: "Article 18 protects theistic, non-theistic and atheistic beliefs, as well as the right not to profess any religion or belief. The terms 'belief' and 'religion' are to be broadly construed."[40] These are clear words. The General Comment goes on: "Article 18 is not limited in its application to traditional religions or to religions and beliefs with institutional characteristics or practices analogous to those of traditional religions." One should add that freedom of religion or belief equally covers the rights of members of large or small communities, minorities as well as internal minorities within minorities, conservatives as well as liberals, converts or reconverts, dissenters or other critical voices and, last but not least, women who typically have marginalized positions within most of the traditional religious communities. This broad conceptualization is deeply anchored in UN documents. As early as 1960, UN Special Rapporteur Arcot

Krishnaswami already argued that the terms "religion or belief" should cover different forms of theism, but also other beliefs, such as agnosticism, atheism, and rationalism.[41]

Such a broad and historically open understanding of freedom of religion or belief can evoke mixed feelings. One reason for unease might stem from fear that freedom of religion or belief would potentially justify dangerous practices occurring in the name of religion, ranging from harmful rituals to fanaticism or even religious terrorism. However, these fears are unjustified. Freedom of religion or belief remains within the overall human rights framework and cannot become the pretext for endangering or abusing the rights and freedoms of others. When adversely affecting other human beings, freedom of religion or belief may require limitations defined by the state which, in order to be legitimate, must be in line with all the criteria prescribed for that purpose. We shall discuss the issue of limitations in the next chapter.[42]

Another objection to the wide conceptualization of freedom of religion or belief concerns the danger that this could lead to invoking various trivial interests.[43] This is a relevant objection. Take the example of a national census conducted in England and Wales in 2001, which revealed that more than 390,000 people (around 0.75 percent) see themselves as followers of a "Star Wars" religion, admittedly following a private internet campaign that had invited the census participants to "do it because you love Star Wars . . . or just to annoy people."[44] Another group of people, who call themselves "Pastafarians," have created a mock-worship of the "big spaghetti monster," and members of that group have invoked a right to use photographs for official documents with a noodle sieve on their heads.[45] Imagine that coffee shop owners in the Netherlands would seek recognition as religious communities in order to be able to sell drugs as part of "religious ceremonies." Could these and similar interests really become cases for human rights concerns? Ronald Dworkin expresses a certain skepticism: "Once we break the connection between a religious conviction and orthodox theism, we seem to have no firm way of excluding even the wildest ethical eccentricity from the category of protected faith."[46] It is generally wise not to jump to conclusions and to assess each case and each situation carefully on their specific merits. Yet the danger of trivialization doubtless exists. People generally opposed to acknowledging a universal right to freedom of religion or belief may even deliberately use mock strategies to demonstrate the absurdity of protecting freedom of religion or belief for everyone.

How can we avoid the pitfalls of trivialization while at the same time keeping the door open for a wide plurality of self-definitions and self-understandings in the area of religion or belief?[47] This is a tricky question. No one should expect an easy way out or a solution that will fit all possible issues coming up in this regard. Neither the UDHR nor the ICCPR define the concepts of religion and belief, and the just-cited General Comment No. 22 merely advocates a broad conceptualization without providing further details. The 1981 UN Declaration on the Elimination of All Forms of Intolerance and of Discrimination Based on Religion or Belief at least gives a hint. The preamble clarifies that "religion or belief, for anyone who professes either, is one of the fundamental elements of his conception of life." This is an open definition, which nonetheless helps to overcome the danger of trivialization. It indicates that religions and beliefs in the understanding of the 1981 Declaration have an existential significance, which permeates the entire self-understanding of a person and his or her way of life. Religions and beliefs can shape a person's identity and create a deep sense of attachment and group loyalty based on shared worldviews, symbols, ethical norms, and practices. It is in recognition of such existential significance that freedom of religion or belief is assigned the rank of an inalienable human right.

The European Court of Human Rights (ECtHR) has developed a similar line of reasoning. In order for a view to fall within the ambit of freedom of religion or belief, the Court states, that view must display "a certain level of cogency, seriousness, cohesion and importance."[48] Again, this is a helpful clarification. On the one hand, the four criteria remain formal and accommodate a broad variety of convictions, religious and otherwise, including views that lie far outside of mainstream religions. On the other hand, the ECtHR makes clear that not any view that someone just happens to have today can claim the status of a serious "belief" or "religion."[49] While the criteria of cogency, seriousness, and importance imply an existential urge based on profound convictions, the element of cohesion requires that the respective position show an impact on a person's identity in a somewhat coherent and holistic manner.

Another proposal comes from Jocelyn Maclure and Charles Taylor. They emphasize the component of "meaning-giving commitments,"[50] thus also using a quite open formulation, which at the same time may help to avoid trivialization. Cole Durham and Brett Scharffs move in a similar direction when borrowing Paul Tillich's concept of a person's "ultimate concern"[51] as a possible point of orientation. Dworkin, who subscribes to a nontheistic religiosity, in the tradition of Spinoza and Einstein, defines religious beliefs as "convictions that one cannot isolate from the rest of one's life. They engage a whole personality. They permeate experience: they generate pride, remorse, and thrill."[52] What these and similar formulations have in common is that they remind us of the identity-shaping significance that religions and beliefs typically have for those professing and practicing them. At the same time, the criteria used to circumscribe the contours of religion and belief remain formal, thus allowing the inclusion of most different forms of existing deep convictions and related (individual and collective) practices.

Although the self-definition of human beings concerning issues of religion or belief remains the necessary starting point, it is not always the end of the story. It must be possible to request from those who claim specific protection that they provide some explanation. The Strasbourg formula ("cogency, seriousness, cohesion and importance") is an attempt to sketch out a viable conceptualization of freedom of religion or belief that combines openness with upholding a certain formal threshold against trivialization. What that means in practice has been developing case by case in the court's jurisprudence. The same happens in the UN Human Rights Committee, which bases its jurisprudence on individual complaints, while also monitoring the practice of all those states that have ratified the ICCPR. Thus, the contours of freedom of religion or belief remain historically open and adaptable to ever-new situations, claims, and requests.

4. "Protestant" Biases in the Conceptualization of Religious Freedom?

While the various criteria and formulas just listed may be helpful to circumscribe the contours of freedom of religion or belief, they can at the same time give rise to a new set of questions and doubts. Already the insistence on self-articulation may actually lead to unintended discriminatory side effects, which warrant critical monitoring. Moreover, the emphasis placed on components like "existential cogency," "meaning-giving commitment," and a person's "ultimate concern" could nourish the suspicion shared by many observers that freedom of religion or belief largely follows a "Protestant" paradigm of religiosity, which privileges individual believing over communitarian rituals and social practices. Is the basic presupposition underlying the human rights approach—namely, that human beings have to play the decisive role of actively defining their religious identities, needs, and wishes—not in itself a manifestation of Protestant theologies and liberal philosophies, which thus gain the upper hand? This is a pressing question. Robert Yelle is convinced that the right to religious freedom actually presupposes a particular notion of religion which, he says, "has commonly—and, I believe, correctly—been traced to tendencies that became dominant during the Reformation, as signaled by the Protestant critique of the Catholic ritual economy of salvation."[53] Elizabeth Shakman Hurd subscribes to a similar view, from which she concludes that, owing to its Protestant bias, the universal promise of religious freedom is illusionary.[54] Ronan McCrea criticizes the jurisprudence of the European Court of Human Rights as being one-sidedly individualistic: "The individualised view of religious freedom . . . is most consistent with a Protestant vision of religion as primarily a matter of the individual's belief and conscience."[55] In her appreciation of Charles Taylor's account of "meaning-giving commitment," Cécile Laborde thinks that the proposed wide and open formula still reflects a Christian, mainly Protestant, legacy.[56] Arvind Sharma, too, problematizes religious freedom, because of its underlying one-sided Western and Christian assumptions.[57]

In contemporary debates on freedom of religion or belief, the term "protestant" frequently figures as a typological concept. Beyond the Christian context, in which the term originally emerged, "protestant" forms of religiosity in this broader understanding may also cover reform movements within Islam, Buddhism, Hinduism, and other traditions.[58] Those who invoke the "protestant" paradigm often focus on three features: (a) the primacy of the internal sphere of believing as opposed to external ritual practice; (b) the emphasis on the individual person; and (c) the organization of religious community life in close analogy to freely chosen associations.

(a) Primacy of the *forum internum*?

Those who presume that freedom of religion or belief privileges the inner dimension of believing prima facie have strong arguments. Article 18 of the UDHR, Article 18 of the ICCPR, and similar international provisions also include *freedom of conscience*, a component that so far has received surprisingly little attention in jurisprudence and academic literature.[59] The term "conscience" defines the nucleus of a person's religious or moral identity, thus indeed highlighting the significance of the internal dimension within freedom of religion or belief.

Even more importantly, the ICCPR provides that the person's inner sphere of holding and forming a religious or belief-related conviction receive absolute legal protection against any coercive interference. Article 18(2) of the ICCPR clarifies categorically: "No one shall be subject to coercion which would impair his freedom to have or adopt a religion or belief of his choice." This part of freedom of religion or belief enjoys an elevated status above any justifiable limitations—unlike external manifestations of faith (acts of worship, individual and communitarian rituals, ceremonies, sermons, teaching, etc.), which can be limited in accordance with certain criteria.[60] Applying a traditional terminology, commentators usually differentiate between the *forum internum* and the *forum externum* dimensions of freedom of religion or belief. Whereas the first dimension receives unconditional legal protection, the latter dimension, while also enjoying strong legal protection, is not immune from possible limitations. Does this not sufficiently illustrate an existing hierarchy between internal and external dimensions of religion or belief—roughly in analogy to the Protestant idea of redemption through faith alone (*sola fide*)?

A closer look into the practice of freedom of religion or belief at least modifies that prima facie impression. The jurisprudence of regional courts and UN bodies as well as the advocacy work of international NGOs actually deal a lot with the *forum externum* of freedom of religion or belief. Examples include the right to wear headscarves, turbans, "burkinis," and other religious garments, the presence of religious symbols like the crucifix in public institutions, the performance of ritual male circumcision, religious initiation and socialization rights of parents, the possibility to obey religious diets and fasting periods during work, discriminatory implications of public religious holidays, the handling of belief-related diversity in public schools, conditions for religious communities to obtain the status of a corporate legal entity, administrative permissions for building houses of worship, regulations concerning the ringing of church bells or the Muslim prayer call, autonomous recruitment of clergy, the running of religious cemeteries, state subsidies for certain religious organizations, legislative measures against collective religious hatred, fair participation in state-funded interreligious dialogue projects, affirmative action programs for members of religious minorities as part of labor or housing laws, demands for official

recognition of indigenous spiritual practices, the running of religious charity organizations, and many other issues. This list of random examples
should suffice to demonstrate that freedom of religion or belief does not
mainly focus on issues of "internal" believing. In practice, it facilitates many
visible and audible—and thus "external"—manifestations of religious life
in all spheres of life.[61]

Nevertheless, the question remains: why the need for an absolute legal
protection of the *forum internum*? Before answering that question, we
should take into account other "absolute" human rights norms, such as
the prohibition of torture and the prohibition of slavery. These and other
categorical prohibitions enjoy the same elevated status as the *forum
internum* of freedom of religion or belief; they too stand above any justifiable limitations, thus demarcating the ultimate boundaries, which the state
can never legitimately cross. When dealing with the "Protestantism" charge,
it is important to bear in mind that the *forum internum* dimension of freedom of religion or belief is by no means unique; it is not the only case of
an absolute prohibition within the ICCPR.

The various absolute prohibitions fulfill an important function for the
understanding and implementation of human rights in general, because
they remind us that the limitation clauses attached to various provisions
should not become entry-points for normative relativism. True, most
human rights provisions—freedom of expression, freedom of peaceful
assembly, freedom of association, and other provisions—can be limited, if
the conditions set out for limitations are all met. This also holds true for
freedom of religion or belief in its *forum externum* dimension. However,
limitation clauses attached to human rights provisions do not permit a
general "balancing" of those rights against public order interests or other
political or legal considerations. The frequently used term "balancing" is
dangerously misleading, because it may superficially justify trade-offs
between human rights and other issues, thereby ultimately undermining
the postulated inalienability, which defines the status of a human right.
Instead of employing the relativistic language of "balancing," it appears
more adequate to interpret limitation clauses in keeping with a *strict justification requirement*.[62] We will tackle this issue in a more detailed manner in
the next chapter. The decisive point for our discussion here is that the
burden of justification always falls on those who deem a certain limitation necessary, not on those who wish to exercise their human right. Moreover, those who call for specific limitations have to demonstrate that all

the criteria prescribed for that purpose are actually satisfied. Justification requirements thus differ from a vague "balancing" semantics in that they are based on the assumption that freedom must remain the rule and limitations can only be invoked as an exception, the necessity of which must be clearly demonstrated in compliance with the criteria set out for that purpose. Finally, the justification logic itself presupposes upholding respect toward those possibly affected by the proposed limitation. This brings us to the "red lines" which can never be crossed. It seems obvious, for example, that torturing or enslaving an individual can never be justified, regardless of the circumstances, since torture and slavery completely nullify the respect that is due to all human beings in their potential of responsible agency. Enslaving persons means to treat them like cattle, and torture reduces the victim to a helpless bundle of pain, shame, and fear. Concerning such phenomena, no exception to the strict prohibitions could ever be permissible. The same is true for practices of brainwashing. Infringing coercively the inner nucleus of a person's conviction-formation means no less than denying the affected individual his or her status as a moral subject. Again, any attempt to "justify" brainwashing or other coercive encroachments into the *forum internum* would be self-contradictory, because that practice is from the outset incompatible with the necessary preconditions of communicative justification in general.[63]

When seen in conjunction with the equally absolute bans of torture and slavery, the strict prohibition of coercive infringements in the *forum internum* of freedom of religion or belief loses much of its alleged "Protestant" flavor. It actually does not indicate an abstract primacy of the internal over external dimensions of human life, as Saba Mahmood claims.[64] The purpose of those absolute norms is the defense, under all circumstances, of the basic respect of human beings in their potential of responsible agency and thus their human dignity, which constitutes the backbone of the human rights approach in general. When applying this insight to the issue at hand, we may thus conclude that the right to freedom of religion or belief in all its dimensions benefits from the absolute protection of its *forum internum* dimension. The *forum internum* is more than just an inner fortress, in which the individual can find his or her ultimate refuge against demands of the external world. By demanding an unconditional respect for everyone's freedom noncoercively to form, develop, change, or uphold his or her authentic convictions, Article 18(2) of the ICCPR at the same time empowers human beings to bear testimony to their convictions, to communicate with others, and freely to participate or not participate in religious community life, and so forth. It thus has beneficial effects on the whole range of guarantees that exist under freedom of religion or belief, including in the *forum externum*.

(b) One-Sided Focus on the Individual?

Another argument demonstrating a "Protestant" bias allegedly underlying freedom of religion or belief is its focus on individuals instead of groups. The charge that human rights favor the individual person at the expense of communitarian values belongs to the traditional arsenal of anti-human-rights polemics—traceable to the anti-revolutionary criticism leveled by conservative authors in the late eighteenth century.[65] A generation later, Hegel drew the picture of a society characterized by "the principle of atoms, of single wills"[66] where individuals merely pursue their selfish private purposes. Drawing on that Hegelian charge, Karl Marx held that human rights were essentially rights of individualistic "separation" of people from each other.[67] In the 1990s, a new version of that type of criticism emerged under the heading of "Asian values," which served the purpose of countering the allegedly one-sided individualism ascribed to the human rights approach by emphasizing the primacy of collective interests.[68]

There is an important element of truth in the assumption of individualism. Human rights empower the *human being qua human being*, prior to any particular group membership. This is a defining feature, without which the very notion of human rights would cease to make sense. Unlike entitlements that originate from particular group memberships, human rights must be respected in all human beings equally, prior to and independent of citizenship documents, family background, or membership in a specific religious community, and so forth. In that sense, one can indeed say that human rights are rights of each individual. However, rights held by the individual are not necessarily "individualistic" in the sense of focusing on the isolated individual while ignoring or even marginalizing the community aspects of human life. Confusing rights held by individuals with an "individualistic" way of life has become the source of countless misunderstandings, not least in the field of freedom of religion or belief.

Actually, human rights always presuppose communities in order to become a reality. To list just a few obvious examples, freedom of expression can only flourish in a discourse community of speakers and listeners. The rights to freedom of peaceful assembly and association are per definition exercised jointly with others. Habeas corpus rights guarantee the maintenance of certain social ties even in situations of arrest and detention, and the right to form trade unions facilitates solidarity among colleagues in the workplace. As the wording of Article 18 of the UDHR and ICCPR testifies, freedom of religion or belief, too, has a strong community dimension; it protects manifestations of religion or belief "in worship, observance, practice and teaching," which may be exercised "either individually or in community with others and in public or private."[69]

Many ideological debates on "individual rights versus community values" construct an abstract antagonism between the two, as if rights of the individual person were per se an onslaught on communitarian loyalty. This is a strange idea. In fact, the critical thrust of human rights does not go against communitarian solidarity; rather, the thrust is against all sorts of authoritarianism. By challenging authoritarian practices in political life, family life, and religious community life—from political censorship to forced marriages and forced conversion—human rights become a positive factor for promoting communitarian solidarity based on respect for everyone's freedom.

Moreover, authoritarianism also manifests itself as forced isolation of individuals, which represents a perverse form of involuntary "individualism." In a climate of fear created by control-obsessed authoritarian governments, dissidents typically face obstacles when wishing to meet, communicate, and form independent political associations. In homophobic societies, gays or lesbians may not dare to "come out" for fear of societal reprisals; they thus cannot live openly together with their partner. Undocumented migrants often avoid contact with members of mainstream society for fear of discovery and deportation. Where governments stage themselves as guardians of religious orthodoxy, converts typically feel compelled to hide their new faith in order not to endanger themselves and others; thus, they also do not dare to meet openly with others. Human rights serve as an antidote to such perverted "individualism," which results from the authoritarian politics of fear. They facilitate the development of free community life, for instance, by broadening the space for public critical discourse, by opening traditional concepts of marriage and family, by providing the conditions for a flourishing civil society, by supporting children in their rights to participation in public life, and by demanding full inclusion of persons with disabilities in a future barrier-free society. Far from being "apathetic to communal aspirations,"[70] freedom of religion or belief is part of that broad enterprise of creating the space for the flourishing of free communities.

(c) Privileging the "Free Church" Model?

Another version of the charge of a Protestant bias holds that freedom of religion or belief fosters voluntary associations based on freely chosen individual membership. This represents a more sophisticated version of ascribing one-sided "individualism" to the right to freedom of religion or belief. The focus is not on an allegedly isolated individual, but on the individual as constituting the final reference point for community organizations defined by voluntary individual membership. Arguably, that type of religious organization historically broke through with the advent of the Protestant "free churches." Is Peter Danchin correct when contending that freedom of religion or belief in its community-related dimensions presupposes "a Protestant understanding of 'the church'"?[71] If this were true, it would mean that freedom of religion or belief would actually privilege a particular historical type of community organization. The universalistic surface would merely hide a particularistic bias.

Religious communities display a broad variety of organizations, ranging from loose networks to membership-based free associations to strictly hierarchical bodies. Moreover, while some communities keep the doors open for new members, others do not admit anyone who has not been born into their community; in that sense they resemble ethnic groups defined by an imagined common origin. Freedom of religion or belief generally accommodates such a broad range of different types of organizations; it does not aim to change membership or admission criteria, let alone replace them by one unified system. When Orthodox Judaism presupposes that a Jew is normally born from a Jewish mother, while other ways of becoming a Jew remain exceptional and connected to certain thresholds, this is fine from the perspective of freedom of religion or belief. Traditionally, Alevites, Yezidis, and Druze stick to even stricter rules when insisting on birth as the only access to the community. Many indigenous people, too, closely link spiritual practices to the idea of a common ethnic origin. Freedom of religion or belief does not intend to alter any of this, nor does it impose a "Protestant"-type membership regulation, roughly on the analogy of Protestant free churches. In particular, freedom of religion or belief does not entitle the state to enforce an opening up of communities with the purpose of allowing converts into all of them. Reforms of membership or admittance criteria remain entirely left to the various communities themselves—provided they wish to embark on such a reform course.[72]

Respect for existing membership regulations is not without one important exception, though, which is the freedom to leave a community. While the criteria for *entering* a religious community—by birth, adoption, marriage, conversion, initiation rites, faith exams, and so on—fall within the autonomy of religious communities, the right to *leave* a community belongs to the nonnegotiable core of freedom of religion or belief. Religious communities have to come to terms with that requirement. They are free to lament anyone's decision to abandon their group, and they may hope and pray for converts to reconsider their decision and come back one day. In that sense, they do not have to fully embrace change. However, they cannot legitimately employ force or intimidation to induce converts to return or to prevent would-be converts from leaving. If necessary, the state has to interfere and protect "apostates" against threats of violence originating from their (former) communities.

The freedom to leave can have disquieting consequences for certain communities, in particular for small and vulnerable groups, not least for indigenous peoples, who often feel exposed to powerful forces of assimilation and disintegration, as a result of economic globalization, urbanization, and modernization processes.[73] Not only may some of their members invoke and use the right to leave; minorities or indigenous peoples may also fear the unfair competition by financially powerful religious groups, which actively recruit new members. From the standpoint of indigenous religions or, as he prefers to call them, "primal religions," Arvind Sharma therefore promotes a right to freedom *from* conversion, which he thinks is currently missing in the conceptualization of freedom of religion or belief. He postulates: "One should be free *not* to convert, and one should remain free from any pressure to convert. In other words, freedom of religion consists as much of the freedom to *retain* one's religion as to change it."[74] Sharma seems to ignore that this freedom has always been part of freedom of religion or belief. What he postulates as innovation has long been recognized, not least by the UN Human Rights Committee, which in its General Comment on Article 18 of the ICCPR *expressis verbis* confirms the freedom also to "retain" one's religion or belief.[75]

The problem is not that freedom of religion or belief one-sidedly focuses on the right to change—at the expense of the right to remain.

Rather, the problem is that vulnerable communities typically lack the resources they need in order to retain their spiritual practices and ideas in the face of powerful forces of assimilation.[76] In such situations, additional support may be necessary. To provide such support is a responsibility of the state, following from Article 27 of the ICCPR. It entitles religious minorities to receive infrastructural measures which they need to strengthen their capacities in key areas, such as education, media presence, political participation, cultural rights, and so on.[77] In 1992, the United Nations General Assembly adopted the Declaration on the Rights of Persons Belonging to National or Ethnic, Religious and Linguistic Minorities, which further specifies the entitlements for minorities. Article 1(1) of the Minorities Declaration demands: "States shall protect the existence and the national or ethnic, cultural, religious, and linguistic identity of minorities within their respective territories and shall encourage conditions for the promotion of that identity." According to Article 4(2) of the Declaration, "States shall take measures to create favourable conditions to enable persons belonging to minorities to express their characteristics and to develop their culture, language, religion, traditions and customs, except where specific practices are in violation of national law and contrary to international standards." In 2007, after years of intensive discussion, the General Assembly finally adopted the UN Declaration on the Rights of Indigenous Peoples, which obliges states regularly to consult with indigenous peoples with a view to identifying adequate ways for them to preserve their distinctive ways of life, including religiosity and spirituality, if they so wish. The last provision—"if they so wish"— remains indispensable, though. Minority rights or indigenous rights do not freeze existing collective identities against further changes; they also do not protect religious or spiritual customs like items in a museum. Within the framework of human rights, the protection of minority rights or indigenous rights always requires respect for people's self-understanding, for their freely articulated self-definitions, and for their free self-development, which in practice can go in quite different directions. Freedom of religion or belief can be, and has become, an integral part of policies promoting minority rights or indigenous rights, respectively. For this to be possible, however, the conceptualization of freedom of religion or belief must further open up to a broad variety of diverse demands, including from people who place themselves far outside the "Protestant" paradigm of religiosity.

5. Paving the Way to a Market Model of Religions?

Apart from the charge of an implicit Protestant bias, critics have also objected that freedom of religion or belief presupposes a "neoliberal paradigm" of a free market for religions and denominations, modeled mainly on the US example. According to Talal Asad, America sees it as its mission to "free beliefs as it frees property, that is, as an object that can be negotiated and exchanged without any legal obstacles."[78] In a similar vein, Elizabeth Shakman Hurd assumes that the hidden agenda underneath international religious freedom is the worldwide promotion of an open market "where the believer or nonbeliever can shop for, among other things, religion."[79]

The central notion to back up that neoliberal interpretation of freedom of religion or belief is the term "choice."[80] No doubt, "choice" plays a crucial role in human rights law in general and freedom of religion or belief in particular. Within Article 18 of the ICCPR, "choice" replaces the term "change," which in spite of heavy opposition made it into the 1948 UDHR. When the 1966 ICCPR was under discussion, delegates agreed on the alternative wording that everyone should be free "to have or adopt a religion or belief of his choice."[81] Within Article 18 of the ICCPR, this formulation even occurs twice. While the first paragraph outlines the general features of freedom of religion or belief, paragraph 2 provides the *forum internum* dimension with the above discussed "absolute" protection by clarifying: "No one shall be subject to coercion which would impair his freedom to have or adopt a religion or belief of his choice."

The term "choice" has attracted criticism, because it seems to stem from the world of the shopping malls. Hence, the impression could arise that religion figures as just another commodity in a spiritual wellness market, where individuals can shop around, as Hurd puts it. Supporters of freedom of religion or belief, too, sometimes express certain unease. For example, Roger Trigg contends: "A religion typically makes demands on its adherents. They are believed to be not only of their making but are obligations imposed on them. That is very different from the 'subjective' choice made because I feel like it, and impose it on myself."[82] In a similar vein Patrick Riordan insists: "Religious faith is not a choice like other choices, and it is of such significance in social life that it warrants particular attention."[83] Julian Rivers, too, finds the term somewhat offensive. He points out: "Focusing on autonomy in the sense of freedom of choice reflects a false view of the person as an unencumbered chooser of what to believe and how to live."[84]

The assumption underneath the various objections just cited is that "choice" implies a particular anthropology, namely the "unencumbered chooser" of spiritual options and commodities. However, this is not necessarily the case. One should bear in mind that within the ICCPR the term "choice" fulfills a *legal* function: it demarcates a sphere that must remain free from any coercion. Given the ubiquitous risk of coercive interferences, the practical significance of providing such legal protection can hardly be overemphasized. Against the danger of manipulation, intimidation, threats, or force, everyone should be entitled to claim his or her right of free choice. However, while "choice" remains indispensable as a legal term, its usefulness for instance in religious phenomenology may well appear questionable. This may be what Patrick Riordan has in mind when pointing out that faith is not a choice like other choices.

Many religious believers may feel that categories like "destiny" or "calling" would more adequately capture the identity-shaping quality of their personal religious convictions, which to them are not just a matter of subjective preference, taste, or "choice." Experiencing an urgent "calling" apparently differs very much from making a "choice" in the everyday understanding of the word; the experience of a calling can even come close to the subjective feeling of having no choice anymore. In other words, what makes sense as a technical legal term may prove much less adequate (in some situations totally inadequate) for describing existential experiences—and vice versa. Legal terminology has its inherent limitations, and it is good to be aware of that fact.

In the above quote, Roger Trigg rightly points to the "demanding" quality that defines any serious religious conviction. However, his conclusion that such demands on the believer cannot become a matter of personal choice would only be plausible, if the term "choice" were to function as a concept of religious phenomenology or religious anthropology. Yet, as pointed out, this is not the case. The important point is that within Article 18 of the ICCPR the term "choice" *only* functions as a legal category. When seen in this light, there is no contradiction between feeling exposed to an unconditional religious demand, on the one hand, and insisting on the legal entitlement to one's personal free choice, on the other. For example, a Jehovah's Witness objecting to serving in the military may feel compelled to follow the "dictates of his conscience" (in that existential sense not just making a choice), while at the same time claiming his legal right to freedom of "choice" against the government. Human life is not one-dimensional.[85]

There is nothing mysterious in the observations just made. They analogously apply to other important spheres of human life. Take the example of marriage or partnership. Many people will agree that "choice" is a somewhat awkward category when it comes to concluding a lifelong relationship upon which so much depends. "Choosing" a spouse like an item from a catalogue would certainly strike most people at least as a little frivolous. Nonetheless, to have a guaranteed human right of free "choice" in matters of partnership and marriage remains highly important, given the ongoing reality of forced marriages or child marriages in parts of the world.

If a young woman who feels under pressure to marry someone imposed on her by her family demands respect for her right to making her personal choice of a spouse, this obviously does not mean that she thereby implicitly subscribes to neoliberal market logic. Insisting on the right to free choice often reflects an existential predicament. The same holds true for freedom of religion or belief. Hurd thus misses the point when contending: "Contemporary international religious freedom advocacy both presupposes and produces the neoliberal religious subject of the religious economies model: a rational, voluntary religious actor who seeks out the religious options that suit her best."[86] This interpretation confuses a specific *legal* category designed to ensure strict non-coercion with a fully fledged neoliberal ideology. In addition to that, the interpretation displays a lack of familiarity with human rights practice. Numerous people across the continents suffer serious consequences just because they remain faithful to their religions, beliefs, or other existential convictions; they face discrimination, stigmatization, or even persecution. Those people obviously do not behave like "consumers" who just "shop around" in a spiritual wellness market to find the "options" that suit them best. Reading a neoliberal market ideology into freedom of religion or belief not only fails to do justice to the significance of this specific right; it also amounts to blatant disrespect for many victims of religious persecution worldwide.

6. Toward a Universalistic Understanding of Freedom of Religion or Belief

No doubt, freedom of religion or belief is a complicated issue. Complications arise not only at the level of its efficient implementation; already the *consistent conceptualization* of this human right is fraught with difficulties, grey zones, and the emergence of ever-new borderline cases.[87] It is all the more important to understand the *human rights logic*, which normatively defines freedom of religion or belief. Instead of protecting religions in themselves, which would presuppose singling out those religions deemed worthy of such protection, freedom of religion or belief aims at *empowering human beings*—and indeed all of them. The guiding principle underpinning human rights in general is equal rights of freedom for all human beings, in recognition of their human dignity. Freedom of religion or belief spells out that guiding idea with regard to the area of religious and belief-related diversity. It protects human beings in their identity-shaping existential convictions and conviction-based practices broadly.

Conceptualizing freedom of religion or belief meaningfully as a "universal" human right proves possible, provided we understand universalism adequately. Two points may be worth reiterating. First, universalism does not aspire to uniformity. The aim is not to come up with a "one-size-fits-all" solution, as Stephen Hopgood wants us to believe.[88] Instead, the starting point of any sustainable conceptualization of normative universalism must be inexhaustible diversity of worldviews, beliefs, and practices. However, it should be a freely articulated diversity, not a mute and silent "otherness." It is exactly this insistence on free and broad articulation which serves as the entry-point for universal rights aimed at safeguarding human dignity, freedom, and equality. Moreover, universalism can only be plausible as a work in progress. This is the second important caveat. Universalism will always remain unfinished business. If "law is no seamless web," as Marc DeGirolami writes,[89] this is certainly true for human rights laws and most particularly for religious freedom as well. In practice, the handling of freedom of religion or belief will never be above the risks of ignorance, complacency, neglect, biases, or blind spots. How could it be otherwise? This is the reason why criticism and self-criticism remain imperative. However, radical alternatives to religious freedom so far have failed to provide any practical guidance as to how to cope with contested issues. Controversies around headscarves in public schools, ritual male circumcision, crucifixes in public classrooms, religiously motivated asylum claims, conversion, missionary activities, and so forth, will not mysteriously disappear once we get rid of the idea of freedom of religion or belief for everyone. In DeGirolami's words, "many people rely on the law to shape and structure their activities, and the loss of an entire body of law—and therefore of legal protection—governing what is still for many a vital part of life would represent a deeply unsettling development."[90] The task remains that one has to come up with fair solutions that respect the significance of religious belief and practice for the people concerned. Moreover, some of the proposed radical counter-positions show a misperception of freedom of religion or belief, whose human rights nature the critics seem to ignore.[91]

Those who cast doubt on the universal aspirations underlying freedom of religion or belief have leveled two main objections. On the one hand, they see the hegemony of a "Protestant" paradigm in operation; and on the other hand, they fear that freedom of religion or belief promotes a "neoliberal" market model in dealing with religious diversity. At a closer look, the ascribed Protestant bias loses much (maybe not all) of its plausibility. Practitioners who work on freedom of religion or belief frequently deal with external mani-festations of religions (*forum externum*) rather than one-sidedly focusing on the internal dimension (*forum internum*) of faith alone.[92] Moreover, given the clear appreciation of community life as an important part of freedom of religion or belief, the ascription of an "individualistic" bias likewise proves questionable. Instead, one of the most vital purposes is to promote the free flourishing of communities. Finally, rather than propagating one particular type of organization akin to the Protestant "free church" model, freedom of religion or belief accommodates a broad range of different types of religious organization, including different membership and admittance criteria as they have developed in conformity with the self-understanding of the respective communities. In short, once we take a closer look at the actual practice of freedom of religion or belief, the charge of privileging "Protestant" types of religiosity loses much of its interpretative attractiveness. Of course, people have actively to articulate their religious claims in order to make it to courts or other fora. Yet this does not mean that the position or practice they wish to see protected necessarily implies a theology or philosophy similar to the "Protestant" primacy of individual faith. The assumption that religious free-dom reflects a neoliberal market model for dealing with religious diversity is even less convincing. This allegation may emerge when one turns the crucial notion of "choice" into an alleged proof of a neoliberal anthropology. How-ever, the purpose of the term "choice" in human rights law is to demarcate a sphere of legal protection against coercive interferences rather than prescrib-ing a particular religious anthropology, let alone promoting a market ideology in the area of religion and spirituality.

Our countercriticism to the above critical objections does not intend to defend the status quo of freedom of religion or belief. Much work remains

ahead of us, already at the levels of awareness building and adequate conceptualization. Here are just a few examples. Although the inclusion of
atheists and agnostics has received clear endorsement in the theory of freedom of religion or belief, this insight has not yet consistently been implemented in human rights practice. Even today, many people express surprise
when learning that atheists, too, fall within the ambit of freedom of religion
or belief.[93] Another issue, which so far has received comparatively little
attention, is the situation of migrant workers, in particular female domestic
workers, many of whom remain "invisible" when taking employment
abroad in private households. Their situation is marked by a combination
of different degrees of vulnerability, such as precarious residency status,
weak labor laws, poverty, invisibility in private households, sex/gender, and
religious minority status. No one can currently even conjecture how many
of them suffer from violations of their freedom of religion or belief.[94] One
of the biggest challenges concerns indigenous spiritual practices, which currently do not seem fully to fit into the normative categories established in
human rights law. As Makau Mutua points out, "The subject of indigenous
religions is one of the most underdeveloped areas of inquiry in human
rights."[95] When it comes to freedom of religion or belief for indigenous
persons or communities, even the insistence on free self-definition and free
articulation, as a requirement for claiming one's rights, may produce unintended side effects and lead to new forms of exclusion unless we develop
sensitivity for alternative ways of articulation outside of the mainstream of
political and judicial practice.[96] Attempts to better adapt the standards of
freedom of religion or belief to the needs and wishes of indigenous peoples
have only just begun.

Hence, much remains to be done and to be discovered. Universalism of
human rights can only work as *universalism in the making.* This is also true
for the right to freedom of religion or belief. Criticism of the universalistic
nature of freedom of religion or belief, including deconstruction of traditional assumptions, can therefore be in the service of the ongoing project.
It can be an antidote to dangers of complacency and dogmatism from
which human rights practice has never been immune. Yet it all depends on
whether such criticism simply declares the universalistic enterprise to be
hypocritical from the start and thus doomed to collapse or whether it leaves
the space open for normative aspirations and experimentations in order to
cross existing boundaries in a never-ending search for common ground in
respect for everyone's inscrutable dignity.

CHAPTER 2

Ambiguities of Freedom

1. Alleged Incompatibilities

From early on, freedom of religion or belief elicited objections among religious traditionalists, who feared that the human rights approach would subject issues of truth, loyalty, and identity to the personal whims, tastes, or preferences of the individual, thus turning the "right" order of things upside down. In his notorious *Syllabus Errorum* (1864), Pope Pius IX even condemned religious freedom as one of the grave errors of modernity. He castigated this right as a way "to corrupt the morals and minds of the people, and to propagate the pest of indifferentism."[1] Just about one hundred years later, with the adoption of the Second Vatican Council's Declaration *Dignitatis humanae* (1965), the Catholic Church abandoned the previous anti-liberal stance thoroughly and became an active supporter of the human rights approach, in particular in the area of religious freedom.[2] Nonetheless, traditionalists from different religions and denominations as well as proponents of religiously colorized national identity politics continue to associate the right to freedom of religion or belief with a general decline of religious traditions or the erosion of community values.

What is more surprising is the observation that freedom of religion or belief can also evoke mixed feelings among liberals and in liberal milieus. Assuming that freedom of religion or belief is a "liberal right" in the broadest sense of the word, a liberal resistance to a liberal right may sound like an oxymoron. Indeed, freedom of religion or belief seems to be the only example of a "classical liberal right" that currently does not receive unanimous applause in liberal circles in the West and elsewhere. Some objections are based on misunderstandings, such as the occasional assumption that freedom of religion or belief provides a pretext for inciting or committing acts of religiously motivated violence. As we will discuss later, this is not the case. Yet ambivalent reactions stem not only from misunderstandings and a lack of knowledge. Being confronted with a religious pluralism that exceeds what is usually considered "normal" may be disturbing also for many people who understand themselves as liberals. Surely, liberal societies define themselves not least by the acceptance of diversity, including in the area of religion and belief. Yet it is not uncommon that believers who manifest their faith visibly and aspire to shape their lives in conformity with their convictions confront inimical reactions, since their behavior does not seem to fit into the proverbial "liberal lifestyle," defined by a dispassionate and perhaps even ironic approach to religious ideas and practices.

Hence, whereas religious traditionalists (or some of them) may have difficulty in fully appreciating the element of *freedom* within the right to freedom of religion or belief, some liberals in turn wonder which role *religion* could possibly play in a modern liberal society. What is the place of religion in an open society, which defines itself by principles of freedom and equality? Could religion play any positive part in a liberal public culture? Some express their doubts. "God is dangerous,"[3] the late sociologist Ulrich Beck pointed out in an article in the German weekly *Die Zeit*, in which he ironically remarked: "Health ministers warn: religion kills. Religion should not be imparted on juveniles below the age of 18." Obviously, this is supposed to be a joke. Yet it illustrates an existing fear that religion could become the entry-point for fundamentalism and obscurantism, thus eroding dearly won liberal and secular achievements.

What skeptics from both camps, religious traditionalism and secular liberalism, have in common is that they both assume that the two components defining the right at issue—freedom and religion—ultimately do not fit together. Winnifred Fallers Sullivan voices such an antagonistic assessment from her point of view when opining: "It is the peculiar nature of religion itself to restrict freedom."[4] And she concludes: "To be religious is not to be free, but to be faithful."[5] Based on this premise, a right to religious freedom cannot make much sense. According to Michael Lambek, religious freedom is an enterprise fraught with an irredeemable contradiction: "Hence, the very idea of freedom of religion is paradoxical; it is the freedom to be unfree in a particular kind of way."[6]

The present chapter challenges the alleged incompatibility of freedom and religion. Section 2 starts with a brief phenomenology of human freedom, whose multiple dimensions cannot be reduced to the aspect of free "choice," which nonetheless remains crucial in human rights law. Subsequently (in Section 3), we deal with the legal contours of the right to freedom of religion or belief. In this context, we inter alia focus on how to handle the relationship between the guarantee of freedom, on the one hand, and the possibility of the state imposing certain limitations, on the other. Section 4 describes current political trends, which in different ways obfuscate the core of this human right—for instance, by twisting it into a protection of the reputation of certain religions, utilizing it for purposes of identity politics, or reducing religion to a merely private matter. The chapter ends with a short résumé (in Section 5).

2. Self-Undermining Freedom?

Can there be a freedom to be unfree? Would it be legitimate to use freedom in such a way that the destruction of freedom is the expected or even intended result? Philosophers of the European Enlightenment discussed this question mainly with regard to slavery and state absolutism. Can human beings sell themselves—and possibly even their posterity—into slavery? Can they surrender to the mercy of an absolute ruler against whom they cease to have any legal claims? To put the question more broadly, are human beings free to forfeit their freedom deliberately once and for all? Kant's categorical response is: no. He argues that if someone were to subject himself totally to somebody else's command, he would thereby abandon his own responsible agency. Without responsible agency, however, the preconditions for any normative practice would ipso facto collapse. Hence, any imagined social contract corroborating the total surrender of a person's freedom would be from the outset null and void. Kant concludes that "every human being still has his inalienable rights, which he can never give up even if he wanted to."[7]

Kant was neither the first nor the only philosopher of his day to insist that fundamental rights of freedom have the peculiar quality of "inalienable rights." In the introductory chapter, we cited a similar statement by Moses Mendelssohn. He more specifically refers to religious freedom when pointing out that "a contract concerning things which, by their very nature are *inalienable,* is intrinsically invalid, and cancels itself."[8] According to Kant, Mendelssohn, and many other thinkers, freedom is something precious; it is profoundly interwoven with issues of personal identity and, even more importantly, with the awareness of one's capacity of responsible agency. From this point of view, human freedom, as recognized and protected through fundamental rights, does not give the individual a carte blanche to discard or destroy that freedom. The opposite is true: human beings owe it to themselves as well as to others to cherish, develop, and defend their freedom. This obligation to cherish freedom provides the moral reason for establishing an order of rights with the purpose of protecting everyone's freedom in line with the principle of equality.[9]

In the framework of human rights, freedom of religion or belief serves the specific purpose of preventing and eradicating all forms of coercion with regard to a person's conscientious positions, religious (or nonreligious) convictions, and the various conviction-based practices, which people often exercise together with others. As the guarantor of this right, the state is obliged to ensure strict noncoercion within society as a whole and, if need be, also in the midst of the religious communities themselves. Threat or use of coercion against dissidents or converts can never be permissible, whatever theological arguments the religious authorities may invoke. The litmus test is the freedom to leave a religious community. Where this minimum condition is not respected, freedom of religion or belief simply does not exist.

In keeping with the logic of the human rights approach, freedom of religion or belief can merely recognize noncoercive forms of religiosity.[10] The prevention of coercion, positively speaking, means guaranteeing everyone's *freedom of choice*. As already briefly discussed in the previous chapter, choice is a crucial and indeed indispensable term in human rights law. Article 18(1) of the ICCPR confirms everyone's "freedom to have or to adopt a religion or belief of his choice." The subsequent paragraph 2 corroborates and further strengthens free choice by proclaiming: "No one shall be subject to coercion which would impair his freedom to have or to adopt a religion or belief of his choice." When interpreting this provision, the UN committee tasked with monitoring the ICCPR pointed out that "choice" inter alia covers the possibility "to replace" one's religion or belief by another religion or by nonbelief,[11] thereby making it crystal clear that the term "choice" functions as an equivalent of the right to "change" a religion or belief, as *expressis verbis* enshrined in Article 18 of the UDHR.[12]

A person's freedom of choice does not disappear after an important choice has been made. Indeed, it never ceases to exist—at least as a possibility—as long as the respective person lives. People remain free to reconsider, regret, revise, or modify their personal choices, including in the area of religion. An individual who has decided to dedicate his life to religious contemplation in a monastery, must have the option to correct his former decision thoroughly and leave the monastery. Freedom of conversion also includes the freedom to reconvert to one's previous religion or to turn to yet another faith or to no faith. Choice remains a possibility, as long as human life endures.

Human freedom would be inconceivable without having choices. It is from this angle that human rights law protects freedom, namely, by recognizing everyone's right to make choices in various areas of life: the choice of a profession, the choice of a spouse, the choice of one's residence, participation in the choice of political representation, and not least the choice of a religion or worldview. Notwithstanding its practical significance, however, the term "choice" cannot fully exhaust all aspects of how human beings experience their freedom. Freedom is more than choice. In the previous chapter we had a short discussion on "choice" as a legal term. The point we wanted to make in that context is that the term choice, when employed within freedom of religion or belief, does not reduce issues of faith to "commodities" in a neoliberal market of religious or spiritual items. When now resuming the reflection on choice, we do so from a slightly different angle. Our interest in the present chapter on freedom is to avoid another form of reductionism, which the insistence on choice can inadvertently produce, that is, losing sight of the existential dimension of human freedom, which transcends the possibility of just having options.

One of the most intensive experiences of freedom comes from being *seriously committed* to one's freely adopted and freely developed profound convictions. Any serious commitment is characterized by a subjectively felt imperative; it has an element of "here I stand, I can do no other."[13] Acting against one's profound religious convictions can amount to no less than a feeling of self-betrayal, which originates from the awareness of not doing justice to one's own religious identity. Failing to honor one's own convictions in practice can literally tear a person apart. This experience is not limited to the sphere of religion. It also concerns the attachment to moral principles, whether they are based on a religious ethos or formulated in secular ethical language. Whoever is serious about certain moral principles will also feel compelled to act in conformity with those principles; otherwise the principles would lack existential significance. People can have similar experiences in other areas of life, too, for example when it comes to partnership, friendship, or family relations. Being faithful to one's dearest and nearest can become a strong existential demand. Now the point we would like to stress is that such *existential demands are part of human freedom,* provided the convictions, principles, significant relationships, and so forth, which have the demanding quality, are freely adopted, freely undertaken, and freely developed.

Reducing freedom to a life devoid of any demanding commitments would amount to a caricature of freedom. Freedom does not mean to lead an undetermined life, that is, a life without existential demands. What is at stake is to *find one's own determination freely,* without external coercion. This is the meaning of "free self-determination." Human rights can only indirectly contribute to facilitating such free self-determination by prohibiting any coercion, thereby ensuring freedom of choice. This is the reason why the term "choice" plays such an important role in human rights law; it is the indispensable entry-point for all rights of freedom. At the same time, the search for meaning and the finding of one's own determination exceeds what the legal order can accomplish. Free self-determination in the sense of finding one's determination freely is a task which only the concerned human being can fulfill in lifelong endeavors. Human rights law can merely improve the external preconditions for this to be possible, namely by eliminating external constraints and obstacles, thus creating and broadening the space for individual "choices."

The emphasis we have placed on freely finding one's own determination should not be misperceived as trivializing the element of "choice," which remains indispensable as long as a person's life endures. Life plans can change thoroughly, convictions once developed can lose their inner persuasiveness, and important decisions taken in the past may require far-reaching revisions in the light of new experiences. Without choices, human life would be frozen in the status quo of what once was achieved. Choice is furthermore the decisive entry-point for human rights law, as already pointed out. In spite of the indispensable role that "choice" has for the realization of freedom, however, it does not—and cannot—capture the whole range of what freedom signifies in human life. Choice is merely the necessary precondition of free self-determination, which itself, if successfully achieved, transcends the aspect of choice. Reducing freedom to having mere choices may actually amount to missing the crucial point that living in harmony with one's freely adopted profound convictions can be the most intense experience of freedom. From the perspective of the concerned individual, the demand to live in accordance with his or her convictions can even come close to a subjective feeling of having "no choice." Although the possibility of changing one's conviction, life plans, and loyalties—and in that sense making new choices—actually continues to exist, it may sink into the background of the consciousness of a fully committed person.

The above-cited remark "to be religious is not to be free, but to be faithful" construes an abstract dichotomy between freedom and faith, which does not match human experience. Remaining faithful to one's convictions, principles, significant relationships, and so on, is fully compatible with human freedom, as long as it remains free from coercion. Living faithfully and in harmony with one's own self-determination may even be the most profound experience of freedom that human beings can make. Again, this is not merely true for the religious sphere, but applies to other important dimensions of human life as well. The demand to be faithful is often spelled out in metaphors like "calling" or "vocation," which at first glance seem to stand in direct contradiction to freedom of choice. However, from an adequately complex understanding of human freedom, that prima facie contradiction ultimately evaporates. There is nothing paradoxical about a convinced pacifist who insists on his legally guaranteed freedom of "choice" when refusing compulsory military service, while at the same time feeling that he has simply to follow the dictates of his conscience. Likewise, for a Baha'i, obeying religious fasting rules may be intimately linked to her religious identity and thus a demand that she wishes to fulfill as part of her personal freedom. For some atheists, public criticism of religion is more than just an intellectual game, namely a personal "calling" as it were, to which they need to respond in order to do justice to their own convictions, principles, and worldviews.

Surely, there may be many cases in which the situation is unclear. Whether a young woman wears the hijab as a manifestation of her personal conviction or whether she merely gives in to social pressure from her religious milieu may remain disputable. In some situations, this may not even be entirely clear to the concerned person herself. When she declares that "she can't do otherwise," this may therefore sound ambiguous in that it can be either a statement on her freely adopted self-determination or reflect a lack of personal freedom. Similar questions arise when a young candidate for Catholic priesthood professes lifelong celibacy—perhaps without fully knowing what he is about to promise. In reality, situations are usually not just black and white, but full of ambiguities. To deal with such grey zones requires sensitivity and a readiness to listen carefully to the concerned individuals.

However, when human beings let themselves be "determined" by a religious, ethical, or other conviction, this is per se neither pathological nor indicative of an absence of personal freedom. Indeed, it may well be a successful manifestation of free self-determination in the sense that they have managed to find their personal determination without coercion. To expel religion from the sphere of freedom, simply because it makes demands on believers, betrays a sadly one-dimensional understanding of freedom. At the same time, this plays into the hands of those anti-liberals who have often discredited rights to freedom as an alleged expression of shallowness and the decline of binding values. "To be religious is not to be free, but to be faithful" is a motto to which the Grand Inquisitor could have gladly signed up.

3. Primacy of Freedom and Criteria for Justifying Limitations

Freedom of religion or belief, as enshrined in Article 18 of the ICCPR and similar human rights provisions, is a complex entitlement. It protects everyone's freedom to search for an ultimate meaning; to communicate their convictions or doubts openly or to keep their faith to themselves; to join a religious group or to stay within the community in which they have grown up; to change or abandon their faith; to invite others to reconsider their religion or belief; to exercise rituals alone and in community with others; to express public criticism of religion or to defend religion against such criticism; to initiate and educate their children in conformity with their own convictions; to receive and impart information on religious issues; to import religious literature from abroad and circulate it; to shape their lives in conformity with religious prescripts; to establish a religious infrastructure, including places of worship, schools, and charity organizations; to recruit clergy in conformity with the self-understanding of the community, and so forth. Freedom of religion or belief is a right of individuals as well as communities, and it has private as well as public dimensions. Against a widespread stereotype, it does not one-sidedly focus on issues of personal conviction or spirituality, but equally covers ceremonial or ethical practices, including dietary prescriptions, dress codes, or collective pilgrimages, as well as institutional and infrastructural aspects of community life.[14] Any list of the various components belonging to that right will necessarily remain nonexhaustive, since freedom of religion or belief receives its practical contours in response to ever-new challenges, which may lead to a "discovery" or "re-discovery" of aspects that had been previously ignored.

Rights of freedom are defined by leaving the decision as to whether and how to make use of that freedom to the rights holders themselves. That is why freedom of religion or belief necessarily includes the right not to profess a religion or belief, not to show any interest in such issues, not to participate in religious ceremonies, not to observe any dietary or other religious rules, not to have one's children educated in a particular religion, and so on. Freedom *from* religion is a logical ingredient of freedom of religion or belief itself, because it follows from the nature of a right of freedom.

It is a truism that rights of freedom cannot be without limitations, since an unlimited freedom would amount to the elbow freedom of those who disrespect the freedom of others. Pointing to the obvious need for some limitations, at the same time, is dangerous, because it may invite arbitrary, discriminatory, or overly broad restrictions. Countless examples demonstrate that this danger is not merely hypothetical. Governments when trying to preserve an existing religious hegemony or being driven by sheer control obsessions, typically invoke an alleged necessity of limiting freedom of religion or belief in the interest of some "higher goods," which they often define as they see fit. Many authoritarian governments rhetorically agree that freedom of religion is a good thing in theory, as long as they have wide leeway to cut down on its practical exercise. Instead of openly saying "no" to human rights, it is more convenient to react in a "yes—but" fashion. The promised respect thus often ends up as just an empty rhetoric. Yet even democratic states have a tendency to invoke limitation clauses in a lax and loose manner, without always presenting compelling reasons as to why certain limitations are really needed and appropriate. Unfortunately, courts, including even the European Court of Human Rights, have not always been straightforward in demanding a precise and diligent handling of limitation clauses.[15] The result is that the contours of freedom of religion or belief and other rights of freedom may get increasingly blurred.

How can we steer a way that pragmatically accommodates certain limitations, when really necessary, without running the risk of selling out the substance of freedom of religion or belief? This is one of the most pressing questions in human rights practice. The general response provided by international human rights law is that limitations must be strictly linked to a number of criteria all of which must be satisfied for a proposed limitation to be justifiable. In case of failure, the proposed limitation will lack legitimacy. It is in that sense that Article 18(3) of the ICCPR specifies the conditions for the justifiability of limitations: "Freedom to manifest one's religion or belief may be subject only to such limitations as are prescribed by law and are necessary to protect public safety, order, health, or morals, or the fundamental rights and freedoms of others." The decisive term within that provision has often been overlooked or neglected, namely the tiny word "only." What it signifies is that states do not have a general permission to impose limitations as they see fit. Instead, it is the other way around in that limitations are generally impermissible—unless and until the said criteria are fully met.[16] Indeed, the whole thrust of limitation clauses is not on permitting limitations but, rather, on limiting the scope for legitimate limitations by linking them to a set of binding criteria. To capture this function, German lawyers have coined the concept of "*Schranken-Schranken*," which in literal translation means "limits to limitations."

According to the criteria listed exhaustively in Article 18(3) of the ICCPR, limitations must be legally prescribed, and they must be obviously "needed" to pursue a legitimate aim—the protection of "public safety, order, health, or morals or the fundamental rights and freedoms of others." In addition, restrictions must remain within the realm of proportionality, which inter alia means they must always be limited to the minimum degree of interference deemed necessary to achieve one of the enumerated legitimate purposes. The measures taken must furthermore be suitable to accomplish the envisaged purpose. These and other criteria serve the purpose of safeguarding the substance of freedom of religion or belief even in situations of conflict with the rights or freedoms of others or other important public interests. Confirming this critical function, the UN Human Rights Committee tasked with the oversight of the ICCPR, has insisted "that paragraph 3 of article 18 is to be strictly interpreted: restrictions are not allowed on grounds not specified there. . . . Limitations may be applied only for those purposes for which they were prescribed and must be directly related and proportionate to the specific need on which they are predicated. Restrictions may not be imposed for discriminatory purposes or applied in a discriminatory manner."[17] Finally, the legitimacy of limitations depends on the availability of legal remedies. Everyone who thinks his or her rights have inappropriately been infringed upon must have access to courts or other mechanisms.

An appropriate understanding and handling of limitations clauses, far from being just a "technicality," is of utmost significance for the flourishing of human rights in practice. Otherwise rights of freedom will end up as empty promises, which can be easily sidelined once conflicting state interests enter the scene. From a human rights perspective, one should always take freedom as the normative starting point against which limitations must be justified. In reality, however, many governments, including democratic governments, do the opposite, for instance when reducing freedom to a "dividend" of successful control politics. This means that freedom will end up as an unreliable "grant" always depending on precarious political circumstances. In the face of this danger, the handling of limitation clauses in theory and practice warrants utmost critical attention. It cannot be left to legal specialists, but should also become an issue for human rights education, political discourse, and awareness raising. In this context, one also should critically tackle the language and metaphors used to circumscribe the conditions of limitations and their (exceptional) justifiability.

A word that all too quickly and all too frequently comes up in discussions on rights and their limitations is the term "balance." It even occurs in countless scientific articles and commentaries on human rights.[18] Whenever a conflict seems to arise between a right of freedom and another consideration, this allegedly becomes a matter for "balancing." However, as Guglielmo Verdirame has observed, "balancing" is a dangerously vague notion, which invites all sorts of trade-offs. How can the elevated status of inalienable human rights survive, once these rights are vaguely balanced against public order interests or other issues that the government deems important? Verdirame's answer is: not at all. He concludes: "A right that is balanceable and negotiable cannot be fundamental."[19] Ample experience illustrates that this critical assessment is correct; as soon as mighty considerations of order, security, or collective identity are put on the weighing scales, rights of freedom will usually lose out.

To counter that danger, the limitation clauses attached to rights of freedom should not be spelled out in analogy to diffuse metaphors like "weighing scales" or "balancing processes." Instead, the criteria for limitations must follow the logic of *strict justification requirements*. The starting point must be everyone's entitlement with inalienable rights to freedom, upon which the whole human rights approach is premised. Accordingly, rights to freedom remain the rule, while a proposed limitation can merely be an exception to the rule, which furthermore requires strong arguments in keeping with all the criteria set out for that purpose. This strict justification logic manifests itself in the wording of Article 18(3) of the ICCPR. As already mentioned, the little word "only"[20] functions as a reminder that any proposed limitation should be considered illegitimate unless and until it meets all the criteria laid down for justifying a limitation. Strangely enough, however, many commentators fail to take the crucial role of the term "only" systematically seriously.[21]

Limitation clauses like the ones contained in Article 18(3) of the ICCPR do not grant states a general permission to "balance out" rights to freedom and limitations in ways that suit their political purposes. It is the other way around in that the state has to meet a high threshold defined by a combination of important caveats. The list of caveats includes presenting compelling empirical and normative arguments, issuing a formal law, persuasively demonstrating the need of such a law for the pursuance of a legitimate purpose, keeping limitations to the necessary minimum, avoiding any discriminatory effects and being willing to defend all of this to the democratic public and before courts. As Jeremy Gunn stresses: "The State . . . should be obligated to prove that the threats to the public order, public health, and the like are real and measurable rather than merely speculative or ideological, as well as that the proposed restrictions would actually reduce the danger."[22]

Additional complications may arise if freedom of religion or belief seems to be colliding with other human rights concerns. Within the list of purposes, in the interest of which limitations can be justified, securing "the fundamental rights and freedoms of others" may be particularly persuasive. But even then, caution is necessary. The first task of legislators or courts is to conduct a precise empirical assessment of the situation. In many cases, it may turn out that the supposed normative conflict does not even exist. One example is the prohibition of the Islamic headscarf undertaken on the empirically questionable assumption that it symbolizes an inferior status of women compared to men. Yet even in situations where a normative conflict in the intersection of different human rights standards apparently does exist, the task remains to do justice to all the human rights claims at issue—*to the maximum degree possible.* The term "balancing" fails to describe this demanding task adequately. Instead, it signals that one should settle for some sort of "middle ground," which remains normatively undefined. This amounts to trivializing the diligence required to uphold the substance of human rights provisions, especially in complicated situations.[23]

Finally, the *forum internum* dimension of freedom of religion or belief even enjoys absolute protection: "No one shall be subject to coercion which would impair his freedom to have or adopt a religion or belief of his choice." This apodictic provision in Article 18(2) of the ICCPR is remarkable for two reasons. First, it confirms a component within freedom of religion or belief that has been—and continues to be—particularly controversial. The freedom to have or adopt a religion or belief implies the possibility of changing one's religion or abandoning any religion. Even sticking to one's inherited religion would cease to be a manifestation of personal freedom, if the option of reconsidering, modifying, or changing did not exist.[24] Second, the protection of the *forum internum* within freedom of religion or belief has received an unusually strong formulation. The prohibition of coercive interferences, including against converts, is one of the few "absolute" norms in international human rights law. It clarifies that not everything can be justified as long as it is based on some more or less plausible pragmatic arguments.

Coercing individuals to profess a faith they do not genuinely believe means nothing less than forcing them to betray themselves. To cite a traditional metaphor coined in the early seventeenth century by Roger Williams, the use of coercion against the nucleus of a person's religious or moral identity would be an act of "soul rape."[25] This can undermine the victim's self-respect beyond repair. Forced self-betrayal furthermore denies the very preconditions of any normative interaction, since it nullifies the due respect for human beings as responsible agents. Brainwashing, too, is a manifestation of total disrespect, comparable to trading and selling people like cattle in a slave market or forcing them to swallow their own excrements, which is a widespread torture practice. Such practices are beyond any conceivable justification.

It is no coincidence that the wording in Article 18(2) of the ICCPR comes close to the formulations used in the absolute prohibitions of slavery and torture. Apart from their practical function as legal safeguards, those absolute prohibitions also fulfill an important symbolic role for the whole system of international human rights protection. They serve as reminders that, in spite of the pragmatic elasticity that human rights norms display in order to be applicable in the real world, not everything is justifiable as soon as strong pragmatic reasons are put on the table. Human rights have the status of inalienable rights after all. This very inalienability implies upholding certain "red lines," which can never be legitimately crossed.[26]

4. Anti-Liberal Distortions of a Human Right

Freedom of religion or belief is a right of *freedom*. This clarification may sound like an utterly trivial remark. Politically speaking, however, it is far from trivial. Various trends obfuscate the defining component of freedom that permeates all aspects of this right: free search for meaning, free articulation of one's belief, free and open communication on religious issues, free religious practice in private and in public, free community developments, and so forth. Strangely enough, even academic commentators sometimes drop the essential component of freedom when employing terms like "the right to religion" or loosely speaking of people's "religious rights." There may be good reasons for using shorthand formulations in human rights law but leaving out the core element of freedom can lead to serious misunderstandings. In recent years, anti-liberal distortions of freedom of religion or belief have emerged under different headings, such as (a) "combating defamation of religions"; (b) protecting collective religious identities; (c) preserving a state-imposed interreligious harmony; or (d) purging the "secular" public sphere of the presence of any visible religion.[27]

(a) "Combating Defamation of Religions"

Until some years ago, one of the biggest challenges to freedom of religion or belief in the United Nations came from demands to fight "defamation of religions." Between 1999 and 2010, the Organisation of Islamic Cooperation (OIC), an intergovernmental body composed of fifty-seven member states,[28] regularly tabled UN resolutions entitled "combating defamation of religions." Although triggering fierce debates, these resolutions in the end always scored a relative majority of votes, albeit with a downward trend as illustrated in the diagram below.[29]

The controversy in the United Nations peaked during the notorious Danish cartoons crisis in 2005–2006. While it is understandable that many Muslims felt offended by those tasteless cartoons, one cannot ignore the danger that political calls for combating such "defamation" could pave the way for authoritarian policies of censorship, criminalization, and other restrictive measures, which would collide with freedom of expression—and with freedom of religion or belief as well.[30] What makes the resolutions on "defamation of religions" particularly confusing is that they convey the message that *religions themselves*—and in particular Islam—should receive

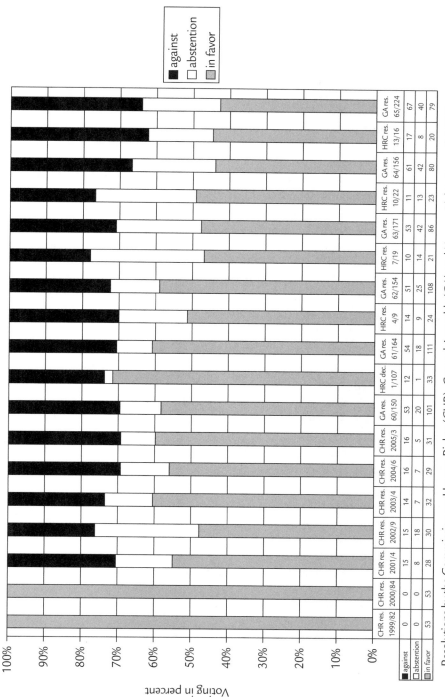

	CHR res. 1999/82	CHR res. 2000/84	CHR res. 2001/4	CHR res. 2002/9	CHR res. 2003/4	CHR res. 2004/6	CHR res. 2005/3	GA res. 60/150	HRC dec. 1/107	GA res. 61/164	HRC res. 4/9	GA res. 62/154	HRC res. 7/19	GA res. 63/171	HRC res. 10/22	GA res. 64/156	HRC res. 13/16	GA res. 65/224
against	0	0	15	15	14	16	16	53	12	54	14	51	10	53	11	61	17	67
abstention	0	0	8	18	7	7	5	20	1	18	9	25	14	42	13	42	8	40
in favor	53	53	28	30	32	29	31	101	33	111	24	108	21	86	23	80	20	79

Resolutions by the Commission on Human Rights (CHR), General Assembly (GA) and Human Rights Council (HRC)

Figure 1. Voting patterns 1999–2010 concerning "Combating defamation of religions"

international legal protection of their reputation. However, the idea of protecting the honor of religions is clearly incompatible with the human rights approach, which institutionalizes respect for the dignity, freedom, and equality of *human beings*. Another problem is that the resolutions appear to legitimize draconian measures, such as anti-blasphemy laws, which typically have intimidating effects on members of religious minorities as well as on religious critics and dissenters. In Pakistan, ill-defined blasphemy offences can even lead to a death sentence.[31]

Owing to their authoritarian spirit, the UN resolutions on combating defamation of religions stand in clear contradiction to a number of human rights, including freedom of religion or belief. Nonetheless, the fact that these resolutions carried "religion" in their title gave rise to superficial perceptions that the whole debate was about the supposedly tense relationship between freedom of religion or belief, on the one hand, and freedom of expression, on the other. The assumption was that while freedom of expression signals "green light" for all sorts of provocations, freedom of religion supposedly functions more like a "stop sign" as soon as religiously delicate issues would be affected. In other words, while freedom of expression was seen as the epitome of a genuinely liberal right, freedom of religion or belief seemed to be a "less liberal" right or even a conservative antidote to an excessive understanding of free speech—or so was the perception.[32] Many years of emotional controversies around the issue of defamation thus contributed to further alienate some liberals from the "liberal" right to freedom of religion or belief.

It was all the more important that Asma Jahangir, UN Special Rapporteur on freedom of religion or belief from 2004 until 2010, clarified that the fight against "defamation" of religions had nothing to do with freedom of religion or belief. She insisted that there can be no right to be free from criticism or even ridicule.[33] Postulating such a right would endanger the very preconditions of an open and pluralistic society, based on intellectual and communicative freedom. Jahangir's successor, Heiner Bielefeldt (Special Rapporteur between 2010 and 2016), followed the same line of argumentation, which also received support from other thematic Special Rapporteurs, most notably Frank La Rue, mandate holder on freedom of expression (2008–2014).[34] Bielefeldt dedicated his last report to the UN Human Rights Council to the "close interrelatedness of freedom of religion or belief and freedom of expression," thus highlighting again that both rights follow the same logic as human rights to intellectual and communicative freedom.[35] The current mandate holder, Ahmed Shaheed, has also called for repealing anti-blasphemy laws as they have a stifling impact both on freedom of religion or belief and on freedom of opinion and expression.[36]

After more than a decade of bitter controversies in different UN forums around this issue, the OIC refrained from tabling a resolution on defamation of religions in 2011. Instead, the organization submitted a resolution titled "Combating intolerance, negative stereotyping and stigmatization of, and discrimination, incitement to violence and violence against persons based on religion or belief." This resolution 16/18 of the UN Human Rights Council was adopted without a vote on 24 March 2011.[37] It has subsequently served as a main reference document in the United Nations. As the complicated title of resolution 16/18 illustrates, the purpose is *protection of human beings* from extreme manifestation of hatred rather than safeguarding the reputation of religions. In this sense, resolution 16/18 signals a step forward. At the same time, caution remains imperative. The anti-hatred legislation in many states is not less vague and diffuse than many of the anti-blasphemy laws, and it can likewise serve as an invitation to employ restrictive measures.[38]

It should be noted in passing that although Western governments mostly voted against the OIC resolutions on "defamation of religions," things are not always clear and consistent in the West.[39] For instance, some European states continue to have anti-blasphemy provisions in their domestic criminal law books.[40] Even some judgments of the European Court of Human Rights remain ambiguous in that they may convey the impression that religious feelings should be protected against offensive expressions deemed "blasphemous" by some believers.[41]

Unfortunately, it currently appears that the debate on "defamation of religions" might reemerge. At a conference held in June 2015 in Jeddah, the old fault lines became again fully visible.[42] During the Jeddah conference, some representatives of the Gulf countries divided the world into states which believe in God and states which believe in freedom of expression. In addition, the Russian Federation has also increasingly pursued a strict anti-blasphemy agenda in recent years. In this context, a superficial "religious freedom" language has been harnessed, with the result that the spirit and letter of freedom of religion or belief, *as a human right of freedom*, becomes increasingly obfuscated. This worrisome trend warrants ongoing critical attention.

(b) Protecting Collective Religious Identities

Another entry-point for profound misunderstandings is the demand for *protecting religious identities*. Whereas the authoritarian overtones of the OIC resolutions on defamation of religions are obvious, demands for respecting collective identities are less clear and have come up in most different political camps. The language of identity can back up right-wing policies of protecting a country's traditional religious hegemony, but it can also be part of left-wing or liberal multiculturalism agendas. Politically speaking, the identity semantics permeates the entire spectrum from nationalistic conservatism to left-wing liberalism and multiculturalism. Be that as it may, the promotion of identity (in the singular) or identities (in the plural) harbors the risk of marginalizing the crucial component of *free choice and free articulation* around which the right to freedom of religion or belief is conceptualized. The warning once raised by Jürgen Habermas against Charles Taylor's multicultural identity semantics, namely that applying ecological categories like the "preservation of different biological species" to human culture would lead to anti-liberal results,[43] has a particular bearing on discussions about religious identities, too. Like other rights of freedom, the right to freedom of religion or belief empowers human beings to freely find their own ways and freely articulate their own convictions, needs, and interests. Freedom of religion or belief cannot be reduced to the recognition or promotion, by the state, of preexisting religious identities. Rather, the state ought to give people the options freely to develop, freely to change, freely to ignore, or freely to defend their individual or communitarian identity and freely to reach out to others and challenge their identities in a noncoercive manner. There is always a risk that the crucial component of freedom gets overshadowed by ubiquitous demands for respecting and protecting identities in themselves.

That danger increases once religious identities get amalgamated with ethnic or "racial" identities. It is true that some religious communities define themselves by an assumed common ethnic origin, with the result that phenomena of ethnic and religious identities overlap. In order to address such overlapping phenomena, the UN Human Rights Council established an ad hoc committee mandated to discuss possible new standards complementing the International Convention on the Elimination of All Forms of Racial Discrimination (ICERD). The idea is that those complementary standards would specifically deal with discrimination faced by religious groups within the context of racism.[44] However, a systematic integration of religious issues into the framework of anti-racism could lead to an "ethnicization" or even "racialization" of religions, with highly problematic implications for the understanding of freedom of religion or belief.

Although at the *phenomenological level* overlaps between religion and ethnicity undoubtedly exist, the *conceptual distinction* between those categories should be kept intact. Unlike ethnic or "racial" group characteristics (or at least to a much larger degree than those), religions and beliefs typically include intellectual ideas—for instance, metaphysical ideas or ethical norms—which can become objects of reflection, communication, and critical comment. They may furthermore be exposed to systematic theological, philosophical, ethical, or jurisprudential argumentation. Such possibility of critical communication constitutes an indispensable core component of freedom of religion or belief. In this regard, religions and beliefs have a different epistemological status than ethnicities. For instance, whereas critical comments on particular ethnic characteristics—an obvious case would be skin color—have met with broad disapproval,[45] critical remarks on religious ideas like, for instance, monotheism, divine revelation, or reincarnation, although possibly deemed offensive by the affected believers, deserve a different assessment. This follows from the explicit recognition of the rights to free choice and free communication in the area of religion or belief. Simply lumping together religion, belief, ethnicity, "race," and other elements of a person's or a group's identity, with the purpose of protecting such identities, implies the serious risk of eroding crucial elements of freedom of religion or belief, in particular the freedom to search, choose, change, reach out, communicate, convert, invite, and peacefully provoke in the field of religion or belief. Ignoring these components in turn can mean that we could too easily fall prey to yet another debate on combating "defamation" of religions or end up with similar conceptual misunderstandings, which conceivably could even arise from within the midst of the human rights community itself.

(c) State-Imposed Interreligious Harmony

Another source of confusion is the amalgamation of freedom of religion or belief with projects of fostering interreligious harmony. Governments when talking positively about the situation of freedom of religion or belief in their countries often conjure up the harmonious relations between the various faith groups, thereby implicitly assuming that freedom of religion or belief is tantamount to such harmony. At a closer look, however, this assumption proves questionable. Surely, human rights are part of a peace project. The preamble of the UDHR proclaims that respect for human rights constitutes "the foundation of freedom, justice and *peace in the world*."[46] However, a peace based on recognizing people's most diverse deep convictions and concomitant practices will always sit uneasy with authoritarian ideas of a state-imposed societal "harmony." Moreover, freedom of religion or belief inter alia protects the rights of minorities, internal minorities within minorities, converts and reconverts, reformers, including feminist theologians, just as it recognizes the rights of followers of mainstream theologies, orthodoxies, or conservative interpretations of religious traditions. Hence, a society respectful of freedom of religion or belief for everyone will inevitably be a religiously diverse society, with shifting boundaries between different communities and subcommunities. Such a society will furthermore accommodate peaceful competition and intellectual controversies on religious and belief-related questions. In other words: if freedom of religion or belief is part of a broader peace project, this will be a not too harmonious peace. What Kant ironically remarked in the introduction to his essay on "Perpetual Peace," namely, that peace should not be mistaken for the tranquillity of a graveyard,[47] likewise applies to the peace facilitated by freedom of religion or belief: it will be a noisy peace, possibly alongside a certain degree of messianic messiness.

Important test cases in this regard are the closely related issues of conversion and missionary activities. Many states—especially in the Middle East and in large parts of Southern and South-Eastern Asia—restrict the possibilities to change a religion or to invite others to reconsider their faith. Restrictive political measures range from social mobbing and structural discrimination in education or the labor market to administrative obstacles and even criminal sanctions.[48] Some governments claim that by prohibiting "proselytism," "unethical conversions," or similar practices they want to uphold societal peace and interreligious harmony. The same argument is also used to back up measures targeting religious dissidents or people holding "deviant" interpretations of their faith. Imposing such prohibitions and restrictions in the name of interreligious harmony, however, has nothing to do with the peace project envisioned in the UDHR, which defines peace by respect for everyone's human dignity, freedom, and equality.

(d) Purging the "Secular" Public Space of Visible Religion

Authoritarian ideas of a state-imposed harmony also occur in the name of "negative freedom of religion" or as some prefer to call it, "freedom *from* religion."[49] Many people associate religion with bigotry, moralistic complacency, community pressure, religious dogmatism, fanaticism, or even violence. Some would therefore prefer to live in a society without any visible and audible religion. The idea is that while in the private sphere everybody should be allowed to think, believe, and practice whatever they wish, the public sphere should remain clear of the "disturbing" presence of religious speeches and symbols and in that specific sense be purely "secular."[50] In his song "Imagine All the People," John Lennon in 1971 invoked such a vision. Verse after verse, the refrain always ends with the words "and no religion, too." One should not underestimate the popularity of such ideas in larger milieus within and beyond Western societies.[51]

As mentioned previously, freedom of religion or belief actually has the "negative" component of also protecting the freedom not to profess a religion or belief, not to attend worship, or just not to care about religious or belief-related issues, and so on. The same holds true for freedom of expression, freedom of peaceful assembly, freedom of association, and other rights of freedom, all of which have their "positive" and "negative" applications. Any attempt to isolate one of those components would undermine the liberating essence of freedom of religion or belief in general. Just as those who exclusively focus on the "positive" application typically marginalize the freedom *from* religion, an undue focus on its "negative" side would likewise lead to anti-liberal results. "Freedom *from* religion," when seen in isolation, is sometimes used to justify authoritarian policies of purging the public sphere of any open religious manifestations. Much of this happens under the auspices of secularism—a term open to most different interpretations, as we will discuss in Chapter 5.

Freedom "from" religion has an indispensable role to play by protecting people against any pressure, especially by the state or in state institutions, to profess a religion or belief or to participate in religious activities against their will. However, freedom from religion does not provide anyone with a legal title against exposure to visible or audible religion in the public sphere. The right to publicly manifest one's religious or belief-related conviction, either individually or in community with others, is enshrined in clear terms in all international guarantees of freedom of religion or belief, including

Article 18 of the ICCPR, which explicitly covers manifestations in public or private. A policy of enforced "privatization" of religion would thus presuppose an authoritarian regime disrespectful of human rights. It would furthermore be at odds with the idea of a pluralistic society.

5. Toward a Complex Understanding of Freedom

In the case of freedom of religion or belief, the principle of freedom warrants highlighting, since this human right has been exposed to practical, ideological, and conceptual distortions. To start with the practical level, many governments loosely and broadly invoke limitation clauses in order to "balance" human rights norms out against all sorts of public order interests. Given the experience of numerous abuses of limitation clauses, it remains important to stress that limitation clauses do not give those in power a carte blanche to restrict freedom of religion or belief as they see fit. It is the other way around in that limitations to rights of freedom should generally be considered illegitimate—unless and until the government presents persuasive arguments in accordance with all the criteria laid down for that purpose. Instead of permitting a general "balancing" of freedom of religion or belief against competing rights and other important interests, the logic of justification requirements should strictly apply in order to safeguard the substance of freedom of religion or belief in situations in which this right collides, or seems to collide, with other important considerations.

Apart from ongoing restrictive practices, freedom of religion or belief has also seen far-reaching ideological distortions. In the past, UN resolutions wrongly confused freedom of religion or belief with authoritarian policies of "combating defamation of religions." Another danger stems from the primacy given to the preservation of collective religious identities or the maintenance of a state-imposed interreligious "harmony." Freedom *from* religion can also become a pretext for twisting freedom of religion into a mere private right, at the expense of manifestations in public life. These and other authoritarian distortions, especially when enacted under the auspices of religious traditionalism, may further nourish a reluctance, which exists on the side of some liberals, to fully appreciate the significance of freedom of religion or belief as part of a holistic human rights agenda.

Finally, distortions also arise from shallow (mis)conceptualizations of freedom itself. Those who reduce freedom to a particular urban, ironic, and religiously dispassionate "lifestyle" miss the point that rights to freedom open up the space for a much broader diversity of convictions and practices, possibly beyond what some liberals may consider "normal." Commentators who even construe an abstract dichotomy between "being free" and "being faithful" fail to do justice to the experience that remaining faithful to one's freely developed personal commitments—religious or otherwise—can be a profound experience of one's *successful self-determination*, provided it remains free from coercive interferences. By challenging such wrong dichotomies, freedom of religion or belief contributes to a more demanding understanding of the multidimensionality of human freedom and thus to a more sophisticated conceptualization of the human rights project in general.

CHAPTER 3

Equality in Diversity

1. Freedom of Religion Versus Equality?

The cover of a report published by the International Network of Civil Liberties Organizations (INCLO) depicts two signposts placed crosswise. While one of the posts points to "Religion," the other points to "Equality," which lies in the opposite direction. The report is entitled: "Drawing the Line: Tackling Tensions Between Religious Freedom and Equality."[1] This wording suggests that the relationship between freedom of religion or belief, on the one hand, and the principles of equality, on the other, is complicated and characterized by "tensions." No doubt, this is correct. The cover picture, however, goes a big step further. It seems to indicate that the two purposes—religious freedom and equality—lie in completely opposite directions. Whoever follows the path of religious freedom will thus necessarily move away from equality, and those who want to pursue agendas of equality and nondiscrimination must break away from freedom of religion or belief—or this seems to be the implicit message the cover picture conveys.

After the discussions on universalism (in Chapter 1) and freedom (in Chapter 2), the present chapter deals with equality and its corollary: nondiscrimination. Equality is yet another pillar upon which the human rights approach is premised. The first sentence of the preamble of the UDHR links everyone's inherent dignity to their "*equal* and inalienable rights."[2] The first sentence of Article 1 of the UDHR likewise emphasizes the significance of equality when proclaiming that "All human beings are born free and *equal* in dignity and rights."[3] The subsequent Article 2 draws the practical consequences by clarifying that "Everyone is entitled to all the rights and freedoms set forth in this Declaration, without distinction of any kind, such as race, colour, sex, language, religion, political or other opinion, national or social origin, property, birth or other status."

When dealing with equality in the context of freedom of religion or belief we have to face two different challenges. One problem concerns the internal inequality within religious communities, many of which continue to be bastions of male hegemony. Until this day, clerical positions in the Catholic Church, in Orthodox and Old Oriental churches, in the traditional currents of Judaism, Islam, and other religions remain reserved to males. We will tackle this issue in the next chapter, which includes a section on gender relations.[4] The second challenge stems from claims for what on the surface may look like "special treatment" of religious minorities. Religious communities, in particular members of minorities, sometimes demand "extras" for themselves, such as additional days off for celebrating their religious holidays or accommodation of special dietary rules in schools and canteens. They may even call for exemptions from generally binding laws and regulations. Much of this happens in the name of diversity. This begs the question to which degree the accommodation of diversity is compatible with the principle of equality. Does the politics of religious diversity in the long run undermine the principle of equality? If taken to its extremes, does the insistence on respect for diversity not imply privileged treatment for some at the expense of discriminating against others? "To continue to use the word [religion] in law is to invite discrimination," the editors of *Politics of Religious Freedom* emphasize in their introduction.[5] The cover picture of the INCLO report seems to illustrate exactly that message.

The purpose of the present chapter is to demonstrate that, from a human rights perspective, the principles of equality and diversity, rather than being antagonistic, actually belong together. In Section 2, we elaborate a "diversity-friendly" concept of equality, which requires taking freedom into the equation. Section 3 highlights that equality can only make sense when consistently applied to human beings as rights holders, not to religions or belief systems themselves. Unpacking indirect and structural discriminations on grounds of religion or belief is the theme in Section 4. When searching for responses to these challenges, we have to look into the potential of "reasonable accommodation" (Section 5), which in the context of the Convention on the Rights of Persons with Disabilities has become a binding requirement (Section 6). The chapter finishes with a short reflection on the idea of "complex equality" (Section 7).

2. A Diversity-Friendly Concept of Equality

What does equality mean in the framework of human rights, and how does it relate to diversity, including religious diversity? If we assume that the principle of equality requires *identical treatment* of all, then equality and diversity will be natural opponents. According to that understanding, any insistence on equality necessarily shrinks the space for diversity, while a preference for diversity, in turn, undermines the principle of equality. There are examples illustrating that such antagonistic ideas of equality versus diversity actually exist. A few years ago, a French mayor announced that the school canteens of his city would no longer cater to the special needs of Jewish and Muslim students. He underpinned his announcement by invoking the principle of "*égalité*," which he implicitly equated with identical treatment, at the expense of diversity.[6] If his policy of equality, understood as sameness, were actually carried out, it would mean that many children from religious minorities would no longer be able to take their meals together with their schoolmates from mainstream society. The politics of equality can thus assume an anti-liberal, restrictive meaning; it can come close to fostering homogeneity or uniformity in society.

Based on such an understanding of "equality as sameness," those who wish to broaden the space for diversity may in turn be tempted to limit the impact of equality. Working for more diversity can thus assume an anti-egalitarian direction. Even today commentators at times cite a formula coined by Aristotle, who in his Nicomachean Ethics demanded that "equal things be treated equally and unequal things be treated unequally."[7] One should note that this Aristotelian formula is very remote from any human rights thinking. Apart from presupposing unequal roles and status positions for men and women, Aristotle even held that some humans were "by nature" slaves, whereas others were "by nature" free and thus entitled to possess slaves.[8] Considering that the proposition "equal things equally and unequal things unequally" historically served to justify slavery, it is somewhat surprising, to say the least, that the Aristotelian formula still occurs in contemporary literature on equality, diversity, and nondiscrimination.[9]

Do we thus face the dilemma of opting either for equality or for diversity? Can we at best strike an uneasy, precarious compromise between the two? In order to overcome this predicament, we have to resort to the concept of freedom, as already discussed in the previous chapter. The principle of freedom is intrinsically connected to both equality and diversity. When seen in that interconnectedness, both notions change their meaning: while equality becomes diversity-friendly, diversity no longer remains in abstract opposition to equality.

In the history of political thought, Kant was one of the first to elaborate the interconnectedness of freedom and equality. In his Metaphysics of Morals, he points out that freedom and equality are inextricably intertwined.[10] Far from representing two separate, let alone antagonistic principles, freedom and equality are actually *interrelated aspects of one and the same principle* or two sides of the same coin, as it were. For it is only in connection with equality that freedom can operate as the guiding principle of the legal order of rights. Rather than being limited by traditions, customs, or other external factors, as it was the predominant understanding in the European history of political thinking, the right to freedom should only be limited by respect for the *equal freedom* of others. In Kant's language, the idea of everyone's "birthright" to freedom necessarily requires equality in the guarantee of freedom.[11] This understanding constitutes no less than a paradigm shift in the conceptualization of freedom, which no longer remains a privilege reserved to those holding particular status positions. Instead, freedom becomes the guiding principle for a legal order of universal and egalitarian rights.

Just as freedom is conceptualized in close connection to equality, the principle of equality in turn is inherently linked to freedom. From a human rights perspective, equality has nothing whatsoever to do with "sameness," uniformity, or homogeneity. As long as the concept of equality is confused with sameness, it will inevitably have an anti-liberal, restrictive, or even authoritarian tone, as illustrated by the abovementioned French mayor who refused to cater to the special needs of religious minorities in school canteens. Highlighting the interconnectedness of equality and freedom changes the picture entirely. Seen from this angle, human rights are *rights to equal freedom of everyone.* They empower human beings freely to pursue their diverse life plans, freely to express their various political opinions, or freely to manifest their different faith-related convictions and practices. Freedom naturally implies accommodation of diversity at all levels. Now, the decisive point is that such respect for freedom and concomitant diversity, rather than privileging certain people of status and rank, is due to everyone equally—in recognition of the universal status position defined by human dignity.[12] This is the innovative shift of meaning in the conceptualization of both freedom and equality. Working for an equal implementation of human rights of freedom for everyone will thus make societies both more egalitarian and at the same time more diverse or pluralistic. In that sense the principles of equality and diversity, including religious diversity, are well compatible with each other. Indeed, they basically reinforce one another. Thus, the Council of Europe was well advised when launching a prodiversity campaign under the egalitarian motto of "all different, all equal."[13]

3. Equality of Humans, Not of Religions

When applying the reflections just undertaken to the more specific context of freedom of religion or belief, we have again to remind ourselves that the principle of equality—like other human rights principles—does not directly relate to religions or beliefs as such. Instead, it relates to *human beings*. Without bearing in mind that human beings are the right holders of freedom of religion or belief, the whole discussion on equality would be doomed to plunge into absurdities, because religions or beliefs as such cannot function as reference points for any meaningful equality claim. Religious views and practices display an inexhaustible diversity. What is considered a sacred duty in the framework of one religion may seem blasphemous from the perspective of another religion. Given the enormous diversity of existing worldviews and practices, there is no common reference point upon which to fix equality claims—unless we focus on human beings. Indeed, human beings constitute the only common denominator that runs through the whole range of different religions and beliefs, both concerning their doctrines and their ceremonial or ethical practices. Consequently, it is human beings who can lay claim to equality, since they are the ones potentially suffering from a lack of such equality. Examples stem from all parts of the globe: the discriminatory exclusion of Baha'is in the Islamic Republic of Iran from any higher education, problems that atheists in Jordan face when wishing to contract a valid marriage within the national family law system, economic boycotts imposed on Muslim minorities in Myanmar, and so on. As different as these phenomena may be, what they have in common is that human beings suffer discriminatory treatment because of their religion or belief.

The UN Declaration on the Elimination of All Forms of Intolerance and of Discrimination Based on Religion or Belief, adopted by the UN

General Assembly on 25 November 1981, also shows a consistent focus on human beings. Article 3 contains an unusually strong formulation when proclaiming that "Discrimination between human beings on grounds of religion or belief constitutes an affront to human dignity and a disavowal of the principles of the Charter of the United Nations, and shall be condemned as a violation of the human rights and fundamental freedoms proclaimed in the Universal Declaration of Human Rights."

The prohibition of discrimination—that is, the corollary of the principle of equality—exists in all major human rights documents. We have already cited the first sentence of Article 2 of the UDHR. Exactly the same enumeration is included in the two Covenants of 1966, the International Covenant on Economic, Social and Cultural Rights (ICESCR) and the International Covenant on Civil and Political Rights (ICCPR). Among the explicitly enumerated grounds of prohibited differentiation they inter alia list "religion." Here is the formulation: "Each State Party to the present Covenant undertakes to respect and to ensure to all individuals within its territory and subject to its jurisdiction the rights recognized in the present Covenant, without distinction of any kind, such as race, colour, sex, language, religion, political or other opinion, national or social origin, property, birth or other status." More recent human rights documents have amended this enumeration by adding disability, age, sexual orientation, and gender identity. Already the 1981 Declaration complements "religion" by adding "belief," a term designed to also cover nonreligious convictions. Admittedly, the term "belief" can cause misunderstandings, since many nonreligious people call themselves "non-believers." The French version of the Declaration is clearer by using the term "conviction" to complement "religion."

4. Tackling Concealed Forms of Discrimination

After the adoption of the UDHR, the international discussion on equality and nondiscrimination has seen enormous strides. Apart from tackling ongoing forms of open and direct discrimination, which occur in all societies across the continents, we have also become more sensitive to concealed forms of discrimination, such as indirect and structural discrimination. The existing norms and structures of a society, even if on the surface applying to everyone equally, typically reflect the implicit standpoints of the majority. More or less inevitably they reinforce majority religions, predominant cultures, hegemonic lifestyles, and so on. In the context of religion, many examples may come to mind, ranging from the seven-day week and public religious holidays to the dress codes prescribed in public institutions or private companies. The everyday rhythm of life, the usual greeting rituals, or the weekly fish served in canteens on Fridays—all of this reflects certain religious traditions, which continue to exercise their influence, far beyond what people usually are aware of.[14]

What members of the majority population may take for granted can cause serious problems for minorities. For example, dress codes in public institutions, which for the majority seem just "natural" or "neutral,"[15] may impose an extra burden on members of certain religious minorities. Work schedules in companies can create difficulties for people who, owing to specific religious prescripts, feel obliged not to work on certain days. Professional duties defined by hospitals or other institutions may collide with deeply held conscientious convictions. The food offered in school canteens may reflect the predominant dietary customs of mainstream society. What should we do about this? Policies of accommodating more diversity can alleviate the indirectly discriminatory implications that existing societal structures may have on (religious) minorities. The question, though, is how far such accommodation should go.

Even a society that aims to fully implement a diversity-friendly equality may face difficulties when wishing to grant maximum accommodation. One typical stumbling block is public holidays originating from a particular religious tradition. From the standpoint of strict equality, one could hypothetically demand that the state either abolish all holidays relating to a liturgical calendar or enlarge the list of public holidays by taking on board the main festivities of all religions and beliefs that happen to exist in the country; most likely, this will be impossible in practice. Moreover, an unqualified accommodation of the special needs of minorities, including by granting exemptions from generally binding regulations, may create unease in the society. If the impression emerges that only members of the majority are supposed to abide by general laws and regulations, while minorities always get exemptions or other "extras," this may in the long run undermine the appreciation of diversity in a society. We obviously need more precise criteria for defining the adequate space for special needs.

5. The Significance of "Reasonable Accommodation"

In 1963, the US Supreme Court decided a case in favor of a Seventh-Day Adventist, Adeil Sherbert, who had lost her employment because of her refusal to work on Saturdays. The administration had rejected her claim for unemployment compensation arguing that she herself had been responsible for the loss of her job. In the end, however, Sherbert won her court case by invoking her right to religious freedom. In its judgment *Sherbert v. Verner*, the US Supreme Court developed a formula which subsequently became known as the "Sherbert test."[16] Under its first prong, the court has to determine whether the person has a claim involving a sincerely held religious belief, and whether the government action has caused a substantial burden on that person's ability to act on that belief. If the first prong is passed, the government must prove that it is acting in furtherance of a "compelling state interest" and that it has pursued this interest in the manner least restrictive, or least burdensome, to the person's religious conviction. The Sherbert case marks the beginning of a whole series of court cases in the United States on religiously motivated claims for accommodation. The outcomes of the judgments differ vastly. Whereas in some cases the courts have shown a high degree of openness for accommodating specific religious needs unless they collide with a "compelling state interest," other cases have led to more cautious decisions.[17] Courts have been particularly reluctant in cases that concern the private sector.

Next to the US, Canada became a field for experimenting with claims for accommodation. The country officially endorsed multiculturalism as part of the Canadian Charter of Rights and Freedoms, adopted in 1982. Section 27 provides: "This Charter shall be interpreted in a manner consistent with the preservation and enhancement of the multicultural heritage of Canadians." Legislators and courts have ever since shown dedication to creating adequate space for the special needs of ethnic, linguistic, cultural, and not least religious minorities. A particularly controversial case concerned a Sikh teenage boy who insisted on keeping his *kirpan* (a dagger with a high symbolic relevance for the Sikhs) when attending school, in spite of the school's clear anti-weapon policy. The Canadian Supreme Court decided in favor of the boy's freedom of religion, while at the same time requesting that his kirpan be safely sewn into his jacket to make sure that it could not be used in a threatening manner.[18]

Even in Canada, a country particularly dedicated to multiculturalism and minority rights, measures of accommodation have met with skepticism in parts of the population, who perceived these measures as privileging minorities. Critics have pointed to the danger that a policy of always "giving in" to minorities might in the end lead to a breakdown of public order and erode the equality of all before the law. In order to dispel such anxieties, the Government of Quebec instituted a commission mandated with clarifying the scope and limits of reasonable accommodation. The "Bouchard-Taylor Commission," named after its two chairpersons (one of whom was the well-known Canadian philosopher Charles Taylor), presented its conclusions and recommendations in 2008. In its report, the commission takes equality as its starting point, while clarifying that equality does not necessarily "have as a corollary uniformity or homogeneity."[19] According to the report, cases of individual adjustment can well be in the interest of an adequately conceptualized equality: "a given right may demand adjustments in treatment that must not be equated with privileges or exemptions since they are intended to remedy a flaw in the application of a statute or a regulation." The commission further notes that "a treatment can be differential without being preferential," which is an interesting formulation.[20] Under the heading of "undue hardship" the commission subsequently addresses a number of limitations to accommodation to make sure that the requested measures remain within the confines of reasonableness: "Accommodation or adjustment requests are . . . limited by: a) the institution's aim (provide care, educate, make profit, and so on); b) the financial cost and functional constraints; c) other people's rights."[21] As was the case with the Sherbert test developed by the US Supreme Court, the Bouchard-Taylor Commission, too, employs a multiperspective approach. Rather than one-sidedly focusing on freedom of religion of certain minorities, the commission also takes into account the fundamental rights and legitimate important interests of other people.

In discussions of reasonable accommodation, the adjective "reasonable" is mostly perceived as a pragmatic caveat to ensure that accommodation remains generally manageable. In that sense, reasonableness inter alia requires avoiding undue financial and managerial burdens placed on employers, companies, or other institutions on which it falls to grant such accommodation. However, the requirement of "reasonableness" could also be interpreted in a more principled manner, that is, beyond its pragmatic function. For measures of accommodation to find broad endorsement, the population at large should be able to see that the proposed measures are based on fair and transparent criteria. Among those criteria, equality must remain the overarching consideration.

With a view to further exploring criteria for the "reasonableness" of accommodation, let us turn to a definition proposed by Gabrielle Caceres. She writes: "Reasonable accommodation aims at relaxing generally applicable rules in order to guarantee a more substantive equality in which the specificities of everyone are taken into account."[22] According to this definition, measures of accommodation serve the purpose of achieving a "substantial equality," which goes beyond a mere "formal equality" by taking into account certain important "specificities"—specific needs, specific vulnerabilities, specific characteristics, and so forth—of certain individuals or groups. What is remarkable is that Caceres at the same time uses the term "everyone" in her definition. That is, in order to be fully reasonable, measures of accommodation must be justifiable within a horizon of egalitarian universalism. This obviously does not mean that everyone can immediately benefit from certain measures of accommodation that have been enacted for the sake of specific religious minorities. For example, a special permission not to work on Saturdays, when being granted for members of the Seventh-Day Adventist Church, remains confined to a comparatively small circle of people; it is not an exemption that everyone can likewise lay claim to. Instead, what the term "everyone" signifies in the above definition is that a specific solution found for a specific situation should be based on universalistic and egalitarian criteria, that is, criteria that would facilitate a similar solution for "everyone," provided they can plausibly claim to be in a similar situation of special need or vulnerability. Thus, the guiding criteria underneath the measures taken in a concrete context, at the same time, must have a bearing also beyond that particular context.

At first glance, measures of accommodation frequently look like exceptions from general rules. However, as Cole Durham insists, "The carve-out made by accommodation is not a distinction made for an arbitrary reason that creates an anomalous legal exception, but one driven by the need to take a fundamental constitutional norm—freedom of conscience—into account."[23] This is an important clarification. Instead of defining accommodation as an "anomalous exception" from given rules, it makes more sense to interpret the measures taken in analogy to a "precedent" within the judiciary, which helps further develop and fine-tune the rules. Although elaborated within a specific context and for the benefit of specific people, they at least implicitly set a "model" that could be relevant for other people as well—ultimately for "everyone" who could plausibly claim to be in a comparable situation. In this sense, the analogy of a "precedent" combines universalism and context orientation. It transcends the mere particularities of a contextualized case by testing the criteria that guide a case-related solution as to whether they could provide guidance for other cases as well— and eventually for everyone who could claim recognition for similar specific needs in similar circumstances.

In Caceres's abovementioned definition the two terms "everyone" and "specificities" are closely intertwined. On the one hand, there is the element of specificities: certain people wish to receive accommodation of their specific needs. On the other hand, for such accommodation to be fully legitimate, it cannot remain a privilege of those who happen to benefit from a particular solution, but should become a broader pattern to which—at least hypothetically—everyone should be able to refer when living in a comparable situation of specific need, specific vulnerability, specific structural discrimination, and so forth. Admittedly, whether and to which degree situations of need are actually comparable will remain contested in many cases. Yet the underlying principle has a solid human rights basis. It requires that measures of accommodation be justifiable in the light of egalitarian universalism in order to be fully "reasonable."[24]

The concept of reasonable accommodation thus understood does not provide a general blueprint for dealing with claims of minorities. Instead, it takes shape in a case-by-case manner. At the same time, it transcends the particularities of individual cases and specific situations by spelling out criteria which themselves do justice to the overarching principles of universalism and equality. This is a demanding concept, which in order to be applicable in practice requires a culture of communication between all concerned parties. In a polarized political climate characterized by cultural wars and growing ideological confrontation, the implementation of reasonable accommodation will always become difficult.

Members of minorities when requesting special measures for themselves should be willing and able to demonstrate that such requests stem from existential interests, the denial of which would expose them to a serious predicament.[25] This requirement should dispel anxieties often existing in mainstream society that policies of accommodation could in the long run open the floodgates to increasingly trivial demands, while at the same time eroding the principle of equality. Accommodation should not be available to just give in to personal tastes, whims, or preferences. People within majority society should thus be able to understand that the purpose of accommodation it not to fulfill a mere "wish list" created by noisy minorities, but to alleviate the effects of indirect and structural discrimination, which frequently occur where existing structures of mainstream society provide the implicit yardstick for regulating societal interaction.

The concept of reasonable accommodation thus understood is based on the intrinsic interrelatedness of equality and diversity, an interrelatedness that is more than a mere external combination of two different principles. We have already elaborated that equality as a human rights principle can only make sense when facilitating diversity. Now we would like to add that this logic also goes the other way around in that *diversity cannot serve as an argument for special treatment or special accommodation unless it remains within the normative horizon of equality.* To cite again one of the formulations of the Bouchard-Taylor Commission: a certain measure of accommodation, while obviously being "differential," should not be "preferential." A diversity-friendly concept of equality and an equality-oriented concept of diversity thus mutually presuppose each other. In other words, measures of reasonably accommodating diversity have nothing whatsoever in common with the Aristotelian formula of "equal things equally and unequal things unequally." Instead, accommodation becomes an essential ingredient of an adequately complex notion of equality based on due respect for everyone's equal dignity and equal freedom.

6. "Reasonable Accommodation" in International Human Rights Law

Unlike in the US and Canada, European legislators and courts have to date been rather reluctant to endorse the concept of reasonable accommodation as part of efficient nondiscrimination agendas. The EU-funded "RELIGARE" project, composed of an international consortium of scholars from different disciplines, concludes that reasonable accommodation within the EU is often rejected even in situations where it would not imply any financial or other costs.[26] Within the RELIGARE research, Katayoun Alidadi undertook a comparative study of the situation in three EU countries—Belgium, the Netherlands, and the UK. She summarizes her findings as follows: "One worrying observation made in the study was that particular religious requests, such as the request to wear a headscarf on the job or to make use of an available space for prayer during break times, can trigger restrictive responses even if they do not actually impede or disturb the running of the business, but because of the 'uncomfortable situation' they create."[27] Things are apparently moving very slowly in Europe, even within the European Court of Human Rights. For example, an orthodox Jew, who had requested that a court hearing on a civil suit should not take place on Yom Kippur, the highest Jewish holiday, remained unsuccessful, even though he had submitted his request more than half a year before the scheduled hearing. When challenging the decision before the European Court of Human Rights, he again lost his case in a four to three judgment.[28] This is an embarrassing outcome. A Polish prisoner was more successful when invoking his freedom of conscience before the Strasbourg Court to request vegetarian food.[29] A British Airways employee, too, won her case in Strasbourg when insisting that, as a practicing Christian, she wanted to wear a necklace with a visible cross over her uniform, even though religious symbols deviate from the airline's general dress code policy.[30] This case of *Eweida v. UK* signals a careful opening up of the Strasbourg Court's jurisprudence for concerns of reasonable accommodation.

Reasonable accommodation has meanwhile become part of an international human rights treaty, namely, the Convention on the Rights of Persons with Disabilities (CRPD), which the UN General Assembly adopted in December 2006. Article 2 of the CRPD defines: " 'Reasonable accommodation' means necessary and appropriate modification and adjustments not imposing a disproportionate or undue burden, where needed in a particular case, to ensure to persons with disabilities the enjoyment or exercise on an equal basis with others of all human rights and fundamental freedoms." That definition already contextualizes reasonable accommodation as part of a policy of ensuring equality, as corroborated in the wording "on an equal basis with others." Article 5 obligates states to create adequate condition for the application of reasonable accommodation, with a view to achieving substantial equality. Its third paragraph reads as follows: "In order to promote equality and eliminate discrimination, States Parties shall take all appropriate steps to ensure that reasonable accommodation is provided." Failure to employ measures of reasonable accommodation in cases where this would not lead to a "disproportionate and undue burden" henceforth counts as discrimination, that is, a violation of equality.[31] While specifically focusing on persons with disability, the CRPD enlarges the understanding of discrimination in general, with repercussions on any future antidiscrimination agenda, not only in the area of disability.[32] One can only hope that this will in the long run have an impact also on policies against discrimination based on religion or belief, which historically played an important role in shaping the very concept of reasonable accommodation.

7. Complex Equality as a Guiding Principle

We started this chapter by citing critics who hold that freedom of religion or belief stands in an inherent contradiction to claims of equality. The objections culminated in the charge that "to continue to use the word [religion] in law is to invite discrimination." Our own reflection comes to the opposite result: not to refer to religion would mean leaving existing hegemonies and discriminatory structures unchallenged, even undiscussed. The relationship between freedom of religion or belief and broader equality agendas may often prove complicated. However, the idea that the two lie in opposite directions, with the result that people would have to make a choice which path to follow, is seriously flawed.

It is no accident that "religion" figures in the discrimination clauses of all major international human rights instruments. In more recent documents, such as the 1981 Declaration on the Elimination of All Forms of Intolerance and of Discrimination based on Religion or Belief, it has been complemented by the term "belief," which represents an inclusive understanding that covers nonreligious convictions as well. Hence, the assumption that freedom of religion or belief privileges religious over nonreligious worldviews is anachronistic, at least at the conceptual level, although in practice nonreligious worldviews may still receive less attention than they should. This must change. Given that equality and freedom belong together, the principle of equality cannot mean sameness or identical treatment. Instead, its function is to ensure that the fundamental rights of freedom be recognized in all human beings equally. The corollary of this understanding is that the principle of equality itself must accommodate diversity. Indeed, in a human rights context, equality can only make sense as a diversity-friendly equality.

When trying to implement equality of rights, the society has to tackle not only open, but also concealed forms of discrimination, such as indirect or structural discrimination, which is a complicated task, especially in the area of religion or belief. Members of religious minorities frequently suffer discrimination from the fact that open or concealed religious hegemonies govern societal norms and institutions thus putting them systematically at a disadvantage when compared to people from majority religions. Measures of reasonable accommodation can help to overcome, or at least alleviate, such discriminatory consequences by giving more space to the existential needs of minorities, provided this does not impose an undue burden on the institutions that are supposed to provide such special measures. Although the application of reasonable accommodation can lead to complicated questions, its general philosophy has a solid human rights basis. Rather than "privileging" minorities and eroding the principle of equality, measures of accommodation serve the purpose of creating suitable conditions for members of minorities who should be able to live in accordance with their religious or belief-related norms and convictions.

If reasonably applied, measures of accommodation will thus bring society more in line with the principle of equality, which in the context of freedom of religion or belief can only mean a *complex equality* based on respect for the existing diversity of human convictions. In spite of all the difficulties that may arise in particular situations, a general denial of reasonable accommodation would mean no less than to freeze existing power relations, hegemonies, and inequalities. As Martha Nussbaum points out from a US perspective, this would amount to a new version of "establishment," which has been strictly prohibited in the First Amendment of the US Constitution. In her words, "the denial of an accommodation for the free exercise of one's own religion is a type of de facto establishment. It means that the majority's religion has been written into law and minorities have been denied the same opportunity to legalize their own practices."[33] Human rights agendas can contribute to overcoming such forms of "establishment" wherever they exist, thus opening up societal structures to the existing and emerging diversity, without compromising the principle of equality.

CHAPTER 4

Awkward Bedfellows? Religious Freedom and Other Human Rights

1. Rights in Conflict

In the previous chapters, we demonstrated that freedom of religion or belief, when adequately conceptualized, can satisfy the principles which define the human rights approach, as summed up succinctly in the first sentence of Article 1 of the UDHR: "All human beings are born free and equal in dignity and rights." Like other human rights, freedom of religion or belief refers to "all human beings" rather than privileging religious believers over nonbelievers. It aims to protect everyone in their profound, identity-shaping convictions and conviction-based practices (see Chapter 1). We have furthermore argued that freedom of religion or belief carries the term "freedom" for good reasons. While providing practical safeguards against unjustifiable infringements, it at the same time contributes to a more demanding understanding of freedom, which itself is a multifaceted phenomenon and includes the possibility to live faithfully in accordance with one's deeply held convictions (see Chapter 2). Finally, freedom of religion or belief also embodies the principle of equality. Rather than eroding equality, as critics have alleged, freedom of religion or belief facilitates a complex understanding of equality. The principle of equality itself, when taken seriously, requires a readiness to accommodate specific needs of minorities, in accordance with universalistic criteria (see Chapter 3). Apart from being fully compatible with the human rights approach, freedom of religion or belief contributes to a more nuanced understanding of human rights and all their defining principles: universalism, freedom, and equality.

Nonetheless, in the eyes of some commentators, freedom of religion or belief has the ambivalent reputation of a right that does not always tie in smoothly with broader human rights agendas. "Freedom of Religion and Human Rights Laws—Awkward Bedfellows"[1] is the title Peter Cumper has chosen for his analysis of tensions between freedom of religion or belief and other human rights. Many examples may come to mind. The autonomy of religious institutions can collide with the rights of employees to form trade unions and go on strike. In many religious communities, women do not have access to clerical ranks or positions of leadership—a situation that contradicts equality of men and women. The right to sexual and reproductive health conflicts with religiously motivated refusals by pharmacists to sell contraceptives. Politicians have harnessed freedom of religion to argue for restrictive anti-blasphemy laws, which are at odds with freedom of expression. People who refuse to acknowledge equal rights for gays and lesbians frequently base their objections on their religious freedom. This list of normative collisions is far from exhaustive. Do we have to conclude that freedom of religion or belief presents an obstacle to the full realization of human rights?

Before exploring the specific relationship between religious freedom and other human rights issues, we should take into account that such normative conflicts do not exclusively arise in the context of freedom of religion or belief. They occur across the broad range of human rights issues. Take the example of freedom of expression. If people utilize their freedom of speech with the intention of spreading prejudices against ethnic minorities, this obviously is at odds with anti-racism agendas. Right-wing movements also use freedom of assembly to protest against the construction of a refugee residence in their neighborhood. To add another example, empirical research projects based on the freedom to perform scientific activities can collide with issues of data protection and the right to privacy. To a large degree, human rights work is a practice of managing conflicts in the intersection of complicated normative configurations. Conflicts involving freedom of religion or belief are no exception in this regard, and there is nothing special about them.

However, it is remarkable that freedom of expression, even though it is sometimes harnessed for racist agendas, continues to enjoy broad appreciation as an "empowerment right," which remains indispensable for any human rights agenda. The same is true for freedom of assembly. The fact that Islamophobic movements such as *Patriotische Europäer gegen die Islamisierung des Abendlandes* (PEGIDA) in Germany, too, make use of that right does not seriously diminish its reputation as an important ingredient of liberal democracy. Obviously, the exercise of rights of freedom cannot be reserved only for the friends of freedom. Although limitation clauses ensure that the use of a certain human right does not directly violate the rights and freedoms of others, these clauses do not prescribe a "liberal spirit" as a precondition for enjoying one's rights to freedom. The human rights movement has generally learned to cope with tensions arising from the fact that rights of freedom are not an exclusive privilege of the liberal friends of human rights. When it comes to freedom of religion or belief, however, some commentators draw different conclusions. The observation that this right, too, can be utilized for anti-liberal agendas, for instance in the area of gender policies, apparently confirms a suspicion that freedom of religion or belief itself may be the problem.[2]

In the following sections, we address two test cases, namely, the relationship between freedom of religion or belief and freedom of expression (in Section 2) and subsequently the relationship with gender issues, which recently have become more prominent in international human rights debates (in Section 3). The chapter will conclude with a summary of the findings (in Section 4). The main purpose we pursue in this discussion is to argue for a holistic understanding of human rights, all of which are ultimately "universal, indivisible and interrelated and interdependent," to cite a famous formula coined by the 1993 World Conference on Human Rights.[3] Ignoring the positive interrelatedness of human rights might lead to increasing fragmentation, which in turn could ultimately erode the legitimacy of the whole system of international human rights protection.

2. Neighboring Rights: Freedom of Religion and Freedom of Expression

Freedom of religion or belief and freedom of expression are "neighboring rights" both in a literal and in a figurative sense.[4] In a number of international, regional, and national human rights instruments they remarkably occur in successive articles. Articles 18 and 19 of the UDHR and Articles 18 and 19 of the ICCPR tie in well with a pattern also found elsewhere: for example, in the European Convention on Human Rights (Articles 9 and 10), the American Convention on Human Rights (Articles 12 and 13), the African Charter on Human and Peoples' Rights (Articles 8 and 9), the EU

Charter of Fundamental Rights (Articles 10 and 11) as well as a number of national constitutions, such as the German Basic Law (Articles 4 and 5). Some constitutions even accommodate the two rights in one and the same article. The First Amendment to the US Constitution (1791) is one of the earliest examples. More importantly, the two rights at issue display far-reaching structural similarities. They both fall within the category of civil and political rights. In many cases they can be invoked in conjunction, for example, against censorship of religious literature. They share the function of protecting people's freedom to develop their own independent thinking and to have, adopt, and openly communicate about their convictions. It is striking that both rights furthermore give special protection to the *forum internum* against coercive interferences.[5]

Given these far-reaching structural similarities, one may wonder why freedom of religion or belief and freedom of expression should even be two distinct entitlements. Why not merge them into one broader right? Why should freedom of religion or belief not just figure as a subcategory of freedom of expression—roughly following the example of the 1789 French Declaration of Human and Civic Rights, which in Article 10 provides: "No one may be disturbed on account of his opinions, even religious ones, as long as the manifestation of such opinions does not interfere with the established Law and Order."[6] The answer is that much would be lost by such a merger. Whereas freedom of expression protects a person's views and positions widely, freedom of religion or belief focuses more narrowly on those views that have an existential significance for the holder, attaining a certain threshold of cogency, seriousness, cohesion, and importance. In that sense, freedom of religion or belief is more specific than freedom of expression. At the same time, however, it is broader, because it also covers practical manifestations of a person's convictions in all spheres of life, for instance, dress code regulations, dietary prescriptions, the celebration of holidays, processions and pilgrimages, the construction of places of worship, the running of charity organizations, the socialization of children, and so forth. These and many other manifestations go beyond mere "expressions" of ideas of all kinds, as they are protected under freedom of expression. For a Muslim woman, it may be important not only to voice her opinion about religious dress codes, but to actually wear the hijab. A Jehovah's Witness will most likely not be satisfied with the possibility to express his opposition to serving in the military; what counts is that he can actually make sure not to be personally involved in any military activities. Thus Patrick Loobuyck misses this point when opining: "Religious freedom ultimately adds nothing to the freedom of expression."[7] The abovementioned examples should illustrate clearly enough that the specific role of freedom of religion or belief, in comparison to freedom of expression, is to recognize *the practical consequences* of a religious or belief-related conviction in all aspects of daily life. Merging this right with freedom of expression could obfuscate its specific function and thus reduce the overall human rights protection.

Although each of the two rights has its specific function, they move in similar directions. They both protect the integrity of individuals in their capacity to hold and form convictions; they jointly facilitate the exchange of ideas, also beyond political, cultural, religious, or other boundaries; and they thereby strengthen discursive democracy, which can hardly flourish without freedom of religion or belief, freedom of expression, and other rights of freedom, like freedom of peaceful assembly and freedom of association.

Against that background, it is surprising that the relationship between freedom of expression and freedom of religion or belief is sometimes perceived as being antagonistic. Not least in the context of debates about "blasphemous" criticism of religion, some commentators assume that the two rights represent opposite interests. While freedom of expression enjoys the reputation of being the epitome of a liberal right, which opens the space for aggressive criticism, artistic experiments, and political provocations, freedom of religion or belief seems to limit or even shrink that very space—or so is the assumption. And while freedom of expression facilitates critical debates on religious themes, freedom of religion seems to call for respecting religious taboos. In other words, although the right to freedom of religion or belief carries "freedom" in its title, it has the awkward reputation of being a less liberal right, which supposedly functions more like a stopper against too lavishly liberal interpretations of freedom of expression.[8]

Such an antagonistic conceptualization of the two rights even underpins some historical judgments of the European Court of Human Rights, which had to decide on a number of blasphemy cases. The best-known example is the case of *Otto-Preminger-Institut v. Austria* (1994). The Austrian authorities had banned a film titled "Das Liebeskonzil" ("The Council of Love"), which puts paramount figures of the Christian tradition into an erotic context. The Otto-Preminger-Institut, a media enterprise, which wanted to show the film in a few selected cinemas, complained about censorship and a violation of freedom of expression as guaranteed in Article 10 of the European Convention on Human Rights (ECHR). However, this complaint was unsuccessful. The Court in Strasbourg held that the measure taken by the Austrian authorities pursued the legitimate purpose of protecting the feelings of Christian believers. The Court argued that the case at stake "involves weighing up the conflicting interests of the exercise of two fundamental freedoms guaranteed under the Convention, namely the right of the applicant association to impart to the public controversial views . . . , on the one hand, and the right of other persons to proper respect for their freedom of thought, conscience and religion, on the other hand."[9] A minority of three judges sitting in the chamber strongly disagreed with that reasoning. In their dissenting opinion, they questioned that the assumed antagonism between freedom of religion or belief and freedom of expression even existed. These judges based their position on a different understanding of freedom of religion or belief, which in their view did not justify restrictive measures like those taken by the Austrian authorities: "The Convention does not, in terms, guarantee a right to protection of religious feelings. More particularly, such a right cannot be derived from the right to freedom of religion, which in effect includes a right to express views critical of the religious opinions of others."[10]

However, in a unanimous judgment of 25 October 2018, the European Court of Human Rights concluded that in the case of *E. S. v. Austria* the domestic courts had carefully balanced the applicant's "right to freedom of expression with the rights of others to have their religious feelings protected, and to have religious peace preserved in Austrian society" and had "discussed the permissible limits of criticism of religious doctrines versus their disparagement, and found that the applicant's statements had been likely to arouse justified indignation in Muslims."[11] In this recent case, the European Court of Human Rights stressed that the domestic courts had a wide margin of appreciation, which they had not overstepped when convicting the applicant of "disparaging religious doctrines."

As already described in Chapter 2, similar debates took place for more than a decade in the United Nations, usually triggered by resolutions on "combating defamation of religions," tabled by the Organization of Islamic Conference (meanwhile renamed as Organization of Islamic Cooperation, OIC). Lack of precision in the definition of what constitutes "defamation" was one of the reasons why these resolutions evoked controversies and political resistance. Given the fact that anti-blasphemy laws usually have chilling effects on the exercise of freedom of expression, a superficial impression emerged that the resolutions on defamation of religions would be a test case illustrating the inherent antagonism between freedom of religion, on the one hand, and freedom of expression, on the other. It was all the more important that Asma Jahangir, UN Special Rapporteur on freedom of religion or belief from 2004 to 2010, publicly contradicted this understanding. She argued that "blasphemy laws and the concept of 'defamation of religions' can be counterproductive since they may create an atmosphere of intolerance or fear and ultimately might establish a normative hierarchy of beliefs."[12] Moreover, experiences from countries like Pakistan,[13] which entertains a particularly draconic set of prohibitions of blasphemy in its criminal code, provide ample evidence that those laws particularly intimidate religious minorities and religious dissidents. In addition to undermining the exercise of freedom of expression, they also violate freedom of religion or belief. Jahangir turned the problematic defamation resolutions into an argument demonstrating that freedom of expression and freedom of religion or belief inextricably belong together in the fight against authoritarian policies. She stressed that "the right to freedom of religion or belief needs other human rights to be fully exercised, including the right to freedom of association or the right to freedom of expression."[14] Measures that threaten freedom of expression often simultaneously threaten freedom of religion or belief, and vice versa. Jahangir's position thus resembles the minority opinion in the abovementioned Otto-Preminger case. Similar to the approach taken by the three dissenting judges she pointed out: "Freedom of religion primarily confers a right to act with one's religion but does not bestow a right for believers to have their religion itself protected from all adverse comment."[15] Asma Jahangir's successors Heiner Bielefeldt (2010–2016) and Ahmed Shaheed (on the mandate since November 2016) have pursued the same line of arguing in their reports to the Human Rights Council and General Assembly.[16]

To emphasize the positive interrelatedness of freedom of religion or belief and freedom of expression does not mean to deny possible conflicts between the two rights.[17] For instance, if polemical attacks occurring in the name of freedom of expression aggressively target certain religious minorities, with the result that members of the targeted groups no longer dare to visibly manifest their faith, this will pose a serious problem from the viewpoint of freedom of religion or belief. In such situations, it may be necessary to limit freedom of expression in the interest of protecting freedom of religion or belief. The purpose of limitations, however, can never be to protect the "honor" of religion against criticism or ridicule (as in the resolutions on "combating defamation of religions") or to protect the "religious feelings" of believers (as in the Otto-Preminger judgment); these two considerations are not covered by the right to freedom of religion or belief. Instead, the purpose must be to defend human beings in their freedom to manifest their religion or belief without fear. Moreover, for restrictions on freedom of expression to be justifiable, the threshold must remain much higher and must be more clearly defined than in the defamation resolutions or in the Otto-Preminger case. What we pointed out in Chapter 2 on the need to handle limitation clauses with caution and diligence, also applies to the limitations clauses connected to freedom of expression. Their invocation can only be legitimate as a last resort and in conformity with all the criteria prescribed for that purpose in Article 19(3) of the ICCPR.

In 2011 and 2012, the Office of the UN High Commissioner for Human Rights conducted a series of expert workshops dedicated to exploring in depth the problem of incitement to hatred, including hatred that targets religious groups. The resulting document has become known as the Rabat Plan of Action on the prohibition of advocacy of national, racial or religious hatred that constitutes incitement to discrimination, hostility or violence, adopted in October 2012 in Rabat.[18] Natan Lerner praises the document as "a timely text, considering the urgency to deal with dangerous manifestations likely to undermine coexistence and threaten the security of vulnerable minorities."[19] While the Rabat Plan of Action acknowledges, as a last resort, the possibility to impose restrictions on freedom of expression in clear cases of incitement to hatred, it generally keeps the threshold for such limitations very high. Based on a proposal submitted by the nongovernmental organization (NGO) "Article 19"[20] and in keeping with respective provisions of international human rights law, the threshold defined in the Rabat Plan contains six elements: (1) the social and political context; (2) the speaker, for example, his or her status and influence; (3) the intent of a speech act (as opposed to mere negligence); (4) its content or form, for example, style, degree of provocation; (5) the extent of the speech, for example, its public nature and the size of its audience; and (6) the likelihood, including imminence, of actually causing harm.[21] It is furthermore remarkable that the Rabat Plan of Action and other recent international documents explicitly call upon states to repeal any existing anti-blasphemy laws.[22]

As the corollary of the high threshold defined for justifiable limitations on freedom of expression, the Rabat Plan of Action advocates for the use of nonrestrictive measures to counter intolerance, stigmatization, and incitement to hatred: "To tackle the root causes of intolerance, a much broader set of policy measures is necessary, for example in the areas of intercultural dialogue—reciprocal knowledge and interaction—or education on pluralism and diversity, and policies empowering minorities and indigenous people to exercise their right to freedom of expression."[23] In a nutshell, the best antidote to problematic uses of freedom of expression is a better use of the same right; this is a key message of the Rabat Plan of Action. It also applies to cases involving Article 18 of the ICCPR, such as manifestations of hatred directed against people on the ground of their religion or belief. This brings us back to the basic insight set out at the beginning of this section, namely the positive interrelatedness of the two rights as enshrined in Articles 18 and 19 of the UDHR and of the ICCPR. Even in complicated situations, their good neighborhood deserves to be cherished.

Incidentally, those who want to counter hate speech chiefly by employing restrictive measures ignore the experience that restrictions often backfire politically. Being summoned before a criminal court can only create a win-win situation for populist politicians who base their campaigns on collective resentments. In case of a judicial victory, they can claim that their aggressive speeches have received the official approval of an independent court. If they end up convicted, they will stage themselves as "martyrs of free speech" against an alleged dictatorship of political correctness. The best strategy against hatred, like that propagated by the PEGIDA movement in Germany, is intelligent and creative counterdemonstrations in order to manifest that entrepreneurs of hatred do not represent "the people" as they like to pretend. At the same time, broad and public demonstrations send important messages of encouragement to targeted minorities who should experience that they are not left alone and that the public space remains safely accessible for everyone.

In a landmark decision of 1958, the Federal Constitutional Court of Germany pointed out that freedom of expression "is in a certain way the foundation of *all* freedoms."[24] Indeed, without freedom of expression, other freedoms like freedom of peaceful assembly, freedom of association, and freedom of religion or belief would be inconceivable. Rights to freedom can only flourish where people have an opportunity to voice their grievances, express their positions, and propose political reforms. In short, what is needed is an open culture of public discourse.[25] That is why freedom of expression is an indispensable asset for democracy and human rights. It is also a precondition for the flourishing of freedom of religion or belief.

3. Tense Relations? Freedom of Religion and Gender-Related Emancipation

Whereas antagonistic interpretations of the relationship between freedom of religion or belief and freedom of expression mostly rest on misunderstandings, tensions between freedom of religion or belief and gender-related human rights claims are more complicated.[26] The term "gender," as we use it here, encompasses a broad range of issues, starting with the equality of men and women. To date, the 1979 Convention on the Elimination of All Forms of Discrimination Against Women (CEDAW) is the most important international instrument demanding such equality. Since the 1980s, international gender discussions have also more and more addressed discrimination on the basis of people's sexual orientation and gender identity.[27] An important, albeit not legally binding, document is the 2006 Yogyakarta Principles on the Application of International Human Rights Law in Relation to Sexual Orientation and Gender Identity.[28] It spells out the whole set of established human rights standards with regard to the specific situations, needs, and vulnerabilities of lesbian, gay, bisexual, transsexual, and intersex persons (LGBTI persons).

Conflicts between gender issues and claims put forward under religious freedom have kept legislators and courts busy. Examples include the refusal of parents to have their children participate in sex education, even though that may be part of the mandatory school curriculum, or parental opposition against coeducation of girls and boys, in particular in sports and swimming classes. Another classic conflict concerns the Islamic headscarf, which in the eyes of critics symbolizes the inferior status of women. In addition, many religious communities prohibit women from accessing clerical and leadership positions. In such cases, too, freedom of religion or belief is used as a main argument to defend an obviously discriminatory status quo. Apart from these more traditional discussions, issues of sexual orientation and gender identity have triggered fierce contestations, at times even culminating in cultural wars. Many of those who oppose policies of nondiscrimination in this field refer to religious freedom to back up their resistance.

For instance, conservative hotel owners refusing to host gay couples or bakers who do not wish to prepare a wedding cake for homosexuals have tried to justify their position by pointing to their own religious convictions. Registrars at local authorities not wishing to get professionally involved with same-sex marriage ceremonies have claimed conscientious objection on religious grounds. Adoption agencies which exclusively cater to heterosexual couples, have likewise grounded their policies on their right to freedom of religion or belief. What follows from these observations? Is freedom of religion or belief an obstacle on the long path toward nondiscrimination in the broad field of gender issues? If so, would it be in the interest of gender-related rights to curtail the influence of religious freedom within the international human rights arena?

A comprehensive assessment of conflicts between gender issues and freedom of religion or belief would go beyond the confines of this chapter. We thus have to limit ourselves to some typological observations, which shed some light on how to tackle assumed or real tensions. After addressing false invocations of freedom of religion or belief, which are often based on misunderstandings (see below *a*), we discuss a few exemplary situations where normative conflicts apparently do exist (see below *b*). Another theme is the discriminatory treatment of women in the internal regulations of religious communities, which cannot be resolved by state interferences; they presuppose internal reforms, including new theological thinking (see below *c*). We finish this section by emphasizing the need to stick to a holistic human rights agenda with regard to freedom of religion or belief and gender issues, in order to do justice to complex wishes and needs of countless people (see below *d*).

(a) False Invocations of Religious Freedom

As a human right, freedom of religion or belief can only protect noncoercive religiosity. Lack of conceptual clarity in this regard has become a source of numerous misunderstandings and many flawed assumptions. Not any act happening in the name of religion can count as a manifestation of freedom of religion or belief. To name a few obvious examples, harmful practices like child marriages, forced marriages, or female genital mutilation (FGM) can never be justified under freedom of religion or belief. Such cruel practices, from which countless women and girls suffer, usually with lifelong traumatic consequences, typically occur within the victim's close social environment or even within the extended family. Whether or not these practices are based on perceived religious prescripts may be contested within and between religious communities. Be that as it may, even if we assume for the sake of the argument that religious motives do cause such practices, they nonetheless remain impermissible. If someone were to invoke freedom of religion or belief with the intention to back up practices like child marriages or FGM, this would become an issue for employing the limitation clause of Article 18(3) of the International Covenant on Civil and Political Rights. Utilizing a human right in order to legitimize brutal human rights violations of others can never be legitimate.[29]

By the same logic, religious freedom does not serve as cover for aggressive homophobic hate manifestations. When radical Christian preachers in Uganda or conservative Islamic ulama in Malaysia instigate hatred against gays and lesbians or even call upon their followers to "take the law into their hands," this has nothing to do with freedom of religion or belief. Surely, people have the right to voice objections against same-sex marriages or other new developments in the context of gender emancipation, which they may find disturbing. They can make use of their freedom of expression, their freedom of peaceful assembly, and—in case religious motives are involved—their freedom of religion or belief to manifest their dissent. However, these rights do not include a license to incite to violence. If the threshold is met, the state must take measures, in line with the respective provisions of international human rights law and the Rabat Plan of Action as elaborated above.

Another issue concerns "sodomy laws," which continue to exist in the criminal law books of several states. In some countries they can even lead to a death sentence. The term "sodomy" alludes to the notorious story of Sodom. Both in the Bible and the Qur'an, the city of Sodom represents a sinful decadence, which eventually led to the destruction of the town and its inhabitants. Given the condemnation of Sodom in the Bible and the Qur'an, religious authorities have called for the application of homophobic "sodomy laws." However, to conclude that these laws could count as a legitimate manifestation of freedom of religion or belief would be a grave misunderstanding, at odds with the human rights nature of religious freedom.

Misunderstandings furthermore exist with regard to state-enforced religious family laws. In many Islamic countries like Egypt, Jordan, Malaysia, Pakistan, or Yemen, but also some non-Islamic countries such as India,

Israel, or Myanmar, family law norms are generally based on the religion(s) to which the couple belongs.[30] For Muslims it means that marriage, divorce, and inheritance issues are guided by the Islamic Sharia; Jews follow the Jewish halacha; Christians have their personal status matters regulated in accordance with the canon law norms of their respective denominations. Other religious communities may likewise apply their own religious norms, provided they have received state recognition. Religious family laws often bestow unequal rights to men and women, usually with discriminatory implications for women. At the same time, they discriminate against atheists, agnostics, or converts, who may face obstacles when wishing to contract a valid marriage at the domestic level. Problems may furthermore occur for "mixed" couples who come from different religions or denominations, since traditional religious family laws do not accommodate all, if any, interreligious configurations. The main problem from a human rights perspective is that in many countries these norms are enforced by the state. However, state enforcement of religious norms per definition implies the threat or use of coercion in religious matters, which raises objections from the standpoint of freedom of religion or belief.

(b) Coping with Complicated Normative Conflicts

While some invocations of freedom of religion or belief are based on misunderstandings, there still remains a broad variety of situations in which normative conflicts between freedom of religion or belief and gender-related rights do exist. Legislators and courts are tasked with deciding on how to solve those assumed or real conflicts or at least strive for viable compromises.

In October 2010, the Parliamentary Assembly of the Council of Europe (PACE) adopted resolution 1763 on "the right to conscientious objection in lawful medical care." The resolution inter alia demands that "No person, hospital or institution shall be coerced, held liable or discriminated against in any manner because of a refusal to perform, accommodate, assist or submit to an abortion, the performance of human miscarriage or euthanasia or any act which could cause the death of a human fetus or embryo, for any reason."[31] While fifty-six PACE members voted in favor of the resolution, fifty-one rejected the text and four abstained from the vote. This narrow outcome testifies to the highly controversial nature of the subject, which had been a matter of fierce and emotional controversies in the weeks preceding the vote. While the pro camp invoked conscientious objection and the autonomy of religious institutions,[32] the contra camp feared for women's access to reproductive health services, which is part of the right to health. A few months after the PACE resolution was adopted, the Swedish parliament explicitly distanced itself from resolution 1763 and called upon Swedish PACE members to try to change the text, even though it had already been adopted.[33] This unprecedented move illustrates the high degree of contestation that the theme can trigger. It polarizes legislators and judiciaries and has even led to splits within the human rights community.

Another controversial theme in the intersection between freedom of religion or belief and gender issues is the refusal on religious grounds to get professionally involved with same-sex partnership or marriage ceremonies. The European Court of Human Rights had to decide on this issue in the famous case of *Ladele v. United Kingdom*. Lilian Ladele, an Evangelical registrar in the UK, refused to solemnize same-sex partnerships, even though this fell within the remit of her professional duties. As a consequence of her refusal, she lost her job. She complained about a violation of her freedom of religion or belief and finally made it to the European Court of Human Rights. In January 2013, however, the Court in Strasbourg decided against her. While a majority of five judges supported the decision, two judges fiercely opposed it.[34] The two judges who were sympathetic to Ladele's claim demanded respect for freedom of conscience. They furthermore pointed to the possibility of pragmatic arrangements, which would have facilitated the full functioning of the institution of the registrar also without involving the claimant in same-sex ceremonies against her will. The judges representing the majority, in turn, pointed to the primacy of the state's nondiscrimination policy, which should not depend on the personal convictions of those discharging their professional duties within an official institution.

There is no general recipe on how to handle such complicated cases in the intersection of different human rights norms. Much depends on the specificities of the case, which should be analyzed with empirical precision and normative diligence. The first step should always be a thorough empirical assessment. In some cases, a careful empirical analysis may lead to doubts as to whether a presumed normative conflict actually exists. One example is the Islamic headscarf, which continues to be perceived by some as indicating an inferior status of women. Such an ascription may prove questionable in the light of credible statements made by Muslim women, including obviously emancipated women, that they wear the headscarf voluntarily and with pride. The German jurisprudence recently changed its position on this issue. Some German *Länder* had adopted legislation that prohibited teachers in public schools from displaying the headscarf in the classroom, inter alia based on the assumption that this garment could be perceived as an implicit statement against the equality of men and women. Another argument was that the headscarf if worn by a person of authority could infringe upon the freedom of religion or belief of students, in particular young girls. In a judgment of January 2015, the Federal Constitutional Court decided against the respective restrictions as legislated in North Rhine-Westphalia.[35] The reasoning of the court was that a mere hypothetical conflict between different rights could not justify far-reaching preventative measures at the expense of female teachers and their freedom of religion or belief. In case of an actual conflict, the court said, the school administration continues to have certain options of restricting the headscarf, if such measures prove necessary, suitable, and adequate.

In situations where a normative conflict apparently does exist, it remains imperative to always consider all the human rights claims at stake. It would not be legitimate to waive one of the claims in the first place by constructing an abstract hierarchy between different human rights norms. Just as it would be wrong to devalue freedom of religion or belief by simply subjecting it to an abstract priority of gender-related rights, it would be equally problematic to dismiss gender-related rights claims when entering the territory of freedom of religion or belief. Positively speaking, the task is to do justice, *to the maximum degree possible, to all the human rights involved* in a particular case or situation in order to produce "practical concordance" of the human rights claims involved.[36] This requires a careful *coordination* of all the human-rights-based concerns at stake in a particular situation. On a conceptual level, we would like to briefly note in this context that the term "coordination" seems better suited to capture the task at hand than the frequently used metaphor of "balancing," which conjures up the idea of two competing goods being placed on the weighing scales. The "balancing" metaphor insinuates a zero-sum conflict as well as the search for some sort of middle ground as the probably most adequate solution.[37] However, the task at hand is not to strike a sort of fifty-fifty compromise between opposite claims, but to coordinate and maximize the competing human-rights-based concerns in a manner that comes as closely as possible to a full implementation for both of them.

School education has always been a particularly sensitive area, where complicated questions arise. Should school authorities interfere when a teacher promotes conservative religious views on gender issues? If so, what should be an adequate threshold for such interference? Should parents have the possibility to refuse having their children participate in mixed sports and swimming classes? Should they also be entitled to claiming exemption for their children from sex education? Or should the school authorities enforce all parts of the curriculum even against certain religious reservations claimed by parents, in order to fully safeguard the child's right to education? In many cases freedom of religion or belief, equality of men and women, parental rights and children's rights, and not least the child's right to education, are interwoven in complex ways. There is usually no easy way out of the resulting predicaments. Measures to accommodate special interests of religious minorities would cease to be "reasonable"[38] if they were tantamount to a general curtailment of the child's right to education. In other words, the space for possible compromises in this context is limited. In exceptional circumstances, however, measures of accommodation may be the only way to spare children being torn between the family and the school.[39]

Additional complications arise if the internal affairs of a religious community are affected. Although the autonomy of religious communities does not exempt religious institutions from general state laws,[40] their autonomy falls within the remit of freedom of religion or belief. In particular, the state should not interfere in the appointment of clergy or other religious leadership positions, which may be important for defining their religious identity; such decisions must be left to the religious communities themselves. For many religious communities, the question of who could and should rise to a clerical leadership position, far from being a mere external "managerial" issue, has profound theological significance. The history of religions is replete with example of schisms that occurred in the wake of conflicts over the legitimacy of clerical and other leadership positions.

From the due respect for the autonomy of religious communities, it follows that the state cannot enforce the principle of gender equality in the appointment of clerics, even though the status quo in many communities obviously discriminates against women.[41] For example, the state does not have a mandate to introduce female priesthood in the Catholic Church, even though the current situation may strike many people inside and outside the Church as anachronistic. Does this mean that freedom of religion or belief at the end of the day claims a priority over demands of gender equality? Does it not presuppose a hierarchy of rights, one of which ultimately does "trump" the other—a position we have just rejected? In order to dispel this impression, we have to take into account that state enforcement is not the only way for human rights to unfold their impact. Human rights "travel" in various ways, not only through enforcement measures taken by the state; they have also begun to penetrate theological reasoning and change the self-understanding of religious communities from within. This brings us to the next section: the role of freedom of religion or belief in facilitating new critical readings of the religious sources, not least with the intention of fostering newly developed sensitivities in the area of gender.

(c) Facilitating New Readings of Religious Sources

Freedom of religion or belief, in conjunction with freedom of expression and other human rights, contributes to opening up religious traditions to systematic questions and debates. By empowering traditionally discriminated groups—including women and girls—to voice their experiences, grievances, ideas, yearnings, and demands, freedom of religion or belief serves as a normative reference for challenging patriarchal structures within religious traditions. The Old Catholic Church, which branched off from Roman Catholicism in the wake of the First Vatican Council (1870),[42] introduced female priesthood in Germany in 1996.[43] In most Protestant churches as well as in the Anglican church, people have meanwhile grown accustomed also to female bishops. For example, the current Lutheran Archbishop of Uppsala and Primate of the Church of Sweden is a woman.[44] Reform movements within Judaism and Islam appoint female rabbis or imams. In April 2017, a first national conference of female imams took place in Indonesia; one of the results was a clear rejection of polygamy.[45] Thus, feminist criticism has at least partially made it into the center of theological debates. As Ayelet Shachar concludes: "The challenges for feminist and other equity-seeking religious interpreters are significant. Beyond gaining access to the historically male-dominated 'temple of knowledge,' they must work within the tradition's hermeneutic horizons so that their re-interpretative claims cannot be dismissed as 'inauthentic'. This path of change-from-within may take years to achieve, but the winds of change are already blowing through the world's major religious traditions."[46]

Women's organizations like Musawah, a global movement for equality and justice in the Muslim family, subject Sharia family law norms to critical scrutiny from a feminist perspective. Zainah Anwar, director of Musawah, writes: "The woman's voice, the woman's experience, the woman's realities have been largely silent and silenced in the reading and interpretation of the text. This human silence was mistaken as the silence of the text, as if God did not speak to women's suffering and questioning."[47] Organizations dedicated to changing the discriminatory religious status quo often face difficulties, and in a number of countries they are not even allowed to exist. Nonetheless, they have gradually become part of international religious reform movements. As discussed above, state-enforced family laws is an area in which many violations of freedom of religion or belief occur, while most of the respective laws at the same time also discriminate against women. Reforms in this regard are therefore in the interest of both freedom of religion or belief and women's rights. This exemplifies that, notwithstanding many normative conflicts, the two human rights standards discussed here frequently point in the same direction. Theological reformers working in this field can thus simultaneously invoke freedom of religion or belief and the principle of equality of men and women to back up their agendas.

In the eighteen commitments on "Faith for Rights" of March 2017, faith-based and civil society actors stressed that religions are necessarily subject to human interpretations and that "critical thinking and debate on religious matters should not only be tolerated but rather encouraged as a requirement for enlightened religious interpretations in a globalized world composed of increasingly multi-cultural and multi-religious societies that are constantly facing evolving challenges."[48] The fifth commitment specifically pledges to revisit those religious understandings and interpretations that appear to perpetuate gender inequality and harmful stereotypes or even condone gender-based violence and harmful practices, for example, FGM, child or forced marriages, and crimes committed in the name of so-called honor. As the fifth commitment is supported by religious quotes from the Talmud, Qu'ran, Bible, Hadith, Guru Granth Sahiba, and 'Abdu'l-Bahá, the High Commissioner compared this approach to "a referential bridge— instead of an ocean of divide—between faith and rights."[49]

We have meanwhile also seen innovative attempts to decipher religious sources and theological concepts from the hermeneutical viewpoint of sexual diversity. "Queer theology" is a very new phenomenon, and those working on this issue may currently represent a tiny minority in many communities. Yet the point is that it has come into existence. The Metropolitan Community Churches, a worldwide Christian movement that started in the late 1960s in Los Angeles, have developed a tradition of blessing same-sex partnerships.[50] The Lutheran Evangelical Churches in Denmark and Norway solemnize same-sex marriages in their church buildings and with active participation of pastors or bishops.[51] Catholic and Protestant theologians have embarked on a new exegesis of the notorious biblical story of Sodom, which according to some new interpretations castigates rape, not homosexuality.[52] A number of Protestant churches accommodate gay or lesbian pastors, some of whom serve the community together with their partners, often with broad approval from their parishes. In an article on the treatment of sexual diversity within an Islamic frame of reference, Javaid Rehman and Eleni Polymenopoulou raise the question: "Is Green a Part of the Rainbow?", that is, whether the color green, which is associated with Islam, is included in the rainbow, the symbol of the LGBTI movement. They stress that "Islam in its early manifestations provided a more egalitarian and positive attitude towards homosexuality and lesbianism than did the other monotheistic religions."[53] Furthermore, organizations such as "Muslims for Progressive Values" seek to reinvigorate the Islamic tradition of *ijtihad* (critical engagement and interpretation of sacred texts) and intellectual discourse,[54] which illustrates that internal discussions have been started.

Concerning theological debates on gender issues, freedom of religion or belief plays an important part, albeit an indirect one. As a human right, freedom of religion or belief cannot privilege any of the theological positions taken within that debate; it cannot favor progressive over conservative religious views. Rather, freedom of religion or belief is a universal human right possessed by all human beings, regardless of whether they subscribe to orthodox, conservative, mainstream, liberal, or feminist religious convictions, or to nonreligious views. Nevertheless, freedom of religion or belief, in conjunction with freedom of expression and other rights of freedom, indirectly contributes to intrareligious reforms by facilitating open debates, including on taboo issues, which over centuries had been shielded against public criticism. This creates a new situation.

What is the role of the state in this regard? Under freedom of religion or belief, the state cannot become a direct promotor of theological reforms. Otherwise, the state would claim for itself a theological mandate, which would be at odds with the necessary self-restraint of a secular state.[55] However, the state can and should create the conditions for religious and theological pluralism to unfold free from fear. This demand is far from trivial, given the reality of mobbing, intimidation, and threats, which reformers sometimes experience within their own communities. Freedom of religion or belief has a key function in this regard by constantly reminding the state of its duty to protect religious pluralism between and within the various religious communities, without mingling in theological affairs.

(d) Overcoming Abstract Dichotomies

The relationship between freedom of religion or belief, on the one hand, and gender-related human rights claims, on the other, remains complicated. One should certainly not expect quick and easy solutions. The human-rights-based assessments of some conflicts are difficult and may go in different directions, which is reflected in many controversies also within the human rights community itself. However, the tensions that have arisen cannot adequately be described as a zero-sum conflict. This is the most important point, which we wish to hammer home. It is simply not true that any victory for freedom of religion or belief equals a defeat of progressive gender issues, or vice versa. In other words, freedom of religion or belief is not per se an obstacle on the long path toward equality of men and women as well as respect for diverse sexual orientations and gender identities. Supporting both freedom of religion or belief and emancipatory agendas in the area of gender is not a self-contradictory "schizophrenic" attitude.

Breaking through the frequently assumed abstract dichotomy between freedom of religion or belief and gender liberation is the precondition for working out viable compromises and searching for possible synergies. Even more importantly, it is the precondition for doing justice to numerous human beings. Public headscarf debates in Western countries have nourished the view that Muslim women allegedly remain stuck between two opposite options, which are thought to be irreconcilable. Allegedly, they have to choose between only two possibilities: either to liberate themselves by abandoning their religious tradition or to stick to their religious upbringing, thereby forfeiting their claims to freedom and equality. Thus, they are supposed to be stuck between tradition and modernity, between religious identity and gender equality, or between religious faith and personal emancipation. Some women may actually feel that such an antagonism adequately describes existing predicaments. Yet what about those who wish to have both: living in harmony with their religious convictions and leading the life of an emancipated woman? There is no guarantee that such wishes and yearning will ever be fulfilled. Yet constructing the relationship between freedom of religion or belief and gender equality as a zero-sum conflict would destroy such hopes and yearning from the outset.

The assumption that one has to make a choice between religious freedom, on the one hand, and gender liberation, on the other, would tear the lifeworld of countless human beings apart, in particular the lifeworld of women. Why should they satisfy themselves with an artificially imposed either-or? Why should they be deprived of enjoying all of their human rights? Surely, some women may gladly turn their back on the religious communities, within which they have experienced discrimination and misogynic prejudices. For some of them, the only interesting aspect of freedom of religion or belief may be freedom from religion. This is a legitimate option. Yet not all women will wish to take such a path. Others will prefer to remain within their religious communities and try to work for internal changes.

Human rights acknowledge diversity. This also includes respect for the diverse paths that women may take toward emancipation and equality. While some women may decide to abandon their religious heritage as too heavy a burden on their way toward personal autonomy and equality, others may decide to work for improving the situation of women within their respective religious traditions, for instance by promoting and implementing alternative readings of the religious sources. Yet others may resort to pragmatic arrangements in order to enlarge the scope of personal life opportunities. Different as these and many other ways may be, they all deserve respect and support.

The same is true for lesbian, gay, bisexual, trans- and intersex persons. Owing to frustrating experiences of homophobic and transphobic stigmatization within religious communities, many of them may actually prefer to be left alone by religion. However, this is certainly not everyone's preference. One can only conjecture that probably tens of millions of people worldwide live in circumstances where they would actually need both: respect for their freely articulated religious identities, in accordance with their religious self-understandings, as well as the freedom to live in harmony with their sexual orientations or gender identities. A dichotomized understanding of the relationship between freedom of religion or belief and the rights of sexual orientation and gender identity would merely reinforce existing boundaries instead of removing them.[56]

During a fact-finding visit to Bangladesh, we met with an organization of gay men who reported that, according to an investigation conducted internally, a clear majority of their members are religiously interested and religiously practicing; many of them regularly attend the Islamic Friday prayer. At the same time, they are exposed to hostile prejudices, including the stereotypical assumption that a gay person must per definition be an "atheist," since homosexual behavior is considered "deviant" from the traditional norms of religious ethics. Obviously, this creates extremely stressful situations, in which many individuals feel literally torn between the various aspects of their personal identity. In Bangladesh, this can actually become a matter of life and death.[57] Furthermore, the spokesperson of gay Muslims in an Eastern European country reported that he often feels excluded from both his religious community as well as the gay community. After coming out as gay, he experienced inimical reactions from his religious environment. At the same time, he often feels antagonism from the gay community, some of whose members presuppose that the only reasonable way for a homosexual person to deal with religion is to turn away from it.

Construing the relationship between freedom of religion or belief and gender-related rights as an abstract either-or dichotomy would betray the yearnings of numerous people whose life situation is characterized by complex needs, complex wishes, and multiple vulnerabilities. It would further deteriorate their prospects to ever reconcile the various components of their identity in order to live in peace with themselves and their social environment. However, as UN Deputy High Commissioner for Human Rights Kate Gilmore pointed out during a workshop in Geneva, it would be very strange to artificially separate the arguably two most existential dimensions of human life: love and faith.[58] To do so in the name of human rights would be utterly absurd.

4. Plea for a Holistic Human Rights Perspective

Back to the initial question: is freedom of religion or belief a strange human right that does not really fit into broader human rights agendas? Does it hinder progressive developments in the area of gender-related emancipation? Are freedom of religion or belief and other human rights "awkward bedfellows," as the title of this chapter suggests (albeit with an important question mark)?

As we have seen in Section 2 of this chapter, antagonistic views of the relationship between freedom of religion or belief and freedom of expression mostly rest on misunderstandings. They often ignore the crucial component of "empowerment," which freedom of religion or belief has in common with other human rights, including freedom of expression. As soon as we adequately conceptualize freedom of religion or belief in keeping with the general human rights approach, it becomes clear that it does not support anti-blasphemy laws or other restrictive measures, which unduly limit freedom of expression. Rather, freedom of religion or belief and freedom of expression largely move in the same direction by protecting the intellectual and spiritual integrity of the individual, facilitating free exchange of ideas, accommodating diversity of convictions and practices, and strengthening the development of democratic discourse.

When it comes to gender issues, as discussed in Section 3 of this chapter, the general constellation is more difficult. Even after the idea of a zero-sum antagonism between gender issues and freedom of religion is refuted, complicated conflicts in the intersection of the two normative standards persist. An adequate handling of the resulting conflicts requires empirical and normative diligence. Constructing abstract either-or dichotomies, however, will never do justice to the complexities of numerous individual cases. Moreover, expecting people to simply make a choice between the supposedly antagonistic rights would betray the needs and yearning of countless people, whose life-situation is characterized by complex identities, complex wishes, and complex vulnerabilities, and it would furthermore ignore the creative potential of people to work for synergies or viable compromises in complicated situations.

No doubt, freedom of religion or belief can become a factor of additional "complications," in particular in the context of gender-oriented anti-discrimination agendas. Yet going the extra mile by tackling such complications might be beneficial for a sustainable nondiscrimination policy. It sometimes happens that those who deconstruct gender stereotypes in the interest of equality and nondiscrimination, at the same time reproduce old, or produce new, stereotypes based on a person's religion or belief, for instance, when accusing headscarf-wearing Muslim women of lending support to patriarchal values. Right-wing populist movements in Europe have meanwhile learned selectively to borrow bits and pieces from a feminist agenda with the intention to exercise pressure on immigrant communities, in particular from Muslim majority countries. Most feminists reject such abuse of feminist semantics.[59] Yet this can hardly be done without taking freedom of religion or belief on board. Sensitivity to religious diversity should therefore become an element of quality management within gender-related nondiscrimination agendas, and vice versa.

In the beginning of this chapter, we quoted the guiding idea that all human rights are "universal, indivisible and interrelated and interdependent." This implies that every human right has an indispensable function to fulfill within the entire system of human rights. While some rights may have been less prominent in the public perception or were even invisible in the past, Special Rapporteurs and intergovernmental bodies have rightly stressed the indivisibility of all human rights which must be promoted and protected in a holistic manner.[60] Neglecting any single human right would not only leave us with a gap, but would furthermore negatively affect the whole range of rights; it would weaken the entire system of human rights protection. For example, without the right to fair access to judicial remedies, the very idea of human rights would cease to make sense in practice. The same is true for freedom of expression, without which people would depend on merciful state authorities rather than being able to bring their grievances to public attention. Already Kant praised "the freedom of the pen" as the "sole palladium of the people's rights."[61] Another example that comes to mind is the right to education, which likewise has an undisputed part to play in raising awareness of everyone's fundamental rights. Our point is that the right to freedom of thought, conscience, religion, or belief has an equally important function to fulfill for the system of human rights. It deals with human beings as holders of profound, identity-shaping convictions. Without acknowledging that important dimension in human life, human rights would fail to do justice to the complexity of the human condition. Indeed, they would cease to be fully humane.

CHAPTER 5

Shades and Modes of Secularisms

Does freedom of religion or belief presuppose a "secular" state, or can it also flourish under the auspices of a religious state? What does the secularity of the state actually mean? Is the alleged "neutrality" of the secular state a mere cloak, which hides the fact that secular governments are no less guided by belief systems than a religious state, albeit without admitting this fact openly? Should the state strictly avoid any involvement with religious issues, or should the government positively engage with religion? If so, what would be an adequate mode for the government to deal with religious issues? These are the guiding questions for the present chapter.

1. Three Country Examples

Those who think that we can easily divide the global political landscape into the two camps of religious and secular states will be surprised at the confusing multiplicity of configurations. Let us take a brief look at three less frequently discussed examples taken from recent country visits of the UN Special Rapporteur on freedom of religion or belief.

(a) Kazakhstan

We are visiting a school in Almaty, the former capital of Kazakhstan.[1] Religion plays a very limited part in the country's official curriculum. The headmaster tells us that at least ninth grade students receive some basic information about religious themes, with much emphasis placed on warnings against religious extremism and "dangerous sects," a term that often remains unspecified. We ask the two female teachers in charge of religious education whether they have ever visited, together with their students, one of the mosques or churches in the vicinity of the school. The women react almost shocked. "We are a secular school," they hasten to assure us. In Kazakhstan, schools as well as other public institutions do not accommodate visible religiosity. Headscarves or other religious signs are taboo. Religious practice remains confined to the private sphere or the spaces specifically licensed by the authorities for that purpose, namely, places of worship and religious institutions. Whoever practices religion outside of those demarked spheres runs the risk of incurring sanctions ranging from fines to imprisonment. In line with this narrow understanding of the place of religion, the army does not employ chaplains. As we learn from the authorities, "we are a secular State, and we have a secular army."

Kazakhstan represents a highly restrictive, almost hermetic type of secularism.[2] In many aspects, it resembles the early phase of Kemalism, when the young Turkish Republic tried to keep religion strictly out of public life, in order to guard against potentially "subversive" tendencies. In addition to this comes the Soviet legacy with its control obsessions. In the Kazakh understanding, "separation" between the state and religious communities is not an effort to strive for mutual independence to the benefit of both. Rather, the separation one-sidedly serves the interests of the state. Whereas the state rejects any public intervention by religious communities, the government subjects the religious groups to tight control measures. When wishing to undertake community-related religious activities, people have to apply for special licenses—for example a license to perform missionary activities, a license to import religious literature, another license to sell such literature, and so forth—which furthermore requires renewal on a regular basis. In this way, the state tightly supervises religious activities to make sure they remain within the narrow channels designed for this purpose. Under such conditions, freedom of religion or belief can hardly flourish.

(b) Bangladesh

"We are a secular Government" is the mantra of Bangladesh's ruling Awami League (AL), which sees itself as the custodian of a secular national legacy.[3] The AL traditionally receives support inter alia from religious minorities—Hindus, Buddhists, Christians, practitioners of indigenous religions, and so forth—who together make up some 10 percent of the population, while the overwhelming majority of the people belong to Islam. In Bangladesh, religion is a ubiquitous reality, not only in private, but also in public life, including in state institutions. A member of the cabinet has decorated his office with verses of the Qur'an to demonstrate his appreciation of Islam. State representatives attach great importance to clarifying that the secular orientation of the government should not be mistaken for hostility toward religion. Unlike some European countries, they also say, the state of Bangladesh will never treat religion as a merely private issue.

In spite of the general pro-secularism rhetoric, the concrete contours of secularism remain somewhat nebulous. For instance, members of the government declared that they would not touch the existing religious family law system—much to the disappointment of women's organizations, who have campaigned for far-reaching reforms. Moreover, the Constitution of the People's Republic of Bangladesh, while enshrining secularism in Article 12, also acknowledges Islam as the religion of the state.[4] The respective amendment (Article 2A) to the constitution was inserted at a time when the current opposition party, the Bangladesh National Party (BNP) was in power. The two main political rivals, AL and BNP, have both left their footprints in the constitution, with the result of irresolvable normative contradictions, not least concerning the relationship between state and religion. That is why any attempt to describe the precise understanding and practice of secularism in Bangladesh is fraught with unsurmountable difficulties. In addition to the said complications, the current government, while formally waving the banner of secularism, wishes to appease conservative Islamic groups in order to win them as allies in the fight against religious extremism. Political rhetoric in Bangladesh is full of ambiguities.

At any rate, secularism *as a concept* in Bangladesh differs very much from the prevailing understanding in Kazakhstan. Indeed, it nearly means the opposite. The guiding idea is that the state should provide space for religious manifestations, not only in private, but also in public. In order to function as a trustworthy custodian of a religiously open space, the government should not take sides with any one of the religious communities, or so is the predominant political rhetoric. In comparison to Kazakhstan's hermetic state secularism, the concept promoted by the government of Bangladesh looks open and inclusive. The country's legacy of secularism, however, is currently in danger of being gambled away politically. In order to keep the opposition out of power, the government makes far-reaching concessions to Islamist movements, which it simultaneously combats and appeases. In the resulting climate of political nervousness, the space for religious minorities, dissidents, and critical internet activists seems to be shrinking more and more.

(c) Denmark

According to the Danish Constitution,[5] the Evangelical Lutheran Church enjoys the special rank of the "People's Church" (*folkekirke*).[6] In spite of a gradual decline of traditional church practice, about 80 percent of the Danish population still formally belong to the *folkekirke*. The church shows typical facets of a state church: it receives a part (around 10 percent) of its annual budget from the state, and the minister for church affairs has direct influence on internal affairs of the church. In political circles, as well as within the church, discussions have begun on whether the privileged status of the *folkekirke* should be abandoned in the long run, which would mean to follow the path that Sweden and Norway took some time ago. Yet it seems that such discussions only find a limited echo in the society. Some of those who defend the historical situation argue that the close relationship with the state has kept the church in touch with the democratic development of modern society, as already advised by the Danish philosopher Grundtvig (1783–1872), whose profound political and cultural influence is still felt today.[7] A recent example is the right for same-sex partners to marry in the church, which the legislation introduced in 2012.[8] Same-sex marriage ceremonies receive broad approval also within the church, including by the vast majority of the clergy.

A term sometimes occurring in theological discussions in Scandinavia is "Lutheran secularity." According to Luther, true faith manifests itself in the person's heart. The resulting radical internalization of faith has redeemed politics from false religious expectations thereby "secularizing" the state and politics as well as other spheres of life. At the same time, Christians should actively shape the secular spheres and fill them with their religious ethos. According to Luther, this is part of their religious calling. The Christian ethos should penetrate society as a whole without compromising the secular logic underneath the various societal areas, including politics. As a consequence of this Lutheran understanding, the secular and the sacred, while being distinct categories in theory, should at the same time come together in practice. These two categories of the "sacred" and the "secular" may indeed blur into a grey area of the "sacrular." The editors of a book on religious issues in Scandinavia thus conclude that there may be "'hidden sacrality' in the secular."[9] They furthermore remark: "From the perspective of Lutheran theology, this 'secularity' makes sense as another way of performing *Christentum*."[10]

In the current Danish context, this peculiar conceptualization of Lutheran secularity can at times assume a polemical significance when being harnessed politically for drawing a sharp line against Islam, which meanwhile constitutes the second largest religious community in Denmark. Critics of Islam hold that, unlike Lutheran Christianity, Islam is a robust and unsophisticated "political religion." Some conservatives go yet another step further; they would like to see the *folkekirke* turned into a cultural bulwark against the growing influence of Islam. In their view, the state-sponsored official church ought to protect the country from the "politicization of religion." The purpose should be to defend the secular nature of Denmark. Obviously, this would amount to a strangely ironic, indeed paradoxical version of secularism.[11] It would mean to endorse one manifestation of politicized religion (i.e., the Christian version) in order to use this in the fight against another manifestation of politicized religion (i.e., Islam). For good reasons, most members of the *folkekirke*, including high-ranking clerics, do not wish to play that political game. Some of them thus plead for a fully autonomous church and the abolishment of its specific constitutional status.

2. Secularism: A Hopelessly Fuzzy Concept?

The three examples just sketched out illustrate that the notion of state "secularity" carries very different, possibly even opposite meanings.[12] This vast variety of different concepts also manifests itself in different institutional arrangements and practices. Indeed, the ways in which more or less secular states regulate their relationship vis-à-vis religious communities differ immensely.[13] The German or Austrian traditions of cooperation between the state and religious communities stand in contrast with the French Republic, which at least in theory sticks to a rather strict separation. Ireland, Italy, Spain, and Poland, although sharing a centuries-long Catholic heritage, have nonetheless each found their own ways of organizing the relationship between state, majority church, and religious minorities.[14] The

United States of America and Mexico spell out secularism in almost opposite ways: while the USA provides the proverbial open market, in which
religious diversity flourishes in sometimes chaotic ways,[15] its southern
neighbor narrowly restricts the public display of religiosity, in particular
in state institutions.[16] Moreover, the above examples of Kazakhstan and
Bangladesh may serve as reminders that secularism is not an exclusively
"Western" theme. Political controversies about the significance and practice
of secularism when taking place in countries such as Tunisia, Senegal, India,
Bangladesh, Indonesia, and so on, have their own contextual features and
can no longer be reduced to just an echo of Western cultural influences.

Given the vast array of definitions, descriptions, views, assessments,
endorsements, rejections, and conspiracy theories in this field, some
observers hold that secularism is "a 'fuzzy', chameleonic, highly misleading
or 'cacophonous concept,'" which we better drop, as Veit Bader advises.[17]
He is convinced that secularism can no longer function as a guiding principle for regulating relations between state and religions. Although sharing
Bader's assessment that the semantic landscape is in fact extremely fuzzy,
we draw a different practical conclusion. Rather than discarding the concept of secularism, we try to further qualify it by subordinating secularism
to freedom of religion or belief. While this right provides the normative
yardstick, the concept of secularism can assume the role of a useful
"second-order principle" in the service of a nondiscriminatory implementation of freedom of religion or belief for all.[18]

In this chapter, we propose a twofold distinction, namely, between
exclusive and inclusive forms of secularism (Section 3), and then between
doctrinal and nondoctrinal versions of secularism (Section 4). The chapter
concludes by elaborating a few consequences derived from our plea for
inclusive nondoctrinal forms of secularism as the most adequate framework
for implementing freedom of religion or belief for all in a nondiscriminatory manner (Section 5). We would like to highlight at the outset that the
purpose of our reflection is *conceptual clarification*, not sociological description. Our attempt at conceptual clarification is furthermore based on strong
normative assumptions. Our starting point and frame of reference is freedom of religion or belief as a human right, which all human beings should
enjoy without discrimination. This is a very specific normative approach,
which has its inevitable limitations. and cannot cover the whole field of
conceptual, let alone empirical, manifestations of secularism. When referring to a number of examples of states from different parts of the globe we

do so in the interest of illustrating our conceptual analysis. We are aware of the risk we run when mentioning concrete examples for the sake of illustration. No real-world example will ever entirely fit into a matrix created for purposes of normative conceptual clarification. That is why we would like at least to emphasize the obvious fact that an adequate sociological study would have to take into account the many contextual factors, variables, historical specificities of each and every one of the states we mention. However, this would clearly exceed the purpose of this chapter, which is specific and limited.

3. Exclusive and Inclusive Forms of Secularism

The first important distinction we propose is between "exclusive" and "inclusive" types of secularism. What they have in common is an element of *distance* that the state maintains vis-à-vis religion. Etymologically, secularity means "worldliness."[19] Hence, the secular state is a "worldly" rather than a religious state. However, the motives for creating and upholding such distance from religion differ very much. *Exclusive secularism* is typically driven by the interest of the state to keep the public influence of religious communities in check or even push religiosity back into a mere private sphere by resorting to restrictive measures. By contrast, *inclusive secularism* aims to open up the space for the free unfolding of religious diversity, not only in private, but also in public. Here, the element of distance itself functions in the service of creating space for all, which requires that the state overcome any open or concealed identification with one particular religion or belief. Although in reality, many grey zones and overlaps exist, the typological difference between exclusive and inclusive forms of secularism remains significant.

The idea that all secular states ultimately fit into the same religious-political camp is an illusion. Assuming that they are all somehow "liberal" would be even more misleading. Nonetheless, this misunderstanding is widespread. For example, commentators expressing concerns at the growing religious and political authoritarianism in Turkey, sometimes associate the tradition of Turkish secularism with a "liberal" legacy that they fear has been lost. However, any equation of the original Turkish secularism with liberalism sounds far-fetched. The Turkish Republic under Mustafa Kemal

Atatürk and his successors, while trying to cleanse politics from any religious interference, frequently employed repressive means to subject religious life to tight political control.[20] While the auspices of Turkish politics have changed thoroughly, the interest in keeping religion under strict state supervision thus provides an element of continuity between the era of early Kemalism and the current government. Another example illustrating the difference between secularism and liberalism is Kazakhstan, which—as briefly described in the opening section of this chapter—represents a rather hermetic type of "exclusive secularism," which is anything but liberal. This type of secularism similarly exists in other former Soviet countries as well, for example in Tajikistan, Turkmenistan, or Uzbekistan, whose track record in terms of freedom of religion or belief has been criticized.[21]

"Inclusive secularism," too, presupposes a clear distance between the state and religion. However, here the element of distance fulfills a different function, because it is part of a project of creating an open space, in which religious diversity can unfold free from fear and free from discrimination. Rather than treating religion as a mere private affair, religious practice can also be manifested in public. At the same time, the distance from the state is supposed to protect religious communities from exploitation by the state for nationalist propaganda or other political interests. In this sense, inclusive secularism represents a policy of deliberate self-restraint: the "worldly" state refrains from mingling with questions of theological dogma, religious identity, and religious norms, thus leaving these and similar issues entirely to the various religious communities and their followers, whose freedom of religion the state respects, protects, and promotes. At least, this is the programmatic aspiration of inclusive secularism.

The United States of America provides a classical example of the inclusive type of secularism. In its foundational mythology, the country praises itself as a safe haven for religious dissidents from Europe. One of the iconic figures within that narrative is Roger Williams, who as early as the mid-seventeenth century strove for peaceful coexistence of people from different faith communities in Rhode Island. He also included indigenous communities in his peace project.[22] Under the protection of the First Amendment (1791) to the US Constitution, a hugely diverse landscape of religious communities emerged. Thomas Jefferson's famous metaphor of "wall of separation"[23] erected between state and religious communities does not aim to fence off religion from the public sphere; it is the other way in that the wall of separation mainly functions as a guarantee of religious freedom against unjustified state interference. In order not to paint too rosy a picture, it should be noted that in reality the US model has been frequently compromised by policies of exclusion and discrimination based on the self-identification of a white, Anglo-Saxon and Protestant nation. The most obvious case of exclusion has been the treatment of indigenous communities and their spirituality, partially up until the present day. Jehovah's Witnesses have experienced pressure and discrimination, for example when refusing to salute the flag. Mormons look back at a history of stigmatization and exclusion. Even Catholics, who today constitute one of the largest Christian denominations in the US, suffered discrimination, well into the twentieth century. In short, the US history, too, illustrates the proverbial difference between a normative model and the reality on the ground. It is important to take both aspects seriously.

Although the ways in which European countries regulate religious affairs differ vastly, many of them may arguably come closer to the inclusive type of secularism, which accommodates religious manifestations in the public space.[24] Germany is a case in point. Since World War II, Germany has developed a tradition of cooperation between the state and religious communities, based on a clear appreciation of functional differences. Yet things are usually not just black and white. With increasing religious diversity, not least as a result of recent waves of immigration, secularism has once again become a matter of political controversies, in which inclusive concepts compete with more restrictive, exclusive readings of state secularism. The French Republic traditionally understands itself as the guarantor of the rights of each individual citizen.[25] This is the reason why the custodians of French republicanism wish to ensure that no political forces stand between the state and the individual, with possibly restrictive implications for manifestations of religious life in public institutions. Well-known examples include the strict headscarf ban in public schools and more recently the general prohibition of the face veil in public life. In Europe, another reason why the space, which a secular constitution is supposed to provide, shrinks nowadays is the fight against religious extremism in the context of combating terrorism and preventing conditions conducive to terrorism. The secular self-understanding of most European countries thus remains an issue of ever-new controversies, adaptations, and reconceptualizations.

Various forms of more or less inclusive secularism also exist outside of the West. We have already mentioned Bangladesh as a country where a secular legacy is currently at risk of becoming increasingly blurred. The same seems to be happening in India.²⁶ While the Congress Party, currently in opposition, continues to wave the banner of secularism, Hindu national- ism has largely occupied the public space in recent years. Muslim and Christian minorities often face hostility as "foreign religions," whose origins lie outside the geographical and cultural territory of India. Advocates of the Indian heritage of secularism have expressed profound concerns at this development. This is just one example illustrating the controversies around the meaning and significance of secularism taking place in most different regional and political contexts, not just in Europe and North America.

4. Doctrinal and Nondoctrinal Secularism

The inclusive concept of secularism as a space-providing principle implies a clear differentiation from doctrinal forms of secularism. This is easier said than done, however, as sediments of cultural and ideological wars have permeated the semantics of secularism to the present day. Organizations dedicated to the promotion of a postreligious, "scientific" worldview mush- roomed especially in the second half of the nineteenth century. Some of them carry the term "secular" in their names. The British Secular Society represents the most famous example. George Holyoake, founder of the organization, liked to use religious terminology when describing his own program. He published a book under the telling title *English Secularism: A Confession of Belief*, in which he furthermore proclaimed: "science is the available providence of man."²⁷

Similar movements developed in continental Europe as well. Toward the end of the nineteenth century, Friedrich Jodl and Ferdinand Tönnies founded the Deutsche Gesellschaft für Ethische Kultur (German Society for Ethical Culture).²⁸ The Monistenbund (Federation of Monists), gathered around Darwin's disciple Ernst Haeckel, promoted its postmetaphysical worldview in a series of "Monist Sermons."²⁹ Here again, the use of reli- gious terminology illustrates the aspiration to replace traditional religions by a new all-encompassing interpretation of the world, which Haeckel mainly presented in his bestseller *Die Welträtsel* (*World Conundrums*). In this book he lamented the premature closure of Bismarck's anti-Catholic *Kulturkampf*, which had torn Germany for many years.³⁰ Haeckel's postreli- gious political vision culminated in the idea of establishing a "*Palace of Reasons* where, owing to our newly won monistic world view, people would venerate the real 'trinity', namely, the trinity of the true, the good and the beautiful," as he phrased it.[31] The natural sciences were supposed to take the role previously filled by religion, and they should harness political power to achieve that purpose. In Haeckel's words: "Our State order can only improve, when breaking through the chains of the Church and elevating our citizens' understanding of the world and of human life through a general *scientific* education."[32]

Another nineteenth-century example of a postreligious scientific worldview is the *religion de l'humanité* developed by the French philosopher August Comte, one of the founding fathers of modern sociology, who coined the concept of scientific positivism. In his vision, trained sociologists should serve as "priests of humanity" and promote the new positivistic gospel of "love, order and progress."[33] Comte expected that a future state would officially adopt his postreligious secular belief system thereby creating a "sociocracy."[34] The "sociocratic State," as envisaged by Comte, is but an alternative version of a confessional state. While replacing religion by a postreligious creed, the confessional structure of the state remains fully in place—or so is the idea. Just as a traditional theocracy employed the instruments of state power to maintain the hegemony of the official religion, Comte wanted to make use of state power in order to shape a new society thoroughly on the tenets of the modern "religion of humanity."

The strong versions of doctrinal secularism that we have just sketched out display an enthusiasm for scientifically based progress, which in the twenty-first century, after many experiences with ambivalent repercussions of science and technology, may sound naïve. However, as Charles Taylor has illustrated in his voluminous study *A Secular Age*, basic assumptions of secularist worldviews have nonetheless become part of mainstream societies in the West, albeit usually in less explicitly "doctrinal" versions.[35] They are often just taken for granted as the "normal" or "neutral" background way of looking at things, possibly connected with a "secular lifestyle" defined by a skeptical attitude toward religion in general. This harbors the risk that the secular self-understanding of the state is confused with doctrinal forms of secularism, in particular the more implicit versions of doctrinal secularism, which are not always easy to detect. This may even happen unintentionally, with no one actively pushing an agenda of doctrinal secularism. People deviating from that mainstream secularism may consequently find themselves in the situation of a minority whose convictions and practices meet with a general lack of sympathy and understanding. One example demonstrating that danger was the partially aggressive debate on ritual male circumcision, which took place in Germany in 2012 after a controversial court decision. What was shocking, however, was the degree of ignorance that many public commentators displayed when calling for a legal ban on male circumcision without even considering how deeply that would affect the religious identities and practices of countless Jews and Muslims.[36]

It thus seems important to uncover and address doctrinal secularism, in particular its concealed forms, in order to overcome its implicitly or explicitly discriminatory repercussions. As Jürgen Habermas points out, this requires efforts on both sides. It should fall not only upon religious people to "translate" their religious views and visions into the secular language of public democratic discourse. Those secular-minded intellectuals who have influence on the public discourse, Habermas demands, should become more accommodating and develop an awareness of the discursive hurdles which religious people have to overcome when wishing to contribute to secular public debates.[37]

It goes without saying that people who belong to secularist movements in the doctrinal understanding of the word can fully enjoy their freedom of expression, freedom of association, and not least freedom of religion or belief when promoting their views. As we have elaborated in Chapter 1, freedom of religion or belief must be broadly conceived, far beyond traditional religions, and it doubtless also covers the freedom to hold and manifest "secularist" doctrinal positions. Those holding such views are furthermore free to try to exercise influence on politics by presenting their positions and demands in public discourse. However, a problem would arise if those doctrinally secular views were to directly guide state activities. This could lead to new forms of confessional, quasi-confessional, or crypto-confessional statehood, with dangers analogous to those connected with traditional state religion, where minorities and dissidents typically suffer discrimination. Accordingly, the requirement to maintain a distance between the state and religion must likewise apply to doctrinal versions of secularism, too. In the words of Jocelyn Maclure and Charles Taylor: "the state should adopt a position of neutrality not only toward religions but also toward the different philosophical conceptions that stand as the secular equivalents of religions."[38] This is a difficult task, because it requires detecting the more subtle versions of doctrinal, quasi-doctrinal, or half-doctrinal secularism, many of which are so deeply interwoven with everyday life in modern societies that they may simply count as "normal" or "neutral."

Doctrinal versions of secularism can also emerge in the context of certain readings of Christian theology. In the beginning of this chapter we

introduced Denmark as a country where secularism is often traced historically to the Lutheran doctrine of the two kingdoms, the worldly and the
spiritual. Some conservative Danish politicians have invoked this theological heritage against the Muslim minority in the country, thus claiming the
modern secular state as an exclusive result of the Christian tradition, in
particular the Lutheran tradition, which they wish to see defended against
the influx of Islam. While there may be good reasons to assume that
Lutheran theology is one of various historical sources of secular thinking in
modern Europe, however, this does not justify exclusive heritage claims on
the secular state. Historically, the secular state in Europe developed in
conflict-driven multiple learning processes, often against the resistance of
the churches, including the Lutheran churches. Moreover, to assume that
Muslims in Denmark are "essentially" prevented from appreciating a secular state, due to the basic teachings of their religion, would be flawed, as
testified by numerous Muslims who explicitly or factually endorse secular
statehood and secular laws. Finally, it would be a special irony to use the
Lutheran Evangelical *folkekirke*, which continues to enjoy a constitutionally
privileged status, as a bulwark for the defense of secularism against Islam.

Such "dialectical turns" exist in many versions. In Germany, conservative politicians have proposed a Christian "leading culture" (*Leitkultur*),
which they wish to see politically protected and defended against increasing
religious pluralization, in particular against Islam.[39] However, by closely
associating the secular constitution with a particular Christian legacy, secularism itself implicitly assumes a doctrinal component, namely, as a proxy
for maintaining the cultural hegemony of Christianity. The most frequently
cited argument in this regard is that Jesus called upon his followers to
"render therefore unto Caesar the things which are Caesar's; and unto God
the things that are God's."[40] Again, it may well be true that elements of
Christian theology are among the various factors which in complicated trajectories historically shaped the understanding of secularism in Germany
and other Western countries. Yet it would be historically far too simplistic
to attribute the modern secular state mainly to the ongoing influence of the
Christian churches. Even more problematic are the systematic implications.
Exclusive Christian ownership claims concerning the genesis of secular
thinking may culminate in a sort of "baptized secularism," which the state
is supposed to defend against possible erosion, most likely with discriminatory consequences for minorities, in particular Muslims. In such a paradoxical approach, the space-providing function of secularism might get entirely

lost. Thus the Beirut Declaration and its eighteen commitments on "Faith for Rights" include the pledge "to prevent the use of 'doctrinal secularism' from reducing the space for religious or belief pluralism in practice."[41]

5. Inclusive and Nondoctrinal Secularism as a Guiding Idea

Can freedom of religion or belief provide orientation within the confusing semantic landscape of secularisms? The answer is yes. However, it is a complicated yes, linked to a number of qualifications. For good reasons, human rights norms do not directly prescribe the secular nature of the state. As a matter of prudence, human rights generally do not provide comprehensive blueprints on how to shape state institutions. Prescribing one mandatory pattern for the whole world would mean to overtax international human rights law and, as a result, erode its legitimacy. There must be space for country-specific diversity and for experimentation as to what the most appropriate solution may look like. This not only concerns issues related to religious freedom; it applies to other human rights issues as well. For example, the right to education can be implemented in different systems of schooling, the right to freedom of expression does not prescribe the details of national media laws, and citizens can exercise their right to political participation within different types of democratic constitutions. Similarly, freedom of religion or belief acknowledges institutional diversity in the ways that states regulate their relationship vis-à-vis religious communities. There is no such thing as the one "best practice example" that all other states should simply emulate.

In its General Comment No. 22, the UN Human Rights Committee even accommodates the possibility for the state to cherish a tradition of an official religion or state religion. Accordingly, official religions are not forbidden in international human rights law. At the same time, the Human Rights Committee stipulates important caveats. Its General Comment No. 22 places special emphasis on the principle of nondiscrimination, which includes nondiscriminatory access to public institutions and positions for people outside the state religion. In the words of the Human Rights Committee, "The fact that a religion is recognized as a State religion or that it is established as official or traditional religion or that its followers comprise the majority of the population, shall not result in any impairment of the enjoyment of any of the rights under the Covenant, including articles 18 and 27, nor in any discrimination against adherents to other religions or

non-believers. In particular, certain measures discriminating against the latter, such as measures restricting eligibility for government service to members of the predominant religion or giving economic privileges to them
or imposing special restrictions on the practice of other faiths, are not in
accordance with the prohibition of discrimination based on religion or
belief and the guarantee of equal protection under article 26."[42] In the light
of these rather far-reaching stipulations, the space for state religions is quite
limited. The Human Rights Committee not only rules out "hard core" versions of state religion; it also prohibits any policy of privileging members
of the official religious, which as its flipside implies discrimination against
others.[43] It seems difficult, if not impossible, that the application of the
concept of an official state religion in practice would not have adverse
effects on religious minorities by way of discriminating against their members.[44] When looking at the wording used by the Human Rights Committee,
the conditional accommodation of official religions in theory comes close
to a prohibition in practice. This has been reiterated by Special Rapporteur
Ahmed Shaheed in his 2018 report to the Human Rights Council, with
reference also to commitment 4 of the "Faith for Rights" framework, warning "against the use of the notion of 'State religion' to discriminate against
any individual or group."[45]

The critical approach to state religions, as taken by UN human rights
mechanisms, suggests an implicit preference for a secular state. Yet here
again the above caveats remain in place. As we have seen, there are many
different versions of state secularisms, ranging from repressive to liberal
types or from hermetically exclusive to broadly inclusive models. A formally
secular state can even turn into a crypto-confessional state, if doctrinal
elements openly or surreptitiously permeate the state apparatus. The discriminatory consequences are not always easy to detect, although they may
be very much tangible for those people who suffer the consequences.
Whereas "exclusive" secularism in its various versions typically restricts the
space for manifestations of religious diversity, the concept of "inclusive"
secularism looks more promising. Within that concept, the "separation" of
state and religion functions as the seemingly "negative" precondition for
what is ultimately a "positive" investment, namely the creation of an open
space in which people can manifest their freedom of religion or belief without fear and without discrimination. This is the guiding idea.

Using the term "separation" between state and religion without further
qualification often leads to misunderstandings. It can nourish the idea that
the purpose would be to cleanse the public sphere of any visible or audible

religious practices. "Separation" may furthermore conjure up notions of a compartmentalization or fragmentation of the human lifeworld. Advocates as well as opponents of the secular state often spell out "separation" in such negative terms, either with the intention of reducing the visible presence of religion in society or in the interest of undermining the legitimacy of state secularity. This has resulted in countless misunderstandings and hopelessly cyclical discussions. As Martha Nussbaum puts it, "The prominence of the bare idea of separation in current debate is a source of confusion, since separation, when not further interpreted through other concepts, may suggest the idea of marginalizing religion or pushing it to the periphery of people's lives."[46] In the interest of clarity, it seems advisable to see the element of distance ("separation") between state and religion as the negative flipside of a positive project, namely, the *provision of an open space for the unfolding of religious and belief-related diversity, in a spirit of freedom and equality.* To cite Nussbaum, "the separation of church and state is, fundamentally, about equality, about the idea that no religion will be set up as *the* religion of our nation, an act that immediately makes outsiders unequal."[47] Without the element of distance, such an open and equal space would be from the outset inconceivable, because a state that understands itself as linked to one particular religion or belief cannot function as a trustworthy guardian of freedom of religion or belief for all without discrimination. However, when trying to fulfill this task of providing place for all, the state has to do more than merely refrain from getting involved with a particular religion. Apart from maintaining the necessary distance or "separation," what is required are active investments in all areas of society, such as education, media work, family laws, interreligious dialogue, and so forth.[48]

The concept of inclusive secularism may also help to eliminate misunderstandings that often arise around the notion of state "neutrality." One typical misunderstanding stems from the equation of neutrality with indifference. Allegedly, the religiously neutral state just does not care about religious issues, thus remaining entirely passive on all these issues. Carl Schmitt's ideological attack against the modern secular state rests on such a negative reading of neutrality as mere indifference. Under the heading of "The Age of Neutralizations," he draws a picture—or rather, a caricature—of the liberal secular state as being merely driven by economic interests and devoid of any higher metaphysical aspirations. By contrast, the idea of inclusive secularism facilitates a much more demanding interpretation of neutrality. Instead of betraying a lack of commitment, state neutrality itself follows from a genuine normative aspiration, namely the nondiscriminatory implementation of freedom of religion or belief for all.[49] Naturally, such a project will always remain "work in progress."[50] No state can ever plausibly claim to have achieved such neutrality in practice.[51] As we have discussed in Chapter 3 on equality and diversity, ideas of "neutrality" often factually cover existing hegemonies, which people may just take for granted. Neutrality in the understanding of a fairness principle, however, requires proactive efforts to detect and overcome hegemonies through ever-new reforms and adaptations.[52]

A state dedicated to inclusive and nondoctrinal secularism should proactively engage with religions and beliefs, for the simple reason that they are part of the society which the state is supposed to serve. Instead of protecting religious truth claims or collective religious identities, what the inclusively secular state ought to protect is everyone's freedom of religion or belief. When engaging with religious communities, the secular state must keep its distance vis-à-vis religions, in order to be able to create, uphold, and defend an open space. This is easier said than done, as elaborated above. Additional complications arise from the demand to also uphold a distance from doctrinal forms of secularism, in particular the "milder" everyday versions of secular beliefs, which many people may simply take for granted. No one has a recipe as to how to avoid the secular state getting mixed up with such versions of doctrinal secularism. An obvious precondition is a culture of open communication between state and communities as well as the readiness to undertake self-critical assessments and ever-new adaptations. Finally, one cannot emphasize enough that the openness of the space provided by the secular state does not mean emptiness. The secular space can and should be filled with a multiplicity of religious symbols, images, and voices, including critical voices.

When discussing universal rights in Chapter 1, we came to the conclusion that normative universalism can never exist in a "pure and simple" format. Universalism can only be credible as an ongoing reform project, which requires dialogue, self-criticism, adaptations, modifications, and exposure to challenges from many different angles. The same can be said about secularism. While we think that secularism, in the way we have further qualified it, can make sense as a guiding idea for the implementation of freedom of religion or belief, no state should ever pretend to have finally made it and in that sense to epitomize the claims of inclusive and nondoctrinal secularism. This issue calls for ongoing critical scrutiny at all levels.

CHAPTER 6

Violations of Freedom of Religion or Belief

1. Multifaceted Impressions

We[1] are standing in front of the ruins of a wooden funeral shed located in a small and remote village in Vietnam. A few weeks ago, the Vietnamese police burned that little shed to ashes. On that occasion, they reportedly also beat up several villagers. Some of them show us their scars and other traces of police brutality. A young woman still lies in a coma. What had happened? The villagers took the liberty of building some wooden funeral sheds, reportedly without asking the administration for permission. It strikes us as strange that a special permission should even be needed for erecting timber sheds consisting of just a few planks in a thinly populated remote region. Maybe this was not the real reason for the police raids. Some time ago, a Protestant preacher had persuaded the people living in this mountainous region to reform their funeral rites, which traditionally can be very costly for the family of the bereaved and may also cause problems of hygiene. The funeral sheds are part of a religious reform project the villagers have embarked upon. However, if people begin to take community affairs into their own hands, this might in the long run undermine the monopoly on politics, to which the Communist Party clings with all its power. In such situations, the government reacts swiftly and harshly to nip the "rebellious spirit" in the bud.

In the Chaco region in Paraguay, a delegation of indigenous peoples complains about the almost total loss of their spiritual heritage. A main reason is the expansion of big agro-companies on the lands traditionally used by indigenous peoples. Apart from undermining their livelihood, this development also erodes their traditional way of life and the spiritual beliefs and practices interwoven with it. The fact that the agro-companies are run by Mennonites, a Christian minority, which itself has a long history of suffering religious persecution, gives the conflict a tragic note. The origins of the Mennonites lie in the sixteenth-century Netherlands and Germany, where they were stigmatized as "Anabaptists." Later on, many of them migrated to Russia. When a new wave of bloody persecution set in under Stalin, large groups of Mennonites migrated again, including to the Chaco region. Given their proverbial industriousness, they developed the land into an economically flourishing business region. Yet what the Mennonites see as a divine blessing is a curse for the indigenous peoples, many of whom end up unemployed or as dependent manual workers. In the regional Bible schools, indigenous children learn that they should turn away from the "pagan" and "superstitious" rites of their ancestors. The intergenerational sense of belonging is dwindling, and many do not see any future for their ways of life, nor for their traditional spirituality.

Refugee children from Syria are crawling through the mud. It has been raining, and the temperature in the Lebanese Bekaa valley is barely above freezing level. Yet there is not enough space in the primitive huts which the refugees have erected "illegally." To describe their improvised settlements as "camps" would be a euphemism. The refugee children belong to the countless victims of a war in which political and religious motives overlap in confusing ways. Not only Sunni terrorist groups commit their atrocities in the name of God; Assad's troops and their supporters, too, invoke religion. More than a million Syrians have taken refuge in Lebanon. The Lebanese government fears that the mass influx of refugees could endanger the precarious religious quota system, which permeates Lebanon's political institutions. What makes the situation even worse is the fact that Lebanon itself has not yet entirely come to terms with its own recent history of violence, which between 1975 and 1990 culminated in a civil war with religious underpinnings.

In Bangladesh's national Hindu temple, a group of elderly women take the floor to lament the deplorable fate of Hindu widows. Owing to an outdated understanding of Hindu family laws, many widows do not inherit, thus ending up destitute and at the mercy of family members. For most of the women, it may be the first time ever to speak in public about the humiliation they have suffered or witnessed. Some of them have to struggle for words. Yet the passion they feel comes through very clearly. The more or less secular government of Bangladesh apparently does not wish to touch the delicate issue of religious family laws, for fear that a reform agenda could antagonize the religiously conservative parts of society. It thus seems that the existing family law systems will remain unreformed in the foreseeable future, in spite of its discriminatory implications, in particular for women from religious minorities.

We are traveling through "Transnistria," the separatist region that has unilaterally declared independence from the Republic of Moldova in 1990 and has been outside the control of the Moldovan government since 1992. Statues of Lenin still dominate the village squares, and the flag decorating the office rooms of the internationally nonrecognized de facto authorities still displays the old icons: hammer and sickle. An elderly Jewish man tells us that night by night he dreams about the Romanian Fascists who he fears could return and deport him once again, thus reliving over and over again the traumas he suffered when he was a child. The older generation in the Transnistrian region remembers Romanian Fascism, German Nazism, the devastations of World War II, the Communist dictatorship under Stalin, the post-Stalin USSR, the decline of Communism, the subsequent civil war, anarchistic capitalism, and exploitation of the country by oligarchs. Having gone through various rapid political "transformations" which repeatedly turned the order of things upside down, most people never had the opportunity to discuss their experiences publicly or to exchange their narratives beyond the small circle of family members and personal networks. A public culture of commemorating the collective traumas of the past does not exist. Some people here assume that the Holocaust of the Jews is an established historical fact while others believe it to be mere fiction. Historical issues remain left to one's personal opinion. The "ghosts of the past" have never been put to rest. This creates a political climate of insecurity and nervousness, with the result that people seek protection from the authorities, whatever their legitimacy may be.

Sierra Leone is an economically impoverished country in Western Africa with the history of a gruesome civil war, which ended in 2002 after more than a decade of extreme violence. The Interreligious Council, in which Muslims, Christians, and others cooperate on a regular basis, plays a crucial role in the ongoing project of rebuilding the nation. The council was a driving force within the Truth and Reconciliation Commission, which after the end of the fighting meticulously documented the atrocities committed by all parties to the conflict. In Sierra Leone, the religious communities live peacefully together, interreligious marriages are a widespread phenomenon, and conversions can go in all directions, not only from Christianity to Islam, but also vice versa. Apparently, not even the civil war could undermine the traditionally relaxed and amicable relationship that exists between religious communities. It is against this background that the Interreligious Council could take up its function as a main facilitator of national reconciliation. Religious communities furthermore support each other in keeping violent extremism out of Sierra Leone. "This is a blessed country," a high-ranking imam emphasizes at a meeting of the Interreligious Council in the capital Freetown. All the others present in the meeting—Sunnis, Shias, Ahmadis, Anglicans, Methodists, and Evangelicals—say "amen."

These briefly sketched scenarios from different countries and contexts may give a first glimpse into the complexity of situations in which violations of freedom of religion or belief occur. One message which those examples should convey is that freedom of religion or belief can never be addressed in isolation. One can be sure that wherever violations of this right occur, other human rights will be affected as well. Another obvious consequence from the above examples is that for a comprehensive empirical analysis of root causes and factors, one has to take into account a host of different variables: political authoritarianism, one-party systems, power imbalances between different groups, economic development or lack thereof, civil wars and historical traumatization, breakdown of state order due to endemic corruption, lack of trust in public institutions, gender stereotypes, outdated family law structures, complicated historical legacies, and countless other contextual factors. Such comprehensive analysis would exceed the confines of a book chapter. What we are going to present in the following is a brief typology of violations of freedom of religion or belief and their underlying motives. While this approach certainly has its limits and problems, the advantage of a typological approach is that it can shed light on different patterns and motives. In order not to remain entirely abstract, we connect typological observations with a few country examples. However, it should be noted that a typological approach will never do full justice to the complexities of any country or any of the specific countries mentioned in this regard.[2] Our main purpose is not to give a global "overview," which we think is ultimately impossible. Instead, we want to sensitize readers to the multifaceted features of violations of religious freedom, many of which remain under the radar of public attention.

2. The Tip and the Iceberg

Violations of freedom of religion or belief take place in most different spheres of society: in court rooms and prisons, in tax offices or immigration centers, in hospitals and psychiatric clinics, in the workplace or at school, in neighborhoods controlled by vigilante groups, and sometimes even in the midst of one's own family. Violations occur through formal sanctions, various types of administrative harassment, discriminatory immigration and naturalization stipulations, unreasonable obstacles to the labor or housing markets, anti-minority stereotypes promoted within the official school curricula, stigmatizing media reports, acts of vandalism and intimidation, and countless other manifestations of prejudice, discrimination, and hostility.

Publicly reported violations are only the proverbial tip of the iceberg. Much remains under the water level, as it were, and even the general size of the iceberg is not fully known.[3] One of the reasons for lack of knowledge is that many types of violations cannot easily be researched. How can we assess a situation where a particular group of people feels constantly harassed by the tax offices? If the permission to renovate a mosque or church has been withheld for an unreasonable time span, this can indicate a lack of bureaucratic efficiency, but it could also be a deliberate act of discrimination. What if children from a certain minority receive lower grades in school than their fellow students? Whether or not this follows from discriminatory stereotypes is impossible to say without in-depth analyses. We frequently move in grey zones, where assessments depend on many variables and remain debatable and controversial.

When it comes to violations of freedom of religion or belief much attention is usually given to restrictive measures that carry their discriminatory intention openly in their titles, for instance, in the case of anti-apostasy, anti-blasphemy, or anti-conversion laws, sometimes called "A-B-C-laws" (for apostasy, blasphemy, and conversion). Criminal law sanctions against apostasy nowadays only exist in some Islamic countries. Examples include Brunei, the Islamic Republic of Iran, Malaysia, Mauritania, Saudi Arabia, Sudan, Yemen, and other states. The circle of states that criminalize proselytism, however, is much broader and also includes countries with a Christian, Hindu, or Buddhist heritage, such as Armenia, Greece, India, Myanmar, or Nepal—to name just a few. Although mainly threatening missionary activities, that is, acts of converting others rather than punishing the act of conversion as such, anti-proselytism laws usually cast a shadow also on the converts themselves, who by implication bear the stigma of naïve or unreliable victims of manipulation, corruption, and seduction. Anti-blasphemy laws, too, exist under the auspices of quite different religions, for example in Bangladesh, Greece, Pakistan, the Russian Federation, and many other countries. What is deemed "blasphemous" often remains quite nebulous, thus granting a broad margin of discretion to law enforcement agencies and national courts. The usual targets of blasphemy laws include atheists, agnostics, members of minorities, but also dissidents within majority religions.

This type of A-B-C laws belongs to the visible tip of the iceberg. Confining the analysis to openly discriminatory laws would thus lead to wrong impressions. In reality, many violations happen through prima facie "neutral" laws, which on the surface do not show any relation to religion. One example is anti-extremism laws, some of which only vaguely circumscribe the offense at issue, with the result that any unwelcome religious practice could fall under "extremism." In the Russian Federation and Central Asian states, this affects the Jehovah's Witnesses and other religious groups. What renders their activities "extremist" remains quite nebulous. Furthermore, in the former Yugoslav Republic of Macedonia, a schismatic bishop was once sent to prison under the domestic anti-hatred legislation, although his "offense" was the establishment of an independent diocese, which he accomplished without any use or threat of violence. The first instance court even argued that he "had instigated hatred toward himself and his followers" and that "the ensuing revolt and intolerance had derived from an infringement of the religious sensibilities of the people who had requested the state authorities to intervene."[4] In Turkey, the charge of terrorism has become rampant; it can target any individual or group who are considered by the authorities as suspicious or unreliable. The Vietnamese criminal code contains a provision against the "abuse of democratic freedoms," which due to the open formulation threatens whomever the government wishes to discipline. Although none of these criminal provisions make reference to religion in their titles, they can be used—and actually are being used—to impose sanctions also on members of religious minorities or dissidents.

An arguably even larger part of the iceberg consists of administrative harassment. In some countries the enjoyment of freedom of religion or belief, in particular in its community-related dimensions, depends on complicated administrative approval procedures. For religious communities, in particular those that the government deems unwelcome, this can amount to an endless struggle with the bureaucracy over signatures, stamps, membership lists, and bank accounts. If some details are found missing or incorrect (which is easy to arrange), this can result in fines, arrests, closures, or confiscations. In countries such as Kazakhstan, Tajikistan, Turkmenistan, or Vietnam, special licenses are needed for performing worship, conducting youth activities, performing missionary work, importing and selling religious literature, and other activities. Sometimes, such licenses are only valid for a particular region or linked to short expiration periods. Hence, people always move in a grey zone of legal insecurity, which has a chilling effect on their activities. Administrative harassment can furthermore exist in the form of nonactivities, for example, when applications for establishing a religious kindergarten remain unanswered or when the issuance of permissions for repairing religious buildings takes unreasonably long. We heard the story that in one country it was apparently easier to first build a chicken farm, which subsequently was converted into a church, than applying for a permission to build a church in the first place.

Structural hurdles for freedom of religion or belief can furthermore exist in family laws. Take the example of Lebanon, where sixteen branches of family jurisdictions exist in parallel, all of which operate on the basis of religious laws.[5] Some interreligious marriage constellations do not easily (if at all) fit into that system. In such cases, the only viable course for a couple to take is by contracting the marriage abroad—usually in Cyprus—and having it approved upon return under the rules of private international law. Moreover, the Lebanese family law does not officially accommodate atheists, who have to find ways to circumvent the system (which at least is possible in a comparatively liberal country like Lebanon). Another problem is legal insecurity in the case that an interreligious marriage breaks up, with the result that existential questions like inheritance and custody for children must be settled. Incidentally, the lack of civil options within some family laws creates strange incentives for people to change their religion, possibly without really meaning it. The fact that Catholic canon law does not acknowledge divorce causes some Catholics officially to convert to Islam, which is the easiest way to get out of an unhappy marriage. This leads to schizophrenic situations, especially if the "converts" continue to feel attached to their old community to which they have officially ceased to belong. This pattern of problems originating from a system of state-enforced religious family laws can be found in many Islamic countries, but also in Israel. Furthermore, in 2015, Myanmar issued restrictive family laws, which serve the goal of protecting the nation's Buddhist hegemony.

Another place of possible human rights violations is the school.[6] We received reports that school students in one country allegedly felt under pressure to perform confessions to a priest who appeared in the premises of a public school during regular school hours. If this were true, it would amount to an unjustifiable infringement of freedom of religion or belief. For good reasons, school education has a mandatory status in most countries—a situation which the government must not exploit to put pressure on children or their parents in order to compel them to perform religious ceremonies against their will. Representatives of the Muslim Uighurs from the Chinese province of Xinjiang reported that during Ramadan school children faced expectations to eat the food provided by the school authorities. By putting pressure on school children, the Chinese government apparently tries to prevent them from experiencing their collective religious identity. Furthermore, the UN Committee on the Rights of the Child expressed concern about reports that in schools in Myanmar students had been converted to Buddhism without the knowledge or consent of their parents.[7]

Concerning religious education broadly speaking, one should differentiate between "religious instruction," on the one hand, and "information about religion," on the other. When it comes to *religious instruction*, that is, an education based on the tenets of a particular faith community, the school has to ensure that no student feels under pressure to participate against their will or the will of their parents, respectively. Exemptions must be easily available and should not be connected to punitive measures or any other disadvantages. By contrast, *information about religion* has a different status and can also become part of the mandatory curriculum, provided it is given in an "objective" manner. In reality, however, the line drawn between instruction and information often remains fuzzy, and claims of "objectivity" in teaching may look far-fetched. Lack of clarity in this regard led to a judgment by the European Court of Human Rights against Norway. The Norwegian government had established a mandatory religious course that was supposed to provide general information on religious issues, while at the same time having a strong focus on Christianity. The Strasbourg Court inter alia criticized the high threshold for getting an exemption.[8] In a judgment on Turkey, the court criticized the way the Turkish authorities had organized school education in "ethics," which de facto is largely based on Sunni Islamic teaching.[9] Whereas Christian students can receive an exemption, Alevi students do not have that option, which according to the claimants shows disrespect for the independence of Alevites. The European Court of Human Rights endorsed this argument and reprimanded Turkey for having violated freedom of religion or belief. In Bangladesh, we received reports that, due to a shortage of qualified teachers, students from religious minorities sometimes receive religious instruction in a faith different than their own. For example, some Christian children ended up sitting in a Hindu class.

In recent years, many of the most atrocious violations of freedom of religion or belief have been committed by terrorist organizations and non-state armed groups. In Nigeria, Boko Haram abducted hundreds of Christian girls, many of whom were apparently converted to Islam and "married" off to their abductors. Followers of the so-called "Islamic State in Iraq and the Levant" (ISIL) videotaped cruelties beyond imagination in order to recruit supporters and cater to international media voyeurism. For decades, the "Lord's Resistance Army" in Eastern Africa has terrorized the population in the name of a bizarre interpretation of Christianity. In India, vigilante groups of the Rashtriya Swayamsevak Sangh and other Hindu nationalists have intimidated members of religious minorities, in particular Muslims and Christians. In general, nonstate actors have a large share in committing abuses of freedom of religion or belief. At times, they receive open or clandestine support from parts of the state apparatus. When places of worship of religious minorities are set ablaze, fire brigades and police sometimes react suspiciously slowly. In a climate of impunity, where prosecution of violent incidents, if taking place at all, typically fails to lead to any tangible results, nonstate actors feel encouraged to continue committing their crimes.

3. Perpetrators and Their Motives

From the multiplicity of motives underneath violations of freedom of religion or belief, we would like to highlight three main patterns: (a) the enforcement of religious truth or purity claims; (b) the defense of a religiously defined national identity; and (c) the control obsessions of authoritarian governments. One should bear in mind, however, that many overlaps between these three patterns exist. Moreover, additional motives, factors, and variables should also be taken into account. We address this under subsection (d).

(a) Religious Truth and Purity Claims

Warfare and acts of terror carried out in the name of religious "truth," death sentences leveled against converts, the systematic persecution of "heretics," aggressive monitoring of religiously "correct" conduct by the police—such phenomena continue to threaten numerous people in the twenty-first century. Restrictive measures mainly target "unbelievers," "heretics," and "apostates," but they ultimately affect all those whose attitudes or behavior is deemed "deviant" from the right path as defined by the dominant forces within the hegemonic religion and their political allies.

Several governments in Muslim-majority countries derive their political legitimacy from their role as self-appointed custodians of religious truth and purity. Members of non-Muslim minorities—Christians, Hindus, Buddhists, or others—when living in these countries cannot actively promote their convictions in public. Similar restrictions affect atheists and agnostics. In Saudi Arabia, non-Muslims are even forbidden from performing any visible religious practices in public. In the Maldives, citizenship remains reserved to Muslims only. In multicultural and multireligious Malaysia, the majority of ethnic Malays, who dominate state institutions, are at the same time defined by their adherence to Islam. In all the countries just enumerated, changing from Islam to another religion or to atheism is de jure or de facto impossible. In the Islamic Republic of Iran, followers of the post-Islamic Baha'i religion face systematic persecution, because the stigma of apostasy seems to hang over the entire community. Baha'is inter alia cannot officially enroll in higher education, and Baha'i cemeteries have repeatedly been bulldozed.

Repressive measures not only target "unbelievers," but also go after intrareligious minorities or dissidents. In some countries dominated by Sunni Islam, this mainly affects Shia Muslims who in Saudi Arabia, Bahrain, and Malaysia suffer increasing discrimination and harassment. In Pakistan, members of the Ahmadiyya Muslim Community are among the most frequent victims of repression and violence. If Ahmadis, who understand themselves as a reform branch of Islam, use the typical Islamic greeting, this may suffice to trigger prosecution under Pakistan's criminal code, which criminalizes any activities by which Ahmadis convey the impression of being Muslims.[10] Sufis are another inner-Islamic group which faces hostility in a number of countries, including around the Persian Gulf.

Apart from correct believing, "correct behavior," too, is subject to tight supervision. Women and girls are among the most likely victims of humiliating control policies, which pretend to measure a person's "virtue" by the inches of hair visible under a headscarf. Holding hands in public with a member of the opposite sex may incur legal sanctions, unless one can prove marriage or close family ties. Countless gays or lesbians go into hiding or even contract fake marriages with a person to whom they may not really feel attracted in order to avoid harassment and persecution. Eating and drinking in public during the fasting period is another punishable offence in some countries. While many of those restrictions occur in Islamic countries, the situation in Israel is in some aspects comparable; secular-minded Israelis as well as Jews not following the orthodox rabbinate, often lament the sticky atmosphere, which encroaches on their personal liberty, not only on the Sabbath or during religious holidays.

Violations of religious freedom in the interest of enforcing "true" faith occur not only through state institutions. Terrorist groups like Boko Haram in Nigeria, Al-Shabaab in Eastern Africa, or ISIL in Syria and Iraq committed atrocities, including killings, abductions, lootings, and acts of vandalism. Among the victims of ISIL were non-Muslim minorities like Yezidis, Mandeans, and Christians, many of whom fled the region or lived as internally displaced persons. After the defeat of ISIL some have begun to resettle in their cities and villages. The Yezidis, whose religious center lies in northern Iraq, still fear for the future of their religious community and identity. Christians still see the legacy of two millennia of church history in the Middle East in jeopardy. Atheists, agnostics, or individuals who criticize the dominant religion only receive limited, if any, support in some countries, where they become victims of violent attacks. Acts of terrorism furthermore target the followers of alternative branches of Islam. Terrorists who see themselves as following the Sunni tradition have attacked Shias or Sufis as "heretics" and destroyed or demolished many of their holy sites. The violence they perpetrate in the name of Sunni Islam may also threaten other Sunnis who do not wish to bow to the pressure of religious conformism or who end up among the many random "casualties" of suicide bombings. While many of the terrorist acts currently occur in the name of Islam— Sunni or Shia Islam—there are also cases of terrorism committed in the name of Christianity. The "Lord's Resistance Army," which is responsible for numerous atrocities, including killings and abductions, in Eastern Africa is the best-known example.

(b) Preservation of National Identity

Whereas violations committed in the name of religious truth or purity nowadays mainly take place in Islamic countries, repression in the interest of preserving a religiously defined national identity occurs in almost all regions and under the auspices of different religions. Many governments invoke a national religious heritage, which they pretend to defend and protect against foreign influences. Followers of nontraditional religions—or religions without a tradition of being present in those countries—frequently find themselves in the position of second-class citizens, and those who abandon the dominant religious tradition risk stigmatization as national traitors or "fifth columns" allegedly operating in the interest of foreign countries and foreign donors.

While the fault line in the above-described pattern—that is, violations committed in the name of religious truth claims—chiefly runs along the dichotomy of true belief versus heresy or nonbelief, a religiously charged national identity politics typically produces the *dichotomy of belonging versus nonbelonging*: what counts is whether or not a religious community fits into the nationalist matrix. Accordingly, repressive measures—including the criminalization of proselytism, restrictive visa regulations, exclusion from citizenship, confiscation of real estate, public anti-sect campaigns, detention and deportation—mainly serve the purpose of preserving the hegemony of the nation's traditional religious heritage.

The national heritage claimed by the state can consist of one religion or a number of religions, including certain old established minorities. In Myanmar, Buddhism plays a major part in defining national identity. The Rohingyas, a Muslim minority in Myanmar, suffer atrocities from nationalist and religious xenophobia drummed up inter alia by radical Buddhist monks. Hundreds of thousands of Rohingyas live outside their home country, many of them victims of "ethnic cleansing" and other atrocities. In Sri Lanka, too, the Singhalese national identity and Buddhism are closely interwoven, with a resulting climate of mistrust toward Muslims, Christians, and other minorities. Hindu nationalists in India accept a broad variety of religious beliefs and practices, including Sikhism, Buddhism, and Jainism, because they have their origins on Indian soil, while attacking

Islam and Christianity as "foreign" religions, whose origins lie abroad. Muslims are often suspected of showing sympathy for India's neighbor Pakistan, and Christians bear the brunt of allegedly representing the interests of the imperialistic West. When "*Dalits*," that is, people from lower-caste backgrounds, convert to Islam or (more often) to Christianity, they may lose their affirmative action benefits, without which they face additional difficulties to get access to higher education or to the labor market.[11]

Harnessing religion as an ingredient of national identity politics also happens under the auspices of Christianity. In the Russian Federation, the nationalistic narrative combines elements of the tsarist history with bits of the bygone Soviet empire, including Stalinism. The common denominator that glues these prima facie irreconcilably different pieces together is an aggressive anti-liberalism, which does not accommodate much religious freedom. In particular, Evangelical denominations and, even more so, the Jehovah's Witnesses face increasing repression. In the wake of a verdict of the Russian Supreme Court in 2017, the nationwide infrastructure of the Jehovah's Witnesses has been dismantled and any religious practice of the community is considered a criminal offence. All this happens in the name of combating "religious extremism." Since the annexation of Crimea in 2014, the Muslim Crimean Tatars, too, have suffered increasing harassment, as they are suspected of not showing sufficient loyalty toward the Russian authorities. Political conflicts over the eastern parts of Ukraine and Crimea have also deepened existing divides and created new ones within the family of Orthodox churches.

In Christian Orthodoxy, ideas of a "symphony" between the nation, the state, and the church have a long tradition. This may further increase the risk that church representatives become complicit in national identity politics. The refusal of some Serbian nationalist politicians to cooperate with the war crimes tribunal in The Hague caused applause in parts of the Serbian Orthodox Church. The European Court of Human Rights had to remind the government of the Republic of Moldova that the Moscow-orientated Moldovan Orthodox Church cannot hold a state-supported monopoly of the Orthodox tradition in the country; the state must also accommodate other churches, such as the Metropolitan Church of Bessarabia, which leans toward Bucharest.[12] In Georgia, too, the Orthodox Church understands itself as a bulwark of the nation, in this case mainly against the traditional political, cultural, and religious hegemony of Russia within the Caucasus region.

Nationalistic tendencies with religious overtones have also become vocal in Western Europe. One example is the treatment of refugees from Syria, Iraq, and other Middle Eastern countries. Various governments in the European Union have articulated xenophobic anti-immigration policies, in particular vis-à-vis Muslim refugees from the Middle East. If accommodating any refugees at all, they declared, they would only take in Christian refugees. The position taken by the current Hungarian government sounds like a re-set of the early modern slogan "*cuius regio, eius religio*," which merged territorial sovereignty with cultural and religious hegemony. Obviously, such a religiously discriminatory policy is not in line with the Geneva Refugee Convention, which protects refugees regardless of their religion.

(c) Control-Obsessions of Authoritarian Governments

Systematic violations of freedom of religion or belief also occur in countries whose governments do not show any attachment to a particular religion or to any religion. What mainly brings them into conflict with freedom of religion or belief is the component of *freedom*, which this right has in common with other human rights. Freedom of religion or belief shows an inherent affinity in particular to freedom of expression, freedom of peaceful assembly, and freedom of association. As a rule, the more authoritarian a government is, the more it typically fears that rights to freedom could become entry-points for "subversive" activities. The usual answer is repression, tight supervision, or even infiltration in order to keep things under strict control. This frequently leads to government-induced splits within religious communities.

Some of the still officially Communist countries, such as Lao People's Democratic Republic or Vietnam, have seen pragmatic reforms in recent decades, including a certain opening up for religious diversity in private and public. Polemical attacks against religion as the "opium of the people" (Karl Marx) or "opium for the people" (Lenin) appear to be a matter of the past. In Vietnam, tourists can visit old and new temples, pagodas, and churches, where people perform their prayers and rituals. To infer from such observations that freedom of religion or belief is no longer a serious problem would be premature, though. Instead, the predominant pattern of repression has changed. While the ideological opposition between religion and atheism seems to have lost much of its former fervor, the obsession to keep all aspects of social life under tight control remains the overall concern of the governing party. The political monopoly, which the Communist Party of Vietnam continues to claim, requires nourishing the illusion that the party and the people have seamlessly identical interests. Public criticism, which could erode this proclaimed unanimity between the party and the people, is per definition "subversive."

Even convinced functionaries of an authoritarian government may from time to time ask themselves whether the publicly staged applause which they regularly receive from the people may not be fully authentic. Enforced loyalty ultimately remains unreliable, and the fact that the opposition cannot articulate their concerns publicly means that much may happen underground. This explains the insatiable control obsessions of authoritarian governments, in particular one-party regimes. In order to keep things under control, they only grant religious practices within tightly monitored official channels, which are specifically designed for that purpose. Examples cover different parts of the globe: from China and Vietnam to post-Soviet Central Asian republics to African states such as Zimbabwe. One example is the management measures imposed by the Chinese government for the reincarnation of living Buddhas in Tibetan Buddhism.[13] Another example is North Korea, where the supreme leader of the Democratic People's Republic of Korea and his ancestors have become objects of enforced political idolatry.

The fault line resulting from excessive state control differs yet again from the dividing lines which we have identified in the two patterns described before. It is neither the dichotomy of true belief versus wrong belief or unbelief, nor the question of belonging versus nonbelonging. Instead, the overarching issue is loyalty to the state and the governing party. Accordingly, the dividing line runs between those communities who credibly demonstrate loyalty by cooperating with the state and those whose loyalty appears questionable. The *dichotomy of loyal versus independent groups* typically runs in the midst of the religious communities themselves, thus causing numerous splits and schisms. In Vietnam it divides for example the official Buddhist Sangha from independent Buddhist groups, such as the United Buddhist Church of Vietnam. In China, some of the Christian churches, both Catholic and Protestant, cooperate within the officially created patriotic associations, while others only meet as unofficial "house churches" or underground churches. Tibetan Buddhists, too, suffer internal splits within a climate of mistrust and suspicion created by tight surveillance, while Muslim Uighurs in Xinjiang province currently face a new wave of brutal repression with mass-scale detentions. It remains to be seen which effects the provisional agreement on bishop appointments, signed on 22 September 2018 between the Holy See and the Chinese government, will have; however, there are good reasons to assume that some currents of underground Catholicism will continue to exist.

(d) Overlaps and Additional Factors

The three patterns just described—(a) "true" belief versus "heresy" or unbelief, (b) national religious heritage versus the influx of "foreign" religions or sects, and (c) loyalty toward the state versus disloyalty and "subversion"—overlap in many ways. The total absence of religious freedom in North Korea stems not only from the control obsessions of a totalitarian government; it follows also from the idolatrous cult of the nation's supreme leader. In the Russian Federation, control interests exist in tandem with a mobilization of nationalism, which includes the invocation of the Russian Orthodox heritage for political gains. Middle Eastern governments, too, combine nationalistic identity politics with the self-appointed role as the custodians of religious norms. China's authorities tighten political control measures by using artificial intelligence, while at the same time staging an ideological campaign in favor of renewed Communist orthodoxy.

The purpose of the typological differentiation just elaborated is not to provide the criteria for neatly structuring the global political landscape. Rather, our main interest is to raise awareness that important differences concerning the motives underneath violations should be taken into account. Lack of such awareness can lead to grave misjudgments. For example, if one approaches the situation of religious freedom mainly from a Middle Eastern perspective, where some countries have established tight monopolies of permissible religious practice, one may be tempted to underestimate the seriousness of human rights problems in India, which mainly stem from the divide between "national" and "foreign" religions. If visitors to Vietnam react positively, surprised to see religious life unfolding in a Communist state, they may have in mind an outdated pattern of ideological polemics against religion as "opium of the people," thus missing the point that the struggle over freedom of religion or belief is far from over, given the ongoing control interests of the political elite with a one-party system. While conversion is a huge problem in Saudi Arabia or Iran, it is possibly less of an issue in China. However, to infer that the Chinese politics is respectful of freedom of religion or belief would be a misinterpretation. The point is that the relevant "test questions" differ from country to country. Many serious misjudgments originate from underestimating the differences of phenomena, motives, and root causes.

. In addition to the three main patterns identified above, one should take note of other relevant variables. An important factor which provides a key to understanding human rights problems in many countries is endemic corruption. When corruption is a daily experience, thus shaping expectations and mentalities, it undermines any trust in the fair functioning of public institutions. In extreme situations, public institutions cease to even deserve the qualification as "public," because they have actually fallen prey to feudal or "mafia" interests. In the absence of trustworthy public institutions, however, people often have no alternative other than turning to their own internal networks, in order to manage their lives. This can create fertile ground for collective "narrow-mindedness," that is, an inward-looking mentality of people who feel under siege in an unreliable or even hostile environment, thus all the more sticking to an "iron-hard" internal loyalty. If the networks happen to be defined along religious or denominational lines, this typically leads to poisoning interreligious relations. Collective narrow-mindedness can culminate in a breakdown of intergroup communication, which in turn increases the likelihood of violent escalation.[14]

The climate of religious freedom furthermore depends on how a country copes with a traumatic history, for example, the history of bloodshed in the wake of the partition of the Indian subcontinent. Memories linger very much in India, Pakistan, and Bangladesh. While Hindu nationalists in India often associate young Muslim men with "extremists" from Pakistan, Islamist movements in Pakistan and Bangladesh in turn connect members of the Hindu minority with India. Christian minorities in South Asia, in particular Evangelicals, suffer the stigma of allegedly representing the former colonial West. Similar problems exist in many countries across the continents—in the ex-Soviet republics of Central Asia as well as in sub-Saharan African countries or in the Middle East. If the "ghosts of the past" have never been put to rest, they continue to shape the perception of contemporary political developments, possibly resulting in dramatic misjudgments and rampant conspiracy projections. It should be noted in this context that old and new conspiracy theories frequently include anti-Semitic stereotypes, in particular in Western countries and large parts of the Arab world.

Land conflicts are another factor underneath many human rights violations. In 2012, more than twenty Buddhist temples located in the Chittagong Hill Tracts, a remote area belonging to Bangladesh, were set ablaze.[15] Most of the Buddhists who live in that region close to Myanmar are indigenous people. As in many parts of the world, indigenous populations encounter problems when requested to provide legal documentation in the modern technical understanding to prove their ownership on the lands their families have used and cultivated for a long time, possibly since time immemorial. Lack of ownership documentation renders them vulnerable to land-grabbing by mafia organizations. The fight over precious real estate does not stop at lands upon which monasteries, churches, pagodas, temples, graveyards, or other religious infrastructure had been erected. The above-mentioned 2012 "Ramu Incident" in the Chittagong Hill Tracts is merely one example.

Finally, one should not forget the impact of misogynic patriarchal structures. Women and girls from minorities often suffer a combination of different human rights abuses. One of the most dramatic phenomena is the abduction of young women from a religious minority, who often are simultaneously converted to another religion and forcibly "married" off, frequently even to one of their abductors. In Bangladesh, we met with Hindu families who were in despair because they had lost their daughters and did not even have the slightest idea of their whereabouts. It was horrible to listen to their stories. Another example is hate speech targeting religious minorities, which in many cases displays a pronounced gender component. In one South Asian country, we heard gossip about an underwear factory run by Muslims, who allegedly tampered with female underwear by inserting a chemical substance, with a view to manipulating the fertility rate of the majority population in order to tip the demographic balance in favor of Islam. Bizarre though this story may sound, it certainly has the potential to drive the targeted company into bankruptcy. It furthermore illustrates that a gender lens is indispensable for a comprehensive analysis of hate manifestations. Images of sexually aggressive minorities are widespread. They typically combine the ascription of "primitive" and despicable instincts with the allegation of long-term demographic purposes, which minorities are thought surreptitiously and strategically to pursue—very much along the lines already displayed in anti-Semitic Nazi propaganda. These images thus mobilize feelings of contempt in conjunction with political hysteria.

4. The Victims

One of the most frequently asked questions concerns the estimated number of victims from different religious backgrounds. Solid answers are difficult, perhaps impossible. It is complicated enough to estimate the number of those who suffer prison sentences for religious reason in a particular country. How should we measure the impact of bureaucratic harassment on certain religious communities and their members? Who would be able to count how many interreligious marriages have been effectively prevented by discriminatory family laws? How many people have personally been victimized by acts of vandalism, smear campaigns, or the destruction of graveyards? How can we quantify the impact of indirectly discriminatory structures in labor or housing laws? The more complex the understanding of violations of freedom of religion or belief is, the more difficult it is to cater to the media interest in getting reliable figures, global maps, and quotable rankings.[16] Governments which effectively employ repressive measures may even be able by and large to avoid visible "cases" of arrest and detention. A climate of constant low-scale intimidation may suffice to keep things under tight control. While producing no "figures," repression may go on unabated.

The Pew Forum on Religion and Public Life, based in Washington, D.C., has therefore decided to focus attention on potential rather than actual violations of religious freedom by estimating the number of people who live in countries with high or very high levels of religious restrictions. According to a study published by the Pew Forum in June 2018, around 83 percent of the world's population falls within that category.[17] This extremely high figure has made many headlines in the media—"bad news is good news." Yet the question remains whether these monstrous figures help to capture realities and if this kind of reporting contributes to an adequate understanding of the issues at hand.[18] We have our doubts.

Among the victims of human rights violations, we can identify people from most different religious and nonreligious backgrounds. Depending on the predominant pattern of repression, they may bear the stigma of "unbelievers," "heretics," "external invaders," "fifth column of foreign powers," "stubborn opposition," or "subversive" forces. Others end up as targets or casualties of violence and warfare. Although no religious community is immune from such victimization, some groups are more likely to become victimized than others. Baha'is in Iran or Yemen, Ahmadis in Pakistan, Falun Gong practitioners in China, Jehovah's Witnesses in Russia and Central Asia are particularly endangered. Jews, too, especially when publicly wearing visible symbols of their religious identity face increasing hostility in some countries, where anti-Semitism seems to be on the rise again, including in Germany, where Jews had suffered the genocidal violence of the Nazi regime. A group of people that have been neglected for a long time are atheists and agnostics. Moreover, we still have limited understanding of the problems of indigenous peoples whose spiritual practices do not fit easily into the established jurisprudence on freedom of religion or belief. Many of their problems, including in the area of freedom of religion or belief, stem from land disputes. In this field, much empirical work and important normative adaptations lie ahead of us. Migrant workers and members of their families, in particular when working in private households, have likewise received comparatively little attention. Many of them live as "invisible minorities" in their host countries, with limited or no opportunities to manifest their religious practices openly.[19] The fact that most domestic workers are women, once again, points to the need of including a gender perspective in any meaningful analysis of root causes, phenomena, and features.

When describing the situation of specific communities, internal theological differences warrant systematic attention; they often play a decisive role. Within Islam, members of the Ahmadiyya Community have suffered systematic persecution, especially since their official "excommunication" from Islam by the Pakistani Parliament in 1974. Another group suffering disproportionately from terrorist violence in Pakistan is Shia Muslims, as testified by hundreds of killings in recent years. In some other predominantly Sunni countries, too, the situation of Shias has deteriorated. Even in Indonesia, a country often praised for its tradition of tolerance, hostility against Shia Muslims seems on the rise. In Bahrain, whose government favors the numerically smaller Sunni branch of Islam, dozens of Shia mosques were demolished. In the Shia dominated Islamic Republic of Iran, in turn, discrimination goes the other way and inter alia affects Sunnis. Incidentally, this illustrates that "Islamophobia" is not an exclusively Western phenomenon, as some commentators have suggested; it also occurs in many predominantly Islamic countries, often in the more specific forms of hostility against Sunnis, Shias, Sufis, Ahmadis, and others.

Internal differentiation along denominational lines also matters when it comes to assessing the situations of Christians. The generic term "persecution of Christians" obfuscates the fact that not all Christian churches are equally affected. In quite a number of countries, Evangelicals attract most of the hostility, since people suspect them of engaging in unwelcome missionary activities and representing the West, in particular the United States of America. In recent years, the internationally known apostasy verdicts leveled against Christians in the Islamic Republic of Iran typically concerned members of Evangelical communities. In the Russian Federation, many of the Protestant and Evangelical churches, especially those with a short history in the country, bear the stigma of "foreign sects." Jehovah's Witnesses, who see themselves as Christians, face resentments, owing to their nonviolent missionary activities and their general conscientious objection to military service. In South Korea, hundreds of Jehovah's Witnesses were imprisoned as a result of their refusal to serve in the military. In Eritrea, some Jehovah's Witnesses have even spent more than twenty years in prison for their conscientious objection to military service.[20]

Christian communities have recently suffered most dramatically in large parts of the Middle East. Hundreds of thousands of Christians have fled Syria and Iraq. This is not only the result of warfare, which affects people from all religious backgrounds. In Mosul and elsewhere, terrorists and their supporters earmarked the houses of Christians with the letter "N" for "Nazareans" before looting and demolishing them. The self-proclaimed "Islamic State in Iraq and the Levant" aimed to erase all traces of religious pluralism in the region. Thus, the old established autochthonous churches— Syrian Orthodox, Chaldeans, Armenians, Assyrians, and others—suffered brutal persecution and tragic losses. Even after the defeat of ISIL, the future of Christian communities in the area remains doubtful. A rich historic legacy of two millennia is in peril. Many Christians from the Middle East feel bitterly disappointed by a lack of solidarity, which they would have expected from the international community, in particular from Europe and America. Side by side with regional Christians, Yezidis have experienced gruesome acts of cruelty. Thousands of Yezidi women and girls live in the captivity of terrorist organizations; many of them reportedly were sold and abused as sex slaves.

Finally, violations of freedom of religion or belief also affect members of religious majorities, in particular individuals who openly voice their dissent or opposition. Critics have castigated fanaticism, vigilantism, and terrorism, the utilization of religion for the purposes of demarking national identity, and the infiltration of religious community life by state agents.

Among those critics are clerics, theologians, monks or nuns, and laypersons. Some of them explicitly base their criticism on the internationally
agreed human right to freedom of religion or belief. Sadly, this does not
protect them from accusations of betrayal or attacks that they suffer within
their own communities. Some of them were killed, disappeared, or ended
up in prison.

CHAPTER 7

Comparing International and Regional Case Law

1. Toward an Emerging Human Rights "Ecosystem"

During a discussion with domestic civil society organizations in an Eastern European country, the issue of the national court system came up. The main question concerned the role of the courts in providing protection of human rights, including freedom of religion or belief. Do the national courts of that country fulfill their function adequately? How do they respond to complaints about human rights violations? Do they cooperate with civil society? Most of the answers given in that session were sarcastic, some almost cynical. "The only court we trust is based in Strasbourg," one participant remarked. Maybe this statement was an exaggeration. Given the generally sarcastic tone of the conversation, it seemed wise to remain cautious and not take such a comment at its face value. Yet it provides an example that human rights advocates may expect much from regional courts and other international mechanisms, in this case the European Court of Human Rights. Are such far-reaching expectations justified? Why should regional courts or international mechanisms function better than national courts? Can they set standards for others to follow, or would that mean expecting too much?

When assessing the contribution of regional courts and other international oversight mechanisms to the implementation of human rights, it is important not to see them in isolation. Courts are only one component (albeit an important one) within a much broader set of institutions, which together constitute a developing human rights infrastructure. Already at the national level, the implementation of constitutional rights provisions is not exclusively left to courts. It is also the mandate of ombuds-institutions and similar mechanisms of informal conflict settlement; National Human Rights Institutions (NHRIs), in some countries called Human Rights Commission or "Defensor del Pueblo"; parliamentary committees tasked with human rights monitoring; expert bodies mandated to carry out unannounced visits in prisons or psychiatric clinics; and so forth. What all those institutions have in common is their public status. Some of them enjoy constitutional rank, or they have at least a legal basis. Not less significant than public institutions, however, is the contribution of independent organizations, usually summed up under the general heading of nongovernmental organizations (NGOs). They comprise single-issue organizations, specialized on the promotion of one particular right or advocating for one particular group of people, as well as organizations working on a broad range of human rights. While many of them are connected to international NGOs, others have their focus more narrowly on domestic issues. Apart from secular NGOs, there are also faith-based organizations, who may fulfill similar functions for human rights.

At the international level, too, the human rights infrastructure presupposes a constant interaction between formal public bodies and nonformal ones. Public institutions include the UN treaty bodies that are tasked with monitoring the implementation of the various human rights conventions and covenants to which they are linked. The conclusions by the UN Human Rights Committee concerning individual cases (called "Views") show "some important characteristics of a judicial decision" and represent "an authoritative determination by the organ established under the Covenant itself charged with the interpretation of that instrument,"[1] even though they do not technically reach the level of judgments by a court. International human rights courts, in the full sense of the word, so far only exist at regional levels, that is, in Strasbourg (for the Council of Europe), in San José (for the Organization of American States), and in Arusha (for the African Union).[2] Without the contribution of international NGOs, which derive their legitimacy from their membership or their expertise, or both, the international and regional institutions of human rights protection would not be able to work. Hundreds of NGOs enjoy accreditation status in the UN or within regional human rights protection systems like the Council of Europe. Their possibilities to contribute include public statements (orally and in writing), amicus curiae briefs, media work, awareness raising, lobbying activities, and so on. The landscape of human rights institutions furthermore includes the Global Alliance of National Human Rights

Institutions (GANHRI) or international networks of parliamentarians, for example the International Panel of Parliamentarians for Freedom of Religion or Belief (IPPFoRB). This list is far from exhaustive.

The practical impact of the human rights infrastructure, as it has developed until now, much depends on whether or not the various levels—local, national, regional, and global—are effectively linked. This is the reason why National Human Rights Institutions play an increasing role. Their mandate includes functioning as a systematic "link" between the international and the national infrastructure. The Convention on the Rights of Persons with Disabilities explicitly demands such a link by obliging states to create a working national infrastructure of implementation and monitoring through one or more independent mechanisms. At the same time, this national infrastructure remains exposed to international supervision based on international standards. This type of linkages has become a success model in human rights practice. In other words, human rights institutions can actually make a difference, provided they cooperate in a meaningful and systematic way.

Now we turn back to the question of regional human rights courts and quasi-judicial international monitoring bodies. The idea is not that they should take over all the relevant human rights complaints. Not only would this be impossible in practice; it would not even make sense in theory. Stephen Hopgood is wrong when ironically invoking the "Tower of Babel" as a symbol of international human rights.[3] Their aspiration is not "to become *The Authority*," as he wants us to believe.[4] Rather, human rights work mainly takes place on the ground, close to where people live. Regional human rights courts, like the Strasbourg Court, and international bodies monitoring the ICCPR and other human rights conventions are not supposed to simply "supersede," let alone replace, national jurisdiction or other actors working on the ground. What they can offer is an additional option for people to submit complaints once they have exhausted all available domestic remedies. By doing so, they furthermore symbolize, as it were, the cross-boundary dynamics of human rights. In that sense their authority actually penetrates national boundaries. Like all judicial authority, however, it remains an authority "on probation," largely dependent on the persuasiveness of the reasoning on which the respective views and judgments are based. For this reason, dissenting or concurring opinions of individual judges and committee members are also made publicly available. Courts can only claim authority when exposing their reasoning to public criticism. Strictly speaking, no one has ever had "the last word" in the sense of being above challenges and public criticism.

The various instruments of human rights protection, as they exist at various levels, should mutually complement each other. However, this requires tireless efforts in coordination and cooperation. The danger of fragmentation not only exists with regard to different themes and different substantial rights, as described in Chapter 4; it also comes with regard to the institutional and infrastructural aspects of human rights. That is why a holistic perspective is imperative, for which César Rodríguez-Garavito has proposed the concept of a human rights "ecosystem."[5] The following observations should be seen in that light. At the same time, they have a specific focus on the necessary coordination between the UN Human Rights Committee and the European Court of Human Rights.

2. Avoiding Forum Shopping

Throughout this book, we have referred to general comments and individual cases that were decided by UN treaty bodies or regional human rights courts. The vast majority of these cases relating to freedom of religion or belief emanate from the Geneva-based UN Human Rights Committee and from the European Court of Human Rights in Strasbourg. A formidable challenge for these international and regional institutions is to avoid diverging and even contradictory jurisprudence on the same or similar matters. Otherwise, the coherence of the human rights framework risks being jeopardized and, in the worst case, opposing jurisprudence may even undermine both the international and the regional frameworks, leading to normative fragmentation. As the former Deputy Registrar of the European Court of Human Rights, Michael O'Boyle, argued in an academic article: "A major risk is that the case law of the different international tribunals can erode the unity of international law, lead to the development of conflicting or mutually exclusive legal doctrines and threaten the principle of universality."[6] This may also trigger so-called forum shopping, when litigants choose to go either to Geneva or to Strasbourg because a particular institution seems more likely to uphold their claims. Furthermore, it is undesirable when states are in a position to pick and choose which interpretation of an international mechanism or regional court suits them best in order to "escape" from their human rights obligations.

For these reasons, double examination of the same matter should be avoided already through procedural safeguards, which have also been contemplated by the drafters of the European Convention on Human Rights (adopted in 1950) and of the Optional Protocol to the International Covenant on Civil and Political Rights (adopted in 1966). Thus the European Court of Human Rights is not supposed to deal with any application that is substantially the same as a matter that *"has already been submitted* to another procedure of international investigation or settlement and contains no relevant new information."[7] By contrast, the UN Human Rights Committee must merely ascertain that the same matter *"is not being examined* under another procedure of international investigation or settlement."[8] This subtle difference, which leaves open the possibility of double examination when the Strasbourg Court has decided a case and then another complaint is submitted to Geneva, is no drafting oversight but was rather introduced on purpose because many UN delegates did not want to imply a hierarchy in which the UN Human Rights Committee would be subordinate to a regional human rights organ. This again reinforces the importance of coordination between regional and international bodies, rather than viewing it as a question of subordination.

In order to situate selected (quasi-)judicial decisions on freedom of religion or belief, the present chapter briefly explains the tasks and competences of the UN Human Rights Committee and the European Court of Human Rights, and then compares their jurisprudence on three specific issues, namely, on religious symbols in public life, religious education, and conscientious objection to military service.

3. The UN Human Rights Committee—
Tasks and Competences

The Human Rights Committee is one of the ten UN treaty bodies that monitor the implementation of the core international human rights treaties. While its name gives the impression that it covered all human rights, the UN Human Rights Committee only monitors whether states parties are implementing the International Covenant on Civil and Political Rights (ICCPR). Several of its provisions are relevant for freedom of religion or belief issues, including with regard to nondiscrimination on the basis of religion (Articles 2, 24, and 26), nonderogability (Article 4), freedom of thought, conscience, and religion (Article 18), the prohibition of incitement to religious hatred (Article 20), and the rights of persons belonging to religious minorities (Article 27).

All states parties must submit regular reports to the Human Rights Committee on the measures they have adopted to implement ICCPR obligations and on progress made in this regard. States parties must report initially within one year after acceding to the ICCPR and thereafter whenever the Committee requests, which is usually every four years. During its three annual sessions in Geneva, the Committee engages in a constructive dialogue with states parties, based on information received from them in writing and orally, as well as from UN entities, national human rights institutions and civil society. The role of nongovernmental organizations in the reporting process is important, including through input at an early stage into the Committee's list of issues, alternative reports on the human rights situation in the country concerned ("shadow reports"), and contributions to the follow-up procedure. The Committee examines each country situation, noting in its "concluding observations" both positive aspects and principal matters of concern as well as making recommendations to the state party. After the adoption of these concluding observations, a follow-up procedure traces information received from the state party within a specified deadline concerning the steps taken, if any, to implement the Committee's recommendations. While the numerous recommendations in concluding observations from different committees to the same state may overlap and at times even contradict each other, the strength of the UN treaty bodies is the open and transparent procedure, which includes input from civil society actors broadly and incentives for coordinated activities by civil society, for example, consolidated shadow reports.

In addition to this regular reporting procedure, the Human Rights Committee may also consider interstate complaints; however, this procedure under Article 41 of the ICCPR has never been used by states so far. Unlike other UN treaty bodies, the Human Rights Committee cannot on its own initiative start inquiries if it has received reliable information containing well-founded indications of serious or systematic violations of the ICCPR.

However, the First Optional Protocol to the ICCPR gives the Human Rights Committee the possibility to examine individual complaints with regard to alleged violations of the Covenant by states parties to this Protocol (116 states as of January 2019).[9] Complaints may also be brought by a third party on behalf of individuals, if these have given their written consent or when they are without access to the outside world, for example in prison or due to enforced disappearance. Individuals must have exhausted all available domestic remedies, which usually include pursuing their claim through the local court system. While mere doubts about the effectiveness of a domestic remedy are usually not sufficient, the Committee can dispense this requirement when domestic proceedings have been unreasonably prolonged or the remedies are unavailable or would plainly be ineffective. If the Human Rights Committee has held a complaint admissible, it then considers its merits and explains in "Views" the reasons for concluding that a violation of ICCPR provisions has either occurred or not. The Human Rights Committee has so far decided more than one thousand cases on the merits, including around fifty complaints that related to freedom of religion or belief issues.[10] While this figure may at first glance look unimpressive, one should not underestimate the significance of handling individual complaints for the development of international human rights law. By dealing with individual cases, the Human Rights Committee remains in touch with paradigmatic problems all over the world, which is a precondition for cherishing international human rights covenants as "living instruments."

Finally, in "general comments" the Committee also publishes its interpretation of the content of specific ICCPR provisions based on the experience gained through monitoring the compliance of states parties and handling of individual complaints. Particularly relevant for our subject matter are the Human Rights Committee's general comments on freedom of thought, conscience, or religion (No. 22 adopted in 1993), on the rights of minorities (No. 23 adopted in 1994), on states of emergency (No. 29 adopted in 2001), and on freedoms of opinion and expression (No. 34 adopted in 2011). Especially the general comments Nos. 22 and 34 have been very influential soft law in shaping the international and national interpretation of freedom of religion or belief, and were utilized for example by the UK Supreme Court in a judgment concerning asylum seekers from Zimbabwe.[11]

4. European Court of Human Rights

The wording of Article 18(1) of the ICCPR is very similar to Article 9(1) of the European Convention on Human Rights (ECHR), which provides that

"Everyone has the right to freedom of thought, conscience and religion; this right includes freedom to change his religion or belief and freedom, either alone or in community with others and in public or private, to manifest his religion or belief, in worship, teaching, practice and observance." Apart from some small edits, the main difference is that Article 18 of the ICCPR refers to the "freedom to have or to adopt a religion or belief of his choice" instead of the explicit guarantee of freedom to "change" one's religion or belief in Article 9 of the ECHR.

The European Court of Human Rights started its work in 1959 and is thus the oldest regional human rights court. Until January 2019, the Court has delivered more than 65,000 judgments on the merits, out of which around 900 cases dealt with freedom of thought, conscience, and religion and in almost 50 percent of these cases the Court found a violation of Article 9 of the ECHR. The subject matter of these cases was wide-ranging and included issues relating to the autonomy of religious communities, blasphemy, conversion, domestic recognition procedures, education, freedom of conscience, gender, holidays, incitement to hatred, proselytism, religious property and symbols, and so forth. In the judgments' chapters on relevant international materials, the Court has sometimes made reference to or even extensively quoted from the UN Human Rights Committee's General Comment No. 22 and reports by the Special Rapporteur on freedom of religion or belief.[12]

The European Court of Human Rights may only deal with a matter after all domestic remedies have been exhausted and within six months from the date on which the final domestic decision was taken. When considering cases brought before it, the Court may sit in a single-judge formation, in committees of three judges, in Chambers of seven judges or in a Grand Chamber of seventeen judges. A single judge may declare inadmissible or strike out of the Court's list of cases an application where such a decision can be taken without further examination, otherwise the application is forwarded to a committee or to a Chamber. Apart from a decision on admissibility, a committee may also render a judgment on the merits if the underlying question in the case is already the subject of the Court's well-established case law. Once a Chamber has rendered a judgment, any party may request within three months a referral to the Grand Chamber. Its judgment is immediately final, whereas a Chamber's judgment becomes final when there is no request for a referral within the deadline or if the request is dismissed. The Court's final judgments are legally binding on the states concerned and have in many instances led to changes in their legislation or administrative practice. The states have a legal obligation to remedy the violations found, yet they enjoy a certain margin of appreciation concerning the means to be used. In some cases, however, the state has refused to comply with the Court's final judgment, which may then trigger execution measures by the Committee of Ministers, made up of representatives of the governments of the forty-seven Member States of the Council of Europe.

The European Court of Human Rights has also received interstate applications in about twenty cases. For example in the fourth interstate case of *Cyprus v. Turkey*, the Court concluded in 2001 that Article 9 of the ECHR had been violated in respect of Greek Cypriots living in northern Cyprus due to the restrictions placed on their freedom of movement which "considerably curtailed their ability to observe their religious beliefs, in particular their access to places of worship outside their villages and their participation in other aspects of religious life."[13] In 2014, the Court held Turkey liable to pay Cyprus more than ninety million euros in respect of nonpecuniary damage suffered by the enclaved Greek Cypriot residents of the Karpas peninsula and the relatives of the missing persons, which has so far not been implemented by Turkey.[14]

It should at least be noted in passing that other regional human rights courts, as they exist in the framework of the Organization of American States (OAS) and the African Union (AU), have to date developed little jurisprudence on freedom of religion or belief. The regional human rights conventions on the basis of which those courts operate, however, likewise contain guarantees of freedom of religion or belief, notably in Article 12 of the American Convention on Human Rights and in Article 8 of the African Charter on Human and Peoples' Rights. Those regional human rights courts have referred to the UN Declaration on the Elimination of All Forms of Intolerance and Discrimination based on Religion or Belief and to the UN Human Rights Committee's General Comment No. 22.[15] Thus, the international recognition of freedom of religion or belief is also reflected in the various regional systems of human rights protection.

5. Religious Symbols in Public Life

While the display of religious symbols in public locations such as classrooms, courthouses, polling stations, or public squares has been the subject of regional and national jurisprudence,[16] the case law of the UN Human Rights Committee has focused so far on the prohibition of wearing of religious clothing and symbols in public. Already in 1993, the Human Rights Committee explained in its General Comment No. 22 that the concept of worship extends to "the display of symbols" and that the observance and practice of religion or belief may also include such customs as "the wearing of distinctive clothing or head coverings." Religious symbols may include garments or ornaments such as headscarves, yarmulkes, crucifixes, collars, nuns' habits, bindi, saffron robes, and turbans.

The jurisprudence in Geneva and Strasbourg differs significantly concerning the expulsion of pupils from public schools in France for refusing to remove conspicuous symbols of religious affiliation during lessons. After the French Parliament had passed a related law in 2004, some Muslim girls went to school wearing headscarves and some young men wore the Sikh *keski* (mini-turban) in order to cover their hair. When the pupils refused to remove the religious symbols, they were denied access to the classroom and finally were permanently expelled by the disciplinary bodies of the public schools.

In the case of *Bikramjit Singh v. France*, the UN Human Rights Committee found in favor of the Sikh complainant because France had not provided compelling evidence that wearing the mini-turban would have posed a threat to the rights and freedoms of other pupils or to order at the school. The Human Rights Committee considered the pupil's permanent expulsion from the public school solely because of his inclusion in a broad category of persons defined by their religious conduct as disproportionate and unnecessary.[17] However, the European Court of Human Rights came to a different result in its decisions on the similar applications of *Ranjit Singh v. France* and *Jasvir Singh v. France*, which were both held inadmissible as manifestly ill founded. Thus the Strasbourg Court considered that the expulsions had been justified and proportionate to the aim of protecting the rights and freedoms of others and public order as well as the constitutional principle of secularity, having regard to the margin of appreciation left to the national authorities in this area.[18]

The diverging jurisprudence in Geneva and Strasbourg is even more apparent concerning restrictions on religious symbols in identity photographs for Sikhs who were denied official documents in France when the picture showed them wearing a turban. Concerning the identity photograph on his driving licence, Shingara Mann Singh saw his application before the European Court of Human Rights held inadmissible in November 2008, but a month later he submitted a separate case to the UN Human Rights Committee, this time concerning the rejection of his application to renew his French passport because he had submitted a photograph showing him with a turban. He argued that the UN treaty body was not obliged to follow the regional case law and that the two cases were distinct. Technically it is correct that the rejections by French authorities of the identity photographs for Mr. Mann Singh's applications for a driving licence and a passport did not relate to "the same matter";[19] however, these two cases are obviously closely related and were brought to Strasbourg and Geneva by the very same person, with different outcomes.

The European Court of Human Rights stressed that identity photographs on driving licences which showed the person bareheaded were needed by the authorities, particularly in the context of checks carried out under the road traffic regulations, and that the requirement for persons to remove their turbans during such checks or for the initial issuance of the driving licence was a sporadic one.[20] However, the UN Human Rights Committee came to the opposite conclusion, because the obligation to remove the turban for the identity photograph would potentially interfere with religious freedom on a continuing basis because the bearer of the passport "would always appear without his religious head covering in the identity photograph and could thus be compelled to remove his turban during identity checks."[21] The UN Human Rights Committee stressed that France must provide Mr. Mann Singh with an effective remedy, including a reconsideration of his application for renewal of his passport and the revision of the relevant rules and their application in practice, as well as take steps to prevent similar violations in the future.

Thus Mr. Mann Singh prevailed in Geneva with his religious freedom claim, whereas his application in Strasbourg had been rejected as manifestly ill founded, taking into account the state's margin of appreciation. This doctrine of "margin of appreciation," which is mainly used in Strasbourg but only rarely in Geneva, thus leads to different levels of protection at the regional and international levels, even though the underlying human rights norms are worded in almost identical terms. In the follow-up to the Human Rights Committee's Views, France stated that it will not amend the relevant rules since neither the national nor regional courts had considered them contrary to religious freedom or to the principle of nondiscrimination.[22] However, the government's argument of merely referring to different domestic and regional jurisprudence is hardly convincing. First of all, international treaties such as the ICCPR are binding on a state party who must perform them in good faith and cannot invoke the provisions of its internal law as justification for its failure to perform the international treaty.[23] Article 55 of the French Constitution even explicitly states that duly ratified treaties shall prevail over acts of parliament. When acceding to the ICCPR, France declared that its articles on freedoms of expression, peaceful assembly, and association will be implemented in accordance with the corresponding articles in the ECHR; however, France made no similar declaration concerning freedom of religion or belief. In addition, the ECHR does not prevail over international treaties, as evidenced by its Article 53 which stresses that nothing in the ECHR shall be construed as limiting or derogating from any of the human rights or fundamental freedoms ensured under any other agreement. Finally, there is no unsolvable contradiction between the outcomes in Strasbourg and Geneva, since the European Court of Human Rights in its admissibility decision had relied on France's margin of appreciation, whereas the UN Human Rights Committee found a violation of religious freedom, and consequently France could follow both mechanisms simply by discontinuing its current restrictive approach concerning religious symbols in public life.[24]

A similar divergence between international and regional jurisprudence can be seen concerning France's ban since 2011 on wearing in a public space any clothing intended to conceal the face. Since this ban mainly affects Muslim women who wish to wear the full face veil, it has been sometimes colloquially dubbed as niqab or burqa ban. In its judgment of 1 July 2014, the Grand Chamber of the European Court of Human Rights gave France a wide margin of appreciation concerning this "choice of society" and found that the impugned ban could be regarded as proportionate to the aim pursued, that is, preserving the conditions of "living together" as an element of the "protection of the rights and freedoms of others."[25] However, in two Views of 17 July 2018, the UN Human Rights Committee concluded that France's criminal ban disproportionately affects the Muslim women who choose to wear the full face veil, and introduces a distinction between them and other persons who may legally cover their face in public that is not necessary and proportionate to a legitimate interest, and is therefore unreasonable.[26] While the Human Rights Committee acknowledged that some women may in fact be subject to family or social pressures to cover their faces, it stressed "that the wearing of the full veil may also be a choice—or even a means of staking a claim—based on religious belief, as in the author's case."[27] The fact that a single judge of the European Court of Human Rights had previously declared their applications inadmissible in Strasbourg did not prevent the Human Rights Committee from taking up their complaints in Geneva, as it could not determine with certainty that their cases had "already been the subject of an examination, however limited, of the merits"[28] in Strasbourg.

6. Religious Education

The issue of religious education in public schools provides another example of forum shopping between Geneva and Strasbourg as well as the possibility of simultaneously submitting complaints to regional and international human rights mechanisms, notably when several persons are affected by a specific situation.

This is precisely what happened in the wake of the introduction in 1997 of a mandatory religious subject in the Norwegian school system, entitled "Christian Knowledge and Religious and Ethical Education." The Norwegian Humanist Association and the parents of eight pupils demanded full exemption from this instruction, which was supposed to provide thorough knowledge of the Bible and Christianity as a cultural heritage and Evangelical Lutheran Faith. After their applications for exemption had been rejected by the schools concerned, they tried to challenge this in the domestic courts, but Norway's Supreme Court rejected their claims. Subsequently, four sets of parents and their children brought their complaint to Geneva, whereas three of the other parents in the national proceedings and the Norwegian Humanist Association went separately to Strasbourg.

Should these complaints be considered as "the same matter" under another procedure of international investigation or settlement? On the one hand, Norway argued that the communications to the UN Human Rights Committee and to the European Court of Human Rights were to a large extent identical and that the parents were seeking a duplicative review by the regional and international bodies of what is essentially one case.[29] On the other hand, the parents stressed that before domestic courts each case had been presented separately and concerned separate administrative decisions as well as that each parent had a right to decide to complain either to the regional or international body.[30] This reasoning was followed by the

UN Human Rights Committee in view of its jurisprudence that the words "the same matter" must be understood as referring to one and the same claim concerning the same individual, as submitted by that individual, or by some other person empowered to act on his behalf, to the other international body. Similarly, the European Court of Human Rights decided that—notwithstanding the common features between the cases in Strasbourg and in Geneva—there was no personal identity between the two groups of families. However, the Norwegian Humanist Association withdrew its application under the ECHR and the European Court of Human Rights declared the applications of the children themselves inadmissible because they had not formally been a party before the national courts and thus had not exhausted domestic remedies.[31] Thus the claimants and the scope of their claims differed to some extent in Strasbourg and in Geneva.

When considering the merits, the UN Human Rights Committee referred to difficulties encountered by the children, some of whom had to recite religious texts in the context of a Christmas celebration although they had been enrolled in the exemption scheme, and concluded that the mandatory subject did not ensure that education of religious knowledge and religious practice were adequately separated.[32] While the European Court of Human Rights only considered the parents' right to respect for their convictions, its majority (in a tight vote of nine judges to eight) held that the system of partial exemption risked unduly exposing these parents concerning their private life and that the potential for conflict was likely to deter them from making any requests for exemptions.[33]

Even though the claimants "won" their cases both in Geneva and Strasbourg, there are subtle differences in the outcomes and the risks of forum shopping are evident. In their separate opinion, two judges bluntly criticized that the European Court of Human Rights had not declared the whole application inadmissible in view of the related case in Geneva: "the risk of contradictory decisions, in which international litispendence has its origin, does exist. This is an example of what the [ECHR] and the Optional Protocol [of the ICCPR] tried to avoid. Unfortunately, their subsequent interpretation by the competent international organs has deprived them of their original sense. The Court's judgment, adopted by nine votes to eight, may lead us to think that the exception of litispendence has been buried, even if—as contradictory as it may seem—in the present case it shows signs of being in good health. This is a pity."[34]

7. Conscientious Objection to Military Service

Another example for changing interpretations and different approaches at the international and regional levels is the jurisprudence in Geneva and Strasbourg on conscientious objection to military service.

Until 1993, the UN Human Rights Committee had held in several cases that the ICCPR did not provide for a right to conscientious objection to military service.[35] However, in its General Comment No. 22, the Human Rights Committee changed its position by arguing that a right to conscientious objection "can be derived from article 18, inasmuch as the obligation to use lethal force may seriously conflict with the freedom of conscience and the right to manifest one's religion or belief." This *forum externum* approach, which leaves the possibility open for states to restrict conscientious objection in line with the limitations clause in Article 18(3) of the ICCPR, was confirmed by the Committee's majority in several cases until 2010.[36] Yet, since 2011, the majority of Committee members have held in numerous cases that the right to conscientious objection inheres in or is inherent to the right to freedom of thought, conscience, and religion.[37] This *forum internum* approach excludes any limitations by the state since the internal dimension is protected unconditionally and must not be impaired by any coercion. In addition, Article 4(2) of the ICCPR prohibits any derogation from freedom of thought, conscience, and religion, even in time of public emergency which threatens the life of the nation. Thus the *forum internum* approach would make it impossible to derogate from or limit any conscientious objection to military service.

The jurisprudence in Strasbourg has made a similar evolution, albeit with some delay and without Geneva's latest change of interpretation. From 1966 to 2010, the European Commission of Human Rights and later the Court had held that freedom of thought, conscience, and religion did not guarantee a right to refuse military service on conscientious grounds.[38] In 2011, however, the Grand Chamber deliberately changed Strasbourg's case law, stressing that the ECHR was a living instrument that must be interpreted in the light of present-day conditions and of the ideas currently prevailing in democratic states. The Grand Chamber explicitly referred to important developments concerning the recognition of the right to conscientious objection in various international fora, most notably the evolution of the UN Human Rights Committee's interpretation in this regard until 2010.[39] Yet Strasbourg did not take on board Geneva's shift to the *forum internum* approach, which the UN Human Rights Committee had released just two weeks before the Grand Chamber judgment of 7 July 2011. Thus, the European Court of Human Rights has been considering a conscientious objector's failure to report for military service to be a manifestation of his or her religious beliefs in the *forum externum*.[40]

What are the main differences between the *forum internum* and *forum externum* approaches as well as the implications of the diverging jurisprudence in Geneva and Strasbourg? In practice, both approaches will most likely lead to the same result, that is, that states must not curtail the right to conscientious objection to military service. Whereas the *forum internum* approach already excludes the possibility of any limitations, in the *forum externum* approach the burden of justifying such a limitation lies with the state but it seems hardly possible to restrict a conscientious objector's freedom to manifest his religion or belief without vitiating or jeopardizing the right's essence. Article 18(3) of the ICCPR must be strictly interpreted and it notably does not allow for restrictions based on the ground of "national security." It was also conceded by the proponents of the *forum internum* approach that the UN Human Rights Committee would never use an analysis of Article 18(3) of the ICCPR to prevent a person from successfully invoking conscientious objection as a defense against legal liability.[41]

The main dogmatic problem with the current interpretation in Geneva is that it privileges certain conscientious decisions that are afforded absolute protection under freedom of thought, conscience, and religion, while completely discarding others.[42] The majority of the UN Human Rights Committee has until now only protected conscientious objection to compulsory military service if the latter cannot be reconciled with the objector's religion or beliefs; however, other pacifist or religious activities could also be considered as worthy of absolute protection. Yet, this would cast the net of the *forum internum* protection too wide and ultimately risks making the limitations clause under Article 18(3) of the ICCPR redundant. Alternatively, if only conscientious objection to military service was to be absolutely protected, this would de facto create a hierarchy of conscientious objection grounds that are considered worthy of protection or not. Thus Strasbourg's approach of strictly distinguishing between the *forum internum* and *forum externum* components seems preferable for the sake of dogmatic clarity. While not precluding the imposition of limitations on the exercise of certain conscientious objections, the Strasbourg approach keeps the door open for most different themes possibly coming into the focus of conscientious claims, including contentious medical issues such as abortion or euthanasia.

Final judgments of the European Court of Human Rights also have the advantage of being legally binding and their implementation is reviewed by the Committee of Ministers of the Council of Europe, which adds another level of supervision in the execution of judgments. Still, from a strategical point of view, it may be more attractive for some complainants to go to Geneva, where their claims of conscientious objection to military service would benefit from the absolute protection of the *forum internum*, albeit with a less powerful follow-up procedure in Geneva compared to the sophisticated supervision machinery in Strasbourg.

8. Coordination and Inspiration

Looking back at five decades of jurisprudence on freedom of religion or belief, more conceptual clarity has been achieved both in Strasbourg and Geneva than some observers had expected in the beginning. There have been some impressive examples of jurisprudential evolution and break-throughs in terms of protection, notably concerning the right to conscientious objection to military service. Yet, there remain also obvious weaknesses, such as the comparatively small number of religious freedom cases decided by the Human Rights Committee and the broad "margin of appreciation" applied in Strasbourg, which seems particularly disappointing from the perspective of certain religious minorities. In this chapter, we have also discussed three examples of thematic areas where the jurisprudence at the international and regional levels either differs slightly or even contradicts each other, with far-reaching legal and practical implications.

Concerning conscientious objection to military service, the Strasbourg approach (which is also shared by UN Special Procedures)[43] seems more convincing than the recent *forum internum* approach of the UN Human Rights Committee's majority as discussed above. Yet, with regard to religious symbols, the jurisprudence in Geneva does not shy away from the substantive questions and appears more consistent than Strasbourg's related case law. Saïla Ouald Chaib commented that she was "happy the Committee chose not to follow the reasoning of the European Court of Human Rights in this case" of *Ranjit Singh v. France* (as adopted by the UN Human Rights Committee on 22 July 2011) and instead she hoped "that the Committee's decision may be a source of inspiration for future Strasbourg case-law."[44]

Double examination should thus not be precluded at all costs, especially from the victims' perspective. Trying to find the lowest common denominator or suggesting any judicial hierarchy at the international and regional levels does not appear conducive either. What is needed instead are more systematic information exchanges, discussion, and coordination among the various international and regional human rights mechanisms in order to develop a holistic "ecosystem" of human rights protection.

The former President of the International Court of Justice, Rosalyn Higgins, put it bluntly in the following three pleas to judges: "We must read each other's judgments. We must have respect for each other's judicial work. We must try to preserve unity among us unless context really prevents it."[45]

CHAPTER 8

Preventing Violence Committed
in the Name of Religion

1. Complex Phenomena

Violence incited, perpetrated, or justified in the name of religion is a shocking reality in different parts of the world, and the brutality displayed in such acts frequently leaves observers speechless.[1] Atrocious acts, which prima facie appear to be "archaic" manifestations of cruelty, are often cynically arranged and purposefully "staged" in order to cater to modern media voyeurism, which adds yet another dimension of humiliation to the suffering of the victims and their families. Violence in the name of religion exists as terrorism, communal violence, civil war, and even international aggression. Perpetrators include different types of nonstate actors as well as state agencies or a combination of both.

A comprehensive analysis of these extremely diverse, complex, and multifaceted phenomena would go far beyond the confines of a book chapter. The intention of the present chapter is more specific. What we chiefly want to explore is *how religious freedom can contribute to preventing violence occurring in the name of religion.* While we do not think that freedom of religion or belief plays the "key" role this regard, we are convinced that freedom of religion or belief, in conjunction with other human rights, can provide the normative framework for broadly designed policies that aim at preventing and overcoming violence in the name of religion.

The human rights approach is relevant not only when it comes to developing practical responses to violence occurring under the auspices of religion; it should already guide the description of phenomena and root causes as well as the choice of adequate categories. Violence and religion is a sensitive theme; it requires a high degree of clarity, diligence, and precision. Apart from being an academic virtue, precision in this field is also a requirement of fairness to human beings. There is no way around: we have to tackle this issue with frankness and honesty, but at the same time with a clear awareness that the language we use when describing violence in the name of religion may have repercussions for many people—followers of various religions, victims of terrorism or other forms of violence, and target groups of prejudice and stigmatization.

Another contribution of the human rights approach is the constant insistence on human agency in the area of violence and religion. This is less trivial than it may look at first glance. In discussions on violence and religion, one frequently faces two attitudes, both of which obfuscate human agency. The first reaction denies any substantial involvement of religions, thus trivializing the responsibility that religious communities—their members and leaders—have to shoulder in the fight against violence (see Section 2). The second type of reaction, by contrast, reads an inclination for violence immediately into the "essence" of certain religions, in particular Islam. While pushing religion into the center of the critical debate, this essentialist approach distracts the attention from the possibilities which human beings have in fostering peaceful interpretations of their religion (see Section 3). The somewhat complicated title chosen for this chapter— "violence committed in the name of religion"—signals distance toward both of these typical reactions. While there is in fact a relevant relationship that warrants serious analysis, this relationship cannot be reduced to a simple equation of only two factors: religion and violence. The passive formulation "committed in the name" accommodates additional factors, the most elementary of which is human agency (see Section 4). We should not lose sight of the simple fact that it is always human beings who bring about the connection between religion and violence, and—even more importantly— that it is also human beings who can actively challenge and "undo" that connection. Whereas religious communities and religious leaders face a particular responsibility to counter aggressive tendencies (see Sections 5 and 6), we also have to take into account political factors (see Section 7). One main factor, which we will further explore, is loss of trust in public institutions, often in the wake of endemic corruption, which creates the fertile ground for the seeds of hatred to take root among broader parts of the population. In Section 8, we will come back to the initial question: what is the specific contribution of freedom of religion or belief to designing adequate responses? We highlight the significance of respect for human rights in any policy of building trust. Freedom of religion or belief further-more encourages projects of cross-boundary communication, a culture of public discourse as well as inner-religious reform agendas.[2]

2. "Nothing to Do with Religion"? Evasive Attitudes

"We have to overcome the state of denial." This was the core message, which Sheikh Maytham al-Salman from Bahrain wished to convey to the participants of a workshop held in the UN-controlled buffer zone in Cyprus.[3] When criticizing a "state of denial," he alluded to an almost instinctively defensive reaction in which many people take refuge whenever they are confronted with violence committed under the auspices of religion. A typical answer is "this has nothing to do with religion." Some go so far as to claim that Islamist terrorism would be outright impossible for the simple fact that the Arabic term "Islam" has the same linguistic root as peace: "salam." According to that logic, any act of violence factually hap-pening in the name of Islam, must per definition be a mere "abuse" of religion by outsiders, be they insane individuals, Machiavellian politicians, or the enemies of Islam. Sheikh Maytham criticized this dismissive attitude for ignoring realities and eschewing responsibility. In particular, religious leaders and intellectuals, he insisted, must face the disturbing experience that terrorist excesses and aggressive propaganda can elicit a positive echo in parts of their communities. Moreover, even the ideologically distorted versions of contemporary jihadism may show certain elements of continu-ity with old traditions of religious polemics. Whereas many invocations of religion in the context of terrorism merely add a superficial semblance of heroic meaning to utterly trivial acts of barbarism, some people may actu-ally believe that violence perpetrated against "unbelievers" and "heretics" could be a God-pleasing act of worship. Violence happening in the name of religion, at any rate, cannot be reduced to misunderstandings, individual madness, and political conspiracies; it deserves to be taken seriously, in particular by the religious communities themselves.[4]

   Maytham al-Salman is a well-known Shia cleric in Bahrain, where the government maintains the hegemony of Sunni Islam, even though the majority of the Bahrainis follow the Shia branch of Islam. While on many occasions speaking out for the rights of Shia Muslims, Sheikh Maytham used the workshop in Cyprus to address acts of horrific violence committed by Shia militias in Syria, Iraq, and elsewhere, thereby setting an example of how to tackle difficult phenomena with honesty.

Although the dismissive mantra "this has nothing to do with religion" is obviously too simple to be true, it may nonetheless be understandable that people take refuge in it. When hearing about atrocities committed by Boko Haram, Al-Shabaab, the Taliban, or the "Islamic State in Iraq and the Levant" (ISIL), many Muslims, indeed the vast majority of the followers of that religion, may not be able or willing to even see a bloody caricature of Islam in such heinous crimes. Christians usually react the same way when being asked about the Norwegian mass murderer Anders Breivik, who staged himself as a lonely Christian crusader against the Islamization of Europe, which he thought was happening in the guise of multiculturalism. The typical refusal to see any real connection with one's religion—or with any religion—demarcates *an abyss of nonunderstanding*, which most people feel when hearing about egregious violence committed against innocent people. At the end of the day, acts of cruelty beyond imagination defy any subtle "interpretation" or satisfactory "explanation." They do not seem to serve a purpose which one would be able or willing really to understand. The typical dismissive reaction—"this has nothing to do with religion"—can be an expression of such ultimate lack of understanding; it is a refusal to read any deeper meaning into manifestations of sheer brutality.

There is yet another aspect worthy of consideration. After the massacres in Paris, Nice, Berlin, London, Barcelona, and elsewhere, perpetrated by individuals who called themselves "soldiers of the ISIL," Muslims in Europe feel exposed to increasing hostility.[5] Insisting that such terrorist crimes have nothing to do with Islam can be an attempt to convey the message: "we Muslims, far from clandestinely applauding violence, are in fact no less shocked than anyone else in the society." The problem is that this message does not always seem to go through. Even worse, the defensive mantra may inadvertently nourish suspicion if conveying the impression that it blocks any serious discussion of root causes and factors. Sometimes there is only a thin line between a spontaneous expression of shock and nonunderstanding, on the one hand, and all too smooth pseudoexplanations, which simply push the issue aside, on the other. Ready-made statements to the effect that "Islamic terrorism" is an oxymoron invented by the enemies of Islam are certainly not suitable to create trust within the society.

This issue is not exclusively connected to Islam. Militant Hindu nationalists are the driving force behind many manifestations of so-called "communal violence" in India, which usually do not "break out" spontaneously,
but often follow a carefully crafted script.[6] In Myanmar, Buddhist groups
such as MaBaTha used dehumanizing and stigmatizing language against the
Rohingya Muslims; in September 2018, the Independent International Fact-
Finding Mission on Myanmar was deeply disturbed by the prevalence of
hate speech, both offline and online, without adequate responses by the
government.[7] Israelis are worried about attacks, including destruction of
property as well as desecration of mosques and churches, reportedly carried
out by a radical minority among Jewish settlers.[8] Christian preachers in
Uganda or Zambia have sparked hatred against sexual minorities, thus paving the ground for homophobic violence, including killings.[9] In the United
States, radical Christian militias prepare themselves for the expected apocalyptic battle against the Antichrist, whom some associate with Islam.[10]

The idea that religious messages are "essentially" peaceful and philanthropic unless being "abused" for inhumane purposes trivializes the
destructive energies that can emerge from the midst of the religions themselves. Surely, religions can create bonds of solidarity and spur people to
move beyond their narrow selfish interests. Numerous international and
regional faith-based organizations show an admirable commitment for
peace, reconciliation, social justice, and human rights. In an empirical
study, Markus Weingardt has put together examples from Mozambique
and Rwanda to Cambodia, India, and the Philippines.[11] Yet religions can
likewise provide justifications for militant superiority claims or the violent
defense of traditional hegemonies. They furthermore deliver apocalyptic
images, which political actors may harness to demonize external rivals and
internal dissidents.

In social reality, religions are ambiguous phenomena.[12] They display
"the ambivalence of the sacred," as Scott Appleby highlights in a book
title.[13] Religions have the potential to open up the hearts, minds, and intellectual horizons of their followers, but they can also foster collective
narrow-mindedness, intolerance, and exclusion. By bringing people
together and creating a profound sense of belonging, religious communities
may at the same time exacerbate existing divisions within society or produce new fault lines. The expectation of internal loyalty can cause people to
erect mental fences against the external world. And the consolation, which
religious messages promise, sometimes goes together with an aggressive lack

of understanding toward those people who stubbornly refuse to accept the blessings of the "true faith."

3. Violence Located in the Core of Religion?
Pitfalls of Fatalism

The evasive mantra "this has nothing to do with religion" conjures up an idealistic "essence" of religion, against the background of which, it seems, violent excesses can only be abuses undertaken from outsiders. "Essentially" religion is peaceful, whatever may factually happen in its name—or this is the assumption of those holding such views. Even more frequently, however, essentialist ideas convey just the opposite message. Instead of exculpating religions from any responsibility for violent acts, they pretend to be able to explain such violence immediately from the "essence" of religion itself. Fanaticism, intolerance, vigilantism, forced conversion, holy wars, violent extremism, and terrorism are said to follow almost logically from basic religious prescripts, orientations, and loyalties. Such atrocities allegedly reveal what religion is all about.

The usual suspect in this regard is Islam. It frequently happens that after a panel discussion on Islam and modernity or similar themes, a reproachful-looking person steps up to the podium in order to hand over a list of Qur'anic verses which supposedly prove the aggressive, intolerant, and violent nature of Islam. The implicit message is that discussing with Muslims is just a waste of time, since their authoritative scripture entitles or even obligates them to perform acts of violence against heretics and nonbelievers. This sometimes culminates in the notorious collective singular: "the Muslim" is like that. Such negative essentialism subordinates hundreds of millions of Muslims, traditionalists and reformers, conservatives and liberals, men and women, to a timeless "essence" of their religion supposedly defined by violent inclinations. Individual faces, individual voices, and individual biographies just disappear, as it were, behind an ascribed collective mentality of fanaticism, narrow-mindedness, and intolerance. From such an essentialist point of view, inner-Islamic diversity and theological controversies become as meaningless as are religious reform agendas, learning experiences, or societal adaptation processes. Phenomena that do not fit into the narrative of an essentially violent religion are waved aside, since they allegedly merely distract from the real issues.

Radical critics of Islam like to depict Islam in sharp contrast to other religions, in particular Christianity or Buddhism, in order to highlight "essentially" different attitudes toward violence. Hans-Peter Raddatz gives an example of such anti-Islamic essentialism when remarking in an interview: "To put it simple, a Christian abuses his religion when employing violence, and a Muslim likewise abuses his religion when *not* employing violence."[14] In other words, whereas acts of terrorism committed by the Taliban or Boko Haram allegedly demonstrate the true and timeless essence of an aggressive religion, similar acts perpetrated by Christian militias like the "Lord's Resistance Army"[15] receive a totally different assessment. Such a way of channeling the phenomena a priori along the line of essentialist categories renders prejudiced views immune against any empirical counter-evidence.

Whereas people often react quite surprised when hearing about mob violence orchestrated by Buddhist monks, because this contradicts the peaceful image that Buddhism widely enjoys, reports about violence in an Islamic context usually do not meet with similar reactions of surprise. They seem to match widespread negative expectations, which thereby receive additional confirmation. Even worse, whenever acts of terrorism occur in an Islamic context, such acts usually receive an implicit or explicit "authenticity benefit" in the sense of corroborating people's views of what Islam is all about. The flip side of this is that all those Muslims who reject and abhor violence or actively work for peace and understanding remain stuck in the mere penumbra of what is perceived to be "real Islam." They sometimes even experience this as a bizarre compliment that, perhaps owing to their successful integration into a modern Western liberal society, they have more or less ceased to be a genuine Muslim: "you are no longer one of those, are you?" From a negative essentialist view on Islam, it seems only logical to infer that liberal and open-minded Muslims, if they happen to exist, cannot be fully authentic.

Ascribing a natural propensity for violence to a religion, in particular to Islam, is the counterpoint to the evasive pattern sketched out above. What both perceptions have in common is the essentialist attitude. Defensive essentialism presupposes a peaceful nucleus of religion, from which it follows that acts of violence can only stem from outsiders. By contrast, reading an inclination for violent militancy into the core of a religion implies that any nonviolent manifestations of that religion must be inauthentic.

While many essentialist ascriptions of violence target Islam, some critics read violent aspirations into the core message shared by all the three traditional monotheistic religions: Judaism, Christianity, and Islam, namely, the existence of only one God. Already David Hume distinguished between intolerant monotheistic and tolerant polytheistic beliefs: "The intolerance of almost all religions, which have maintained the unity of God, is as remarkable as the contrary principle of polytheists."[16] In a book entitled *The Price of Monotheism*, Jan Assmann recently reformulated this criticism.[17] In his view, Moses stands at the beginning of a history of three thousand years of militant monotheism, which crystallized around the sharp dichotomy between the one true God and the many false demons. In the wake of Assmann's books, Peter Sloterdijk even accused the monotheistic religions of imposing an "obligation to exercise cruelty" on their followers.[18]

At times, the critique even moves beyond the confines of monotheism and targets religion as such. An example is John Lennon's famous song "Imagine All the People" (1971), which paints the picture of a peacefully united humanity without state borders, but also without any boundaries drawn by religions. Apparently, many people associate religions with unpleasant phenomena, such as moralistic resentment, bigotry, self-righteousness, narrow-mindedness, fanaticism, and not least a propensity for violent action. This nourishes the utopia of a future society in which religions should cease to exercise any influence on public life.

4. Overcoming Essentialisms

The two versions of essentialism just described differ very much on the surface, as they imply opposite assessments of the issue at hand. The first version of essentialism is evasive, in the sense of denying any relevant connection between religion and violence. The second version, by contrast, nourishes fatalistic thinking, since it ascribes a propensity for violence to the very "DNA" of certain religions, if not of religion in general. In TV talk shows dedicated to this theme, proponents of the two opposite tendencies—evasiveness and fatalism—often play into each other's hands, thus making sure that the controversy goes on forever, usually in a cyclical manner and without yielding any new insights.

In spite of their obvious opposition, however, the evasive and the fatalistic versions of essentialism share a number of common features. They do not care much about nuanced analyses. Why should they? Precise descriptions of the relevant phenomena, an account of internal religious diversity, and explorations of theological reform agendas appear to be just a waste of time. More importantly, essentialist perceptions in all their versions ultimately obfuscate the responsibility that human beings have whenever it comes to acts of violence and their justification. The dismissive standpoint denies that religious communities—that is, their members, representatives, leaders, and intellectual supporters—have much, if anything, to do with the issue at hand. According to the fatalistic pattern of essentialism, things may at first glance look quite different. However, terrorists and others who commit acts of violence merely seem to carry out what allegedly lies in their "religious DNA." While they are doubtless the ones performing these evil acts, the evil itself is located at a different level, namely at the level of their religious upbringing and orientation rather than within their own sphere of responsibility.

As we have emphasized throughout the chapters of this book, freedom of religion or belief always focuses on *human beings as responsible agents*. Accordingly, one important contribution—or rather metacontribution—of freedom of religion or belief to the analysis on violence is its insistence on *taking human agency seriously*. Many of the images used in discussion of violence in the name of religion appear to downplay this elementary insight by drawing on the analogy of natural catastrophes. One cannot emphasize enough that violence in the name of religion does not "break out" like a volcano. It is not true that the "hot lava" of collective religious hatred has always existed underground and is doomed to "erupt" as soon as authoritarian governments release their iron grip on societies. Violence is not a "natural" phenomenon. To say it with Nelson Mandela's famous words: "No one is born hating another person because of the color of his skin, or his background, or his religion."[19] Violence happening under the auspices of religion results from many political, historical, sociological, and not least religious factors, which we have to analyze carefully in order to design suitable counterstrategies based on the understanding that human beings, within and outside religious communities, can always make a difference.

5. Responsibility of Religious Communities

Religion is not beyond human agency and thus human responsibility. Human agency is already involved in the interpretation of religious traditions, dogmas, laws, practices, or identities. Religious sources and normative codes of conduct always accommodate different readings undertaken by human beings, whether they are aware of it or not. In practice, any lived religion is inevitably interpreted religion. This is even the case in religious communities which in theory deny the space for human interpretation of divine revelation, as it is the case in major currents of Islam and in a number of Christian denominations. While the denial of interpretative space obviously hampers the development of critical hermeneutics, it does not alter the fact that interpretation nonetheless takes place. As stressed by Norani Othman, a founding member of the reformist movement "Sisters in Islam," there is no understanding of religious texts without human interpretation: "we in the present have to read those texts in order to understand them at all; but in seeking to understand them we—like all Muslims throughout history—bring to our own reading of those past texts the frameworks of understanding of our own time and place. So we are always, like all the great ulama of the past—even though they were not aware of it—both reading the present back into the past from which we seek contemporary guidance, and also left with the problem . . . of deciding *how* we are now to implement or proceed upon that understanding."[20] Whoever denies the space for human interpretation of religious texts, thereby actually monopolizes it by turning his own interpretation into the only possible way. While such denial often stages itself as religious humbleness, it usually amounts to an authoritarian imposition of tenets.

Interpretation is not the exclusive business of experts in exegesis or religious law. It also happens through everyday religious practice of ordinary believers and other laypersons. Moreover, interpretation is not even necessarily a deliberate effort. Maybe only few Christians have a theologically sophisticated view on St. Paul's command: "let your women keep silence in the churches."[21] Most liberal Christians simply disregard that verse as an outdated and somewhat awkward position, which actually does not bother them too much. Such disregard can also count as a mode of "interpretation" in the broadest sense. Implicit interpretation through disregard, however, can only work as long as the larger community goes along with it. Once questions are being raised, the merely implicit answers will no longer suffice and must be complemented by explicit clarifications and proactive interpretative efforts.

Concerning the relationship between violence and religion, too, interpretation always takes place, not only by experts, but also in the everyday religious practice of ordinary members of religious communities, whether they are aware of their interpretative activities or not. Religious communities usually accommodate a broad range of different attitudes toward violence, from clear rejection to conditional acceptance to heroic celebration.[22] The majority of believers usually react with horror when being confronted with acts of terrorism happening in the name of their religion—or of any religion. However, there are also people who glorify violent militancy as a way of showing strong religious commitment. Yet others may think that violence could be justified under certain conditions, for example, as the last resort when it comes to defending one's religious community. In any case, the decisive point is that violent attitudes and ideologies do not directly flow from an assumed perpetual "essence" of any particular religion (or of a particular type of religions). They always presuppose human beings who actively perpetrate, silently condone, explicitly applaud, or theologically endorse violence.

Whenever violence is committed or justified in the context of religion, the relevant religious ideas, concepts, images, narratives, and so on, deserve meticulous analysis. Although they should not be seen in isolation from broader political factors (which we will discuss in Section 7 of this chapter), it would be wrong to dismiss polarizing religious interpretations as merely "external" excuses for acts of aggression whose "real" motivations supposedly lie elsewhere. At the same time, it is imperative to avoid the pitfalls of essentialism, which in all its versions trivializes human responsibility. Just as it is human beings who bring about the connection between religion and violence, it is also human beings who can challenge that connection, for instance when they refuse to listen to hate-inciting sermons, articulate their abhorrence to violence, openly contradict ideological justifications, and actively care about young people who seem to turn away from society. In short, it is human beings who link religion and violence, and it is human beings who can also delink the two.

Critical analysis of religious influences, in particular when undertaken from within the religious communities themselves, is an arduous task. Religious concepts, metaphors, norms, and codes of conduct can be so deeply interwoven with daily practices that it may sometimes be almost impossible to develop the intellectual distance needed to put such influences to a critical scrutiny. Human beings are not fully transparent to themselves, especially when it comes to assessing the impact that religious socialization processes have on their self-understandings. Those who embark on a serious religious criticism may furthermore experience hostility within their immediate social environment. Yet believers within all religious traditions have nevertheless begun to tackle this task. A main issue warranting critical reflection is a dogmatic understanding of religious truth, which has divided human beings into those who follow on the right path versus those who allegedly remain stuck in ignorance and error. History is replete with examples of bloodshed resulting from such dichotomized views, which sometimes blend with apocalyptic expectations of a forthcoming battle between the disciples and the enemies of God.[23] Many religious communities also face a history of entanglement with national identity politics, which typically nourishes religious xenophobia. Another theme is gender stereotypes and their religious justification. One example of negative stereotyping in the intersection of religion, nationality, and gender is rumors, which we heard in various parts of South Asia about a "love jihad" allegedly waged by Muslims. The assumption is that Muslim boys approach Hindu or Buddhist girls with the strategic purpose to tip the demographic balance in favor of a future Muslim hegemony. This example demonstrates that hate propaganda often has a pronounced gender dimension.[24] Yet another issue is religiously motivated homophobia. Ultraconservative Christian preachers in Uganda or the US invoke the story of Sodom and Gomorra, which in the book of Genesis epitomizes sinful and self-destructive decadence. This illustrates the necessity to engage in critical rereadings of the foundational scriptures, and other religious texts. In short, the themes that deserve critical scrutiny are manifold. They include issues of faith and doubt, truth and error, moral guidance and conscientious opposition, the glorification of martyrdom, old and new gender stereotypes, expectations of group loyalty, and theological justifications of power.

Tackling difficult religious and theological legacies is the precondition for discovering—or rediscovering—the positive potential inherent in religious traditions for preventing and eradicating violence. Religions can open horizons; they can motivate people to overcome selfishness and narrowmindedness, to develop empathy and practice solidarity—also beyond the confines of their own groupings. Religious traditions contain ideas of human dignity, social justice, and peace, often in the shape of metaphors and parables, which directly speak to people's hearts. While acts of violence committed in the name of religion currently attract broad media coverage, peace-building activities of religious actors, both domestically and internationally, receive much less, if any, public attention. The first step for changing this must be an enhanced awareness within the religious communities themselves, as Markus Weingardt points out: "First of all, the religious communities themselves are called upon to become much more aware of their peace-building competences, to solidify these competences and make them widely known."[25]

6. The Role of Religious Leaders: From the Rabat Plan of Action to the Beirut Declaration

The role and responsibility of religious leaders and faith-based actors have been developed further in documents following broad consultations, which took place under the auspices and with the support of the United Nations, in particular the Office of the High Commissioner for Human Rights (OHCHR). The 2012 "Rabat Plan of Action on the prohibition of advocacy of national, racial, or religious hatred that constitutes incitement to discrimination, hostility, or violence" already laid out some of religious leaders' core responsibilities against incitement to hatred. The Rabat Plan of Action explicitly states that religious leaders should refrain from inciting violence, they should speak out firmly and promptly against hate speech, and they should clarify that violence can never be tolerated as a response to incitement to hatred.[26]

Expanding those responsibilities to the full spectrum of human rights, the faith-based and civil society actors participating at the OHCHR workshop in March 2017 (fully gender-balanced with 50 percent women and 50 percent men) adopted the Beirut Declaration and its eighteen commitments on "Faith for Rights."[27] The Beirut Declaration considers that theistic, nontheistic, atheistic, or other believers should join hands and hearts in articulating ways in which "Faith" can stand up for "Rights" more effectively so that both can enhance each other. The corresponding eighteen commitments on "Faith for Rights" articulate specific commitments, which are also supported by quotes from various religious, philosophical, and human rights texts. For example, the "Faith for Rights" framework includes the commitments to prevent the use of the notion of "state religion" to discriminate against any individual or group; to revisit religious interpretations that appear to perpetuate gender inequality and harmful stereotypes or even condone gender-based violence; to stand up for the rights of all persons belonging to minorities; to publicly denounce all instances of advocacy of hatred that incites to violence, discrimination, or hostility; to monitor interpretations, determinations, or other religious views that manifestly conflict with universal human rights norms and standards; to refrain from oppressing critical voices and to urge states to repeal any existing anti-blasphemy or anti-apostasy laws; to refine the curriculums, teaching materials, and textbooks; and to engage with children and youth who are either victims of or vulnerable to incitement to violence in the name of religion.

While the Rabat Plan of Action and the Beirut Declaration were not adopted by states and do not have the status of legally binding norms according to the established sources of international law (that is, hard law), they could arguably be considered as—potentially—behavior-affecting soft law[28] or at least as "softish law" in the making. In Rabat and Beirut, the texts were drafted and adopted unanimously by faith-based and civil society actors working in the field of human rights, including relevant UN Special Rapporteurs and members of UN treaty bodies. These aspirational texts, which elaborate (self-)"commitments" by nonstate actors rather than "obligations" adopted by states, have been frequently referred to in UN reports and resolutions. For example, more than 180 UN documents by human rights mechanisms, civil society organizations, and states have referred to the Rabat Plan of Action until September 2018; this means that in the first six years after its adoption, every twelve days a UN document was published with a reference to the Rabat Plan of Action. Also at the intergovernmental level, it has left its imprint, notably in resolutions. The General Assembly has noted the conclusions and recommendations of the OHCHR expert workshops contained in the Rabat Plan of Action in several resolutions on freedom of religion or belief and on combating intolerance. The UN Human Rights Council repeatedly encouraged the government of Myanmar to increase efforts further to promote "peaceful coexistence in all sectors of society in accordance with Human Rights Council resolution 16/18 of 24 March 2011 and the Rabat Plan of Action."[29] Similarly, in a thematic resolution, the Council recalled both "as important tools to counter violent extremism in all its forms and manifestations."[30] This is remarkable since the Council thereby puts the guidance provided by its own resolution 16/18 on the same level as the expert-led Rabat Plan of Action. At the regional level, the European Court of Human Rights in its judgment on the Pussy Riot case referred to the Rabat Plan of Action under "relevant international materials" as well as in its summaries of submissions from Amnesty International, Human Rights Watch, and the NGO Article 19, as did Judge Elósegui in his separate opinion.[31]

Similarly, the Beirut Declaration has been quoted by the Secretary-General, High Commissioner, and Special Rapporteur on freedom of religion or belief in several thematic or country-specific reports to the Security Council, General Assembly, and Human Rights Council.[32] Furthermore, in its concluding observations on Nigeria, the Committee on the Elimination of Discrimination against Women recommended to "expedite the repeal or amendment of all discriminatory laws identified by the Nigerian Law Reform Commission following its comprehensive audit of discriminatory laws in the State party and include religious leaders in the process of addressing issues of faith and human rights, so as to build on several 'faith for rights' initiatives and identify common ground among all religions in the State party, as acknowledged by the delegation."[33] When referring to the Beirut Declaration in September 2017, the then UN High Commissioner Zeid Ra'ad al Hussein reiterated his conviction that religious leaders, with their considerable influence over the hearts and minds of millions of people, could and should be consequential human rights actors in the world today, with real positive impact on the human rights landscape, while at the same time refraining from politicizing religious beliefs.[34]

7. Political Actors and Factors

While religious communities face a special responsibility when being confronted with acts of violence committed in their name, their responsibility is not exclusive.[35] Not even the Thirty Years' War (1618–1648), which in countless textbooks represents the culmination of European religious warfare, can adequately be described along religious lines only. The same is true for many of the contemporary manifestations of violence with religious underpinnings; they usually involve numerous nonreligious motives as well, which we can broadly subsume under the heading of "politics." Pointing to the role of politics does not reduce the responsibility of religious actors, which we have just highlighted. There can be no political "utilization" of a religious community unless parts of that community are willing to play that game. Even the most cunning Machiavellian politician would not be able to mobilize religious sentiments for political gains without having at least some support from within the respective religious communities themselves. Abuse of religion can never be merely external; it is always at the same time an abuse from within.

Depending on specific situations, political factors can include difficult historical legacies, long-term repercussions of colonial "divide-and-rule" policies, a climate of political authoritarianism, social inequalities or caste hierarchies, ethnic fragmentation, rapid demographic changes, migration processes, a widening gulf between urban and rural development, the breakdown of meaningful public discourse, lack of fairness within a stratified education system, precarious political legitimacy, hate messages in social media, a misogynic and homophobic "macho" culture, the weakness of civil society organizations, experiences of racist exclusion, processes of increasing gentrification, fear of economic and social decline in a shrinking middle class, lack of prospects for youths in the face of mass unemployment, endemic corruption and political cronyism, widespread disenchantment with government, general loss of trust in public institutions, a climate of impunity as a result of inefficient state reactions, proliferation of weapons and international arms trade, proxy wars, and countless other problems. Any specific incident of violence committed in the name of religion warrants a careful interpretation of relevant factors, including the broader political environment in which such acts have taken place.[36]

It would not make much sense to go through the list of all the many actors and factors that appear relevant for an adequate analysis and a comprehensive counterstrategy, which in any case must be specific and contextual in order to make a difference. Instead, we would like to focus on one factor and elevate it to the level of more abstract "typological" analysis, namely, the loss of trust in public institutions. There are two reasons for us to single out this specific factor. First, lack of trust in public institutions, especially extreme forms of resulting mistrust, often creates the fertile ground for the seeds of hateful and polarizing religious messages. Our second reason follows from the human rights approach, on which our whole analysis rests. Human rights are not just "values"; they also aim at the establishment of public infrastructure at various levels: local, national, regional, and global. One of the specific contributions of human rights in general and freedom of religion or belief specifically stems from their institution-building function.[37]

Loss of trust in public institutions often starts as endemic corruption and political cronyism. In the long run, this can lead to increasing disenchantment in larger parts of the population with the state and a concomitant societal fragmentation, with likely spillover effects on the religious communities. This problem is particularly acute in weak, highly corrupted, or failing states, some of which provide the territorial bases for terrorist organizations. The recent experience that terrorist groups strategically use the internet to spread their hate messages should not make us lose sight of the fact that they at the same time need a territorial base to conduct their military operations. It is usually failing states that provide such a base: Afghanistan, Somalia, Yemen, Libya, or Iraq. The Iraq war undertaken by former US president George W. Bush and his "coalition of the willing" in the guise of a supposed "war on terror" was a key root cause enabling the rise of the self-appointed "Islamic Caliphate" of ISIL.[38] This is just one example demonstrating that the forces of violence cannot be exclusively attributed to local or regional agents; one should also take the relevance of global power dynamics and hegemonies into account.

When people lose any trust in the fair functioning of public institutions, owing to daily experiences of corruption, they will manage their lives by resorting to their own support networks. Where else should they turn? In many cases, such networks happen to be defined along ethnic or religious lines or a combination of both. Expectations of group loyalties will gain more and more importance, while the overall framework of public institutions may increasingly lose its relevance. The resulting societal fragmentation processes can reinforce inward-looking mentalities, collective anxieties, and general suspicion against everything happening outside of the narrow boundaries of one's own groupings. While the sphere where people invest trust is shrinking more and more, the external world seems to become more and more hostile. This may result in a mentality of being "under siege" in an increasingly opaque broader environment.

Without functioning public institutions, there can be no public space which all individuals and groups could access without fear. Under such conditions, it is nearly impossible to experience religious and other pluralism as something "normal," let alone enriching. Rather, the coexistence of different religious groupings may resemble the way in which competing mafia organizations shape their precarious coexistence, namely, by demarcating and jealously protecting their respective "influence zones." Every inch occupied by a rival means lost territory for one's own group—or this is the typical perception. In order to prevent being driven out of one's turf, religious communities observe one another with growing suspicion. Thus, in a society without trustworthy public institutions, the danger increases steeply that religious communities, too, develop an attitude of mistrust not only vis-à-vis the state and its agencies but also toward one another. They thus may get infected by what Martha Nussbaum termed "the politics of fear."[39]

In the absence of trustworthy public institutions, it is furthermore nearly impossible to develop or uphold a culture of public discourse. Instead, people will mainly listen to their own networks and trust the narratives spread internally. Rumors, gossiping, personal traumas, and negative expectations largely remain unchecked by potential counternarratives or any facts-based counterevidence. This can further contribute to a prevailing atmosphere of collective narrow-mindedness, that is, a mistrustful attitude of people who feel they are under siege in an unreliable, unpredictable, and hostile environment. Expectations of unconditional group loyalty become all the more important and often override issues of faith.[40] Under such circumstances, a sudden crisis, an unforeseeable incident, or mere gossiping can ignite violent reactions. The end of this vicious cycle is a climate of political hysteria, in which militarized groups fight each other by using all available means.

It would be wrong to infer that religious communities are merely passively exposed to such societal fragmentation processes; they can function as additional actors and factors of violent escalation, for example, when turning group loyalty into a sacred duty, celebrating the "martyrdom" of war heroes, and invoking apocalyptic pictures of perpetual enmity. Religious images of heroes and demons can become the matrix for interpreting contemporary conflicts in an unreliable political environment. Political hysteria and religious apocalypse may thus mutually reinforce each other, thereby further speeding up the vicious spiral of mistrust, paranoia, and violent escalation.

In his study on *Terror in the Mind of God*, Mark Juergensmeyer points to the highly symbolic dimensions of some violent acts, which "refer to something beyond their immediate target: a grander conquest, for instance, or a struggle more awesome than meets the eye."[41] At the end of the twentieth century, Serbian paramilitaries saw themselves as reliving the legendary Battle of Kosovo against Ottoman Muslims in 1389. The Irish Republican Army cherished memories of collective victimization throughout the centuries. Similarly, the current regional conflicts in the Middle East are often thought to originate from theological disputes that started in the first decades of Islamic history over the question of who should succeed Prophet Muhammad as leader of the *ummah*. The use of mythological and essentialist categories for interpreting and describing contemporary conflicts lends an additional layer of fatalism to the occurrences, thus further shrinking the discursive space for political conflict management.

8. Contributions of Freedom of Religion or Belief

Freedom of religion or belief does not provide the magic key for solving all multifaceted and multidimensional problems just touched upon; such a general key does not exist. However, freedom of religion or belief, in conjunction with other human rights, plays an indispensable part in setting the normative framework for any anti-violence agenda, which ultimately must involve all areas of politics: education, media, migration and integration, labor market, housing market and urban planning, domestic security, justice, gender equality, youth, foreign relations, defense, and development cooperation. A precise description of the tasks ahead can only make sense in response to specific contexts, which exceeds the confines of a book chapter. Hence, we have to limit ourselves to a few general observations.

(a) A Component of the Rule of Law

In our sketchy analysis of political causes of violent escalation, we have highlighted the loss of trust in public institutions as one of the factors typically accounting for processes of violent escalations. Endemic corruption, lack of accountability, mafia practices, and related phenomena of crisis prepare the fertile ground for the seeds of hatred to take root and grow quickly. Consequently, one of the main preventative tasks is to cultivate, build, or rebuild institutional trust. Principles of transparency, accountability, and the rule of law provide necessary orientation, and human rights are an important part of this. The interplay of national constitutions, courts, and oversight institutions in line with international standards can help bring about more stability and reliability based on respect for everyone's equal rights.

The rule of law requires constant cultivation even in old established democracies. After the massacres perpetrated by Islamist terrorists in Paris in November 2015, the French government imposed a state of emergency, which gave law enforcement agencies broad leeway to impose restrictions, in particular on freedoms of expression, peaceful assembly, and association, as well as the right to privacy.[42] The assumption underlying such restrictive policies, namely, that principles of rule of law in general and human rights in particular are obstacles, which in situations of crisis should succumb to the primacy of an efficient security management, has all too often proved wrong. Although security concerns and human rights sometimes do collide, one should not underestimate the positive contributions of human rights for and within comprehensive security agendas. As stressed by the former High Commissioner for Human Rights, effective counterterrorism measures and the protection of human rights are complementary and mutually reinforcing objectives, both of which must be pursued by states as part of their duty to protect individuals within their jurisdiction.[43] Furthermore, the strict criteria prescribed for justifying limitations to human rights have beneficial effects on security politics, because they help to keep the focus narrowly on the real issues at hand.[44]

Like other human rights, freedom of religion or belief requires that any limitations imposed by the state in the interest of, inter alia, public order or safety be *precisely and narrowly defined*. Notably, freedom to manifest one's religion or belief cannot be limited on the ground of "national security," which means that the purpose for imposing restrictions must be spelled out more specifically concerning a permissible limitation ground.[45] For limitations to be justifiable, they must furthermore be actually suitable to achieve the said purpose and should be kept to the necessary minimum, that is, the least far-reaching intervention from all available options. These and other requirements help to prevent restrictive measures from growing out of proportion. Ample experience demonstrates that restrictive measures do not necessarily improve public safety. Instead of tackling the real threats, such measures arbitrarily target broader communities, exacerbate existing or newly emerging fault lines and create an atmosphere of mistrust, often at the expense of minorities, critics, and dissidents. This certainly does not serve purposes of trust building and peace.

Democratically elected politicians, too, frequently succumb to the temptation of imposing unreasonable and disproportionate restrictions in the interest of demonstrating strength and resolution. One blatant example was the harassment of "burkini" wearing women in France in the aftermath of the terrorist attack in Nice, in July 2016. The mayor of Villeneuve-Loubet instantly issued a formal prohibition of the burkini on the territory of his municipality. It is certainly understandable that a horrified population wished to see the authorities take action against terrorists. However, exposing women who walk on the beaches in gowns and with headscarves (not even wearing face veils) to humiliating control procedures obviously fails to serve any justifiable purpose. If those measures had any effect, they might quite likely have exacerbated feelings of collective victimization in parts of the Muslim population in France, while at the same time reinforcing stereotypical images of Islam in the larger society. In response to complaints lodged by civil society organizations, the Conseil d'État eventually declared the ban null and void.[46]

Human rights are not a luxury for times of peace and tranquility. Although at times conflicting with the immediate interests of law enforcement agencies and their political supporters, human rights, including freedom of religion or belief, actually prove particularly important in situations of crisis and instability. Within the broader framework of the rule of law, they oblige the state to present compelling arguments that certain limitations to freedom of religion or belief and other human rights, if deemed necessary, remain strictly in line with all the criteria stipulated under international human rights law. The population at large and in particular those who are mainly affected by such restrictions, should be able to understand which purposes these measures pursue, in which way they are suitable to serving the said purposes, why they are really necessary, and what the government does to avoid discriminatory effects, for instance against certain religious minorities. This certainly places a burden on governments, legislators, and judiciaries. Yet if the authorities shoulder that burden, they at the same time serve the overarching purpose of building institutional confidence in society. This is an important investment on the long path toward peace.

(b) Toward a Facts-Based Culture of Public Discourse

One of the typical repercussions of loss of trust in public institutions is a decline of public discourse. If it is true that the absence of public discourse typically breeds narrow-minded attitudes, it follows that the development of public communication is another crucial component of any meaningful counterstrategy. The abovementioned Rabat Plan of Action calls upon states, the media, civil society organizations, and other stakeholders to respond to incitement to hatred, including religious hatred, chiefly through communicative counter-action. According to the Rabat Plan of Action,[47] the best antidote to hate speech is "positive speech." This includes public demonstrations of solidarity for victims and targeted communities, fair professional journalism, active accommodation of marginalized groups within the media, in particular public media, and other initiatives. If the targets of hate speech experience broad solidarity, thus feeling they are not left alone in society, this will also reduce the danger that some of their members resort to violence as a supposed means of "self-defense." The Rabat Plan of Action presupposes a positive interplay between the rights to freedom of religion and freedom of expression, which in practice should mutually reinforce each other.[48] Similarly, the Beirut Declaration regards speech as fundamental to individual and communal flourishing. While acknowledging that war starts in the minds and is fueled by often hidden advocacy of hatred, the Beirut Declaration stresses that positive speech is also the healing tool of reconciliation and peace building in the hearts and minds. Thus, the supporters of the Beirut Declaration identify "speech" as one of the most strategic areas of their responsibilities they commit to assume and support each other for implementation on the basis of the thresholds articulated by the Rabat Plan of Action.[49]

"Positive speech" should not be mistaken for painting rosy pictures and shying away from complicated questions—on the contrary. An efficient counterstrategy against hostile stereotypes cannot consist of mere "image campaigns," which seek to replace negative pictures by positive pictures. Such image campaigns might even inadvertently nourish mistrust in parts of the population, since people may suspect that the intention is merely cosmetic. A more promising approach aims to overcome stereotyping through fact-based reporting, which in turn requires adequate conditions for professional investigative journalism. The purpose is to solidify or restore experience-based common sense, including on issues of religious diversity and interreligious coexistence. Building trust is a complex task, which also includes *building trust at the level of carefully investigated facts.* Trust is impossible without honesty, and honesty mainly manifests itself by taking complicated realities seriously.

Hannah Arendt already addressed this theme in the 1960s.[50] The point she wanted to make is that facts play a foundational role in constituting people's common political lifeworld; they also provide the precondition of any meaningful communication, in particular in politics. Communication is not only a process of exchanging messages between communicators and recipients; it is always communication "about" something, that is, it requires content, which itself presupposes the possibility of agreeing on certain elementary historical and political facts. If this possibility disappears, for example, as result of ubiquitous "fake news" and massive manipulation, communication itself may eventually lose its "worldliness," that is, being grounded in a common lifeworld. This was Arendt's main concern. Consistent lying, she wrote, "pulls the ground from under our feet and provides no other ground on which to stand." One possible result, which we currently can witness on a daily basis, is an endless series of unilateral "tweets," which merely cause confusion without conveying any real information or meaning. Against this increasing danger, the development of political common sense based on cultivating factuality must be a priority. Hence, taking facts seriously becomes yet another indispensable element of building confidence.

It is in the interest of solidifying facts-based common sense to admit that coexistence among people of different religious and nonreligious orientations is not always easy and can produce tensions and other unpleasant side effects. Misunderstandings, feelings of frustrations, and other negative experiences are part of human life. When merely told within internal circles or hermetic chatrooms, such negative stories create the breeding ground for a climate of mistrust, resentments, or even fully fledged conspiracy projections. By contrast, sharing experiences, including negative stories, in public debates, provides opportunities for exposing such experiences and concomitant feelings to possible counternarratives, countercriticism, and counterevidence based on carefully investigated facts. The perspectives of women and people from different generations should always be broadly accommodated in such projects. Only then can fact-based reporting help to prevent negative experiences from growing out of proportion and hardening into hermetic prejudices.

Criticism of religion is a natural part of any culture of frank public discourse. The space for such criticism must be broad and naturally includes the possibility to raise difficult questions about religion and violence—a theme that worries many people, who wish to see it discussed frankly and with honesty. Such criticism should not be stigmatized, let alone criminalized, as "blasphemous." Both the Rabat Plan of Action and the Beirut Declaration urge states that (still) have anti-blasphemy laws to repeal them, since such laws have a stifling impact on the enjoyment of freedom of thought, conscience, religion or belief, as well as on healthy dialogue and debate about religious issues.[51] The eighteen commitments on "Faith for Rights" also include the pledge "not to oppress critical voices and views on matters of religion or belief, however wrong or offensive they may be perceived, in the name of the 'sanctity' of the subject matter."

Critics may thus openly challenge religious communities and publicly expose evasive attitudes, wherever they exist. However, critique of religion can only be fair when paying adequate attention to intrareligious diversity, internal controversies, theological learning processes, reform agendas, societal transformations, as well as historical and political facts. Much depends on the choice of adequate, that is, nonessentialist categories. Essentialist ascriptions, which pretend to derive a propensity for violence from supposedly immutable "core messages" of certain religions, subject many millions of people to a supposedly timeless "essence" of a particular religion, thereby obfuscating the diversity of individual biographies as well as personal convictions, faces, and voices. Moreover, essentialist ascriptions frequently feed fatalistic attitudes. This warrants serious countercriticism. In most cases, the spread of essentialist messages may still fall within the scope of what freedom of expression permits. Yet while censorship cannot be an option, other activities, in particular communicative counterstrategies, are all the more important.

(c) Encouraging Religious Reform Agendas

Is it not bitterly ironic that militant nationalists use Buddhism, which sees the human self as a mere illusion and a hurdle on the long path to salvation, as an ideological tool for policies of collective selfishness? How can Hinduism with its vast cosmos of diverse philosophies, theologies, mythologies, and spiritual practices reinforce the trivial bifurcation of "us" versus "them"? How is it possible that the Islamic prayer call "God is above all" has become the battle cry of terrorists, whose acts of cruelty belie any faith in a merciful God? How can Christian preachers incite hatred against LGBTI persons, which obviously runs counter to the gospel's command to "love thy neighbor"? These are questions that puzzle many observers. According to Scott Appleby, religious extremists—while pretending to show particular religious zeal—typically have a rather limited, superficial, and selective understanding of religious traditions. "Ironically, extremists—who often claim to be upholding the 'fundamentals' of the religion—tend to be highly selective in choosing which sub-traditions to embrace and honor."[52] Based on empirical case studies from different parts of the world, Andreas Hasenclever comes to a similar conclusion: "many contemporary faith-related conflicts are not really about religion in a more demanding understanding. . . . The available findings indicate that religion and violence

can only come together, if the complexity of religious traditions is systematically ignored and the public debate on adequate interpretation is denied."[53]

It is crucial that criticism of selected, one-sided, and distorted interpretations of religious ideas, concepts, and traditions come from the midst of
the religious communities themselves. The good news is that this actually
happens—at least to a certain degree. Organizations of Buddhist monks in
Myanmar and Sri Lanka publicly attack the amalgamation of Buddhism
with aggressive nationalism as a distortion of Buddhist teachings. In India,
intellectuals from a Hindu background have exposed the shallowness of
Hindu nationalist ideologies. Muslim reformers have built networks across
state borders to support one another against the rise of religious narrow-
mindedness. Raising awareness about ambiguous attitudes toward violence
within the Christian tradition has become part of theology curriculums.

Religious reformers have often been termed "moderates" as opposed to
extremists or radicals. Not everyone subscribes to this terminology. It actually seems to give violent extremists the credit of promoting a strong and
heroic interpretation of religion, while reformers apparently have to satisfy
themselves with merely sending out defensive signals. Even worse, "moderate religion" may actually sound like a merely lukewarm version of faith.
Appleby thus has an important point to make when questioning this usual
way of labeling reformers. "Contrary to the misconceptions popular in
some academic and political circles, religious actors play this critical and
positive role in world affairs not when they moderate their religion or marginalize their deeply held, vividly symbolized, and often highly particular
beliefs in a higher order of love and justice. Religious actors make a difference when they remain *religious* actors."[54]

Religious reformers with a pronounced anti-violence agenda often show
a simultaneous commitment to human rights as well.[55] The main goal
underlying human rights, after all, is the facilitation of peaceful coexistence
based on respect for everyone's equal dignity and equal rights.[56] Reformers
within various religious communities can therefore locate themselves
within this overarching international peace project, if they wish. The awareness of being in tune with a worldwide human rights movement across
religious, denominational, cultural, and ideological divides can be particularly important for people who face difficulties within their own religious
communities. It may encourage them to continue working for reforms in
spite of obstacles and resistance. In this context, the eighteen commitments
on "Faith for Rights" can give additional encouragement, because they

stress the shared conviction that interpretations of religion or belief should add to the level of protection of human dignity. The third commitment specifically pledges that "critical thinking and debate on religious matters should not only be tolerated but rather encouraged as a requirement for enlightened religious interpretations in a globalized world composed of increasingly multi-cultural and multi-religious societies that are constantly facing evolving challenges."

Apart from providing general encouragement, how can freedom of religion or belief foster religious reform agendas? What is the role of the state in this regard? Does freedom of religion or belief oblige the state to promote religious reforms, or would the state, when mingling with such issues, trespass into the autonomy of religious communities? The answer to these questions is complex. As a secular human right, freedom of religion or belief cannot serve as a quasi-theological or crypto-theological standard.[57] While entitling human beings to hold, develop, express, and manifest their various views in this area, freedom of religion or belief does not endorse any of these views. It cannot function as a yardstick for assessing the persuasiveness of theological or philosophical arguments. In respect for everyone's freedom of religion or belief, the state, too, should not mingle with theological reform agendas and their underlying interpretations of religious sources. Instead, what the state ought to do is *ensure a safe and open space*, in which the diversity of positions and practices can manifest itself freely and without fear. In order to be able to fulfill this function credibly, however, the state has to exercise strict self-restraint and cannot claim any theological authority for itself.[58]

Hence, the way in which freedom of religion or belief contributes to intracommunity reform agendas can only be an *indirect* one. This is very much in line with the peculiar indirectness, in which freedom of religion or belief generally relates to religions or beliefs, namely, by approaching them from the angle of human beings, who are the ultimate right holders. This indirectness also defines the mode in which freedom of religion or belief relates to religious reform agendas in the area of counterviolence. By empowering human beings to develop their own thinking and express their own positions, human rights help to subject religious traditions to critical questioning, internal discussions, expressions of doubts, new readings of sacred texts, as well as innovative religious self-understandings. This is a significant contribution. Surely, to a certain degree, religious traditions have always been arenas of internal contestation. Yet with the advent of freedom of religion or belief as an international human right, this has become clearer and more explicit than before. In conjunction with other human rights, freedom of religion or belief can thus facilitate the elaboration of innovative positions within religious discourses.[59]

Creating and upholding an open space in which inter- and intrareligious diversity can unfold freely und without fear remains a core responsibility of the state. This includes the guarantee that this space remains strictly free from coercion. While being obliged to exercise self-restraint concerning religious or theological controversies, however, the state cannot remain "neutral" if internal critics, dissidents, or converts feel under threat. In such situations, the state has to intervene and provide active protection based on the clear understanding that freedom of religion or belief can only acknowledge noncoercive forms of religiosity.

(d) Promoting Intergroup Communication

Interreligious communication is another important component in any policy of building or rebuilding trust in society. Surely, it would be naïve to expect that resentment, suspicion, or other negative feelings will disappear as soon as people start talking to each other. Depending on the context, communicative encounters may even inadvertently expose insuperable limits of mutual understanding, and they may dig out complicated legacies or irreconcilably different worldviews. Yet people who meet, talk, and listen on a regular basis, will in the long run most likely realize that they have also much in common. Seeing *real* human faces and hearing *real* human voices provides the most promising antidote against "abstract" conspiracy projections, which ascribe a supposedly totally "alien" and negative mentality to members of another group. Intergroup dialogue is thus an important preventative strategy and helps to manage existing conflicts.

In order for interreligious communication to unfold its potential of building confidence, adequate circumstances are of the essence.[60] Broad participation, the accommodation of diversity not only between, but also within religious communities, a climate of security, and encounters on an equal footing are among the most important factors. Much depends on agenda setting and the choice of topics. States can and should play an active role in facilitating interreligious and other forms of cross-boundary communication under appropriate circumstances. This is part of their promotional obligations under freedom of religion or belief.[61]

The importance of regular intergroup communication becomes obvious in situations when it is actually missing. During one of our fact-finding missions in Eastern Europe, the government had invited the country's religious communities to a nonpublic consultation on a new draft law. When entering the room, one immediately felt the tense atmosphere. While the representatives of the religious communities used the opportunity to voice their own interests and concerns, they mostly refused to react to the points expressed by others. Almost everyone spoke just for themselves and their own group. People typically avoided eye contact with others and kept their eyes strictly focused on the desk in front of them. Some participants articulated hostile and prejudiced views of other religions or denominations, whose representatives were sitting only a few meters next to them in the same room. Although the coexistence of different religions in that country had been generally tranquil, the tangible atmosphere of mistrust in the absence of a culture of regular intergroup communication felt quite worrisome.[62]

By contrast, in a mission to Lebanon we experienced a country with a highly developed culture of interreligious communication.[63] From 1975 to 1990, Lebanon was torn by a civil war, with active involvement of the religious communities, although almost everyone agrees that the root causes of warfare were mainly of a political nature. During a visit to Beirut, we attended the "*Rencontre spirituelle islamo-chretienne,*" an interreligious celebration held on the day of St. Mary's Annunciation (25 March). Mary's Annunciation is of religious significance for Christians and Muslims alike. The religious communities had therefore agreed to celebrate this day as an interreligious national holiday. The ceremony started when a Muslim cleric cited verses from the Qur'an against the background of ringing church bells. Subsequently, Muslim and Christian teenagers performed an improvised dance around the altar to express their determination to work together against violence. One should not underestimate the significance of such ceremonies, in particular when conducted on a regular basis and with broad participation. Other interreligious projects in Lebanon pursue more practical purposes, such as providing humanitarian assistance to people in need. An organization for example aims at building trust between different religious communities and their local leaders, while others cooperate in reaching out to prison inmates to support their spiritual and social needs as many could become easy prey to religious radicalization due to their living conditions and lack of prospects.

Particularly impressive were experiences from Sierra Leone, an economically poor country with a history of violent political turmoil and the historical legacy of a gruesome civil war, which only ended in 2002.[64] Muslim and Christian denominations—Sunnis, Shias, Ahmadis, Anglicans, Baptists, Methodists, and others—cooperate on a regular basis, not only in the capital, but also in the provinces. In general, religious violent extremism is not much known in Sierra Leone. Members of the Interreligious Council mentioned one strange case, when a Christian woman claimed to have dreamed about the late Muhammad Gaddafi whom she allegedly saw being punished in hell. Based on her dream, she publicly called for the destruction of a mosque sponsored by Gaddafi. On the request of the Muslim members of the Interreligious Council, the Christian churches reacted swiftly and publicly rejected the woman's antagonistic message. Apparently, they were successful, because the situation remained calm.

The prevailing atmosphere of interreligious cooperation in Sierra Leone has many roots, including education in public and private schools, where students from different religious backgrounds learn together. We visited a school in Freetown run by the Ahmadiyya Muslim Community, which takes students from Ahmadi, Sunni, Shia, and Christian backgrounds. The teachers, too, came from diverse faith communities. This is only one example of communication taking place outside of formal interreligious dialogue settings. Informal communication of people who work or learn together without being required permanently to identify themselves as followers of this or that religion has the advantage of also taking individuals on board who feel unable or unwilling to express their views in theological language.

The Interreligious Council in Sierra Leone acted as the driving force within the Truth and Reconciliation Commission (TRC) established shortly after the civil war, which ended in 2002. Already in 2004, the TRC presented a report which meticulously describes the atrocities committed by all parties to the conflict. The religious communities were able to take this important peace-building role, because the paranoia of the civil war had only limited spillover effects on the relationship between the religious communities themselves. This may be the result of the broad appreciation of religious pluralism, which in Sierra Leone is ingrained in people's everyday lifeworld, where Muslims and Christians live together, intermarry, and even convert to another religion, usually with the blessings of their communities.[65] Within Islam, Sunnis, Shias, and Ahmadis coexist and cooperate, and the same is true for the various inner-Christian denominations. Such

experience of amicable coexistence provides the most powerful counterevidence against the fatalistic assumption that members of certain communities are at the end of the day "doomed" to hate each other.

Interreligious communication with the purpose of building peace also
exists in an organized fashion at the international level. For example, in
October 1970, the World Conference of Religions for Peace convened for
the first time.[66] As a worldwide NGO with broad membership and accreditation status with the United Nations, the coalition Religions for Peace
brings together people from different faith communities. While their religious orientations remain different, they share a commitment for peace,
understanding, and reconciliation promoted in the name of religions.
Interreligious dialogue can help to strengthen the peace-building capacities
that religious communities may have also in situations where religious
motives are obviously not part of the conflict. As Rüdiger Noll emphasizes,
"Even in conflicts without a religious component, it is often the religious
organizations or religious personalities that have the credibility from the
people to mediate."[67] As one famous example, he cites the South African
archbishop Desmond Tutu, who played a crucial role in reuniting a country
that had been haunted over generations by the apartheid system, the politics of fear, and massive obstacles to interethnic communication.

In a comprehensive political study entitled *God's Century*, Monica
Duffy Toft, Daniel Philpott, and Timothy Samuel Shah analyze conditions
on which prospects for success of religious actors striving for mediation
and peace depend. Among the various relevant factors, they highlight the
independence of religion from political power as well as clear theological
anti-violence agendas. Hence, their conclusion that "religious actors are
most successful when they are independent of the state—and, in the case
of peace mediation, of opposition forces as well—and espouse a political
theology of peace or reconciliation."[68]

Just as religions can become a factor of conflict and violent escalation,
they can also become a driving force for peace and solidarity. Mary Robinson, former UN High Commissioner for Human Rights, once called upon
the religious communities to take that role and use their freedom of religion
for the betterment of societies: "The major religions, while concerned with
ultimate questions, frequently present themselves as protectors and promo-
tors of human dignity. They see themselves in particular as defenders of the
deprived, the poor, the discriminated against. So their religious freedom is
a freedom in society not merely to believe and to worship, but also to

uphold the cause of the deprived."[69] The key message of the Beirut Declaration and its eighteen commitments points in a similar direction: "faith" and "rights" can and should become mutually reinforcing spheres. When human rights are effectively protected, this may lead to the flourishing of free individual and communal expressions of religions or beliefs, and human rights may in turn benefit from deeply rooted ethical and spiritual foundations provided by religions or beliefs. The approach of the "Faith for Rights" framework is broad and inclusive, since believers are defined—in line with the Human Rights Committee's General Comment No. 22—as holders of "theistic, non-theistic, atheistic or other" convictions. Thus, the Beirut Declaration reaches out to persons belonging to most diverse religions and beliefs from all regions of the world, in order to enhance cohesive, peaceful, and respectful societies on the basis of a common action-oriented platform open to all actors who share its objectives.

CHAPTER 9

Custodian Against the Sacralization of Human Rights

1. Human Rights and Religion(s)

After analyzing, in the previous chapters, how human rights tackle "religion," we now explore the relationship from the opposite angle. How do religious communities position themselves to human rights? Can they contribute to a culture of human rights? Should they adapt their internal structures to modern principles of freedom and equality? Can the state, directly or indirectly, facilitate reforms within religious communities, or would this amount to trespassing? What is the significance of freedom of religion or belief in all of this?

Clarifying the relationship between human rights and religions is important for both sides. If religious communities wish to have an impact on public political life, they nowadays have to develop a clear position toward human rights. After World War II, human rights have become an international normative framework, which is not only binding upon states, but—albeit in a different way—concerns societal organizations as well, including faith-based actors and organizations. At the same time, it is obvious that the frequently invoked normative consensus on human rights remains precarious. Apart from the proverbial cleavage between normative aspirations and stubborn realities, which has always existed, the very concept of human rights has recently come under renewed pressure. Whereas in the past, criticism of human rights often came from the political left, objections against human rights today frequently occur in the guise of "traditional religious values." Not least for this reason, it is also in the interest of human rights to clarify the relationship toward religion.

We first describe basic affinities and conflicts between human rights and religions (Sections 2 and 3). We then analyze one of the core functions that define the human rights approach—that is, shaping peaceful coexistence under circumstances of pluralism by empowering human beings, in respect of their human dignity (Section 4). This empowerment function explains the specific normative authority that human rights can claim, including when dealing with religious communities, as well as certain limitations inherent in the human rights approach (Section 5). The combination of authority and modesty should guide the state in its role as the formal guarantor of human rights. While the state is obliged to eliminate all forms of coercion between and within religious communities, the state can only indirectly contribute to the broader religious and theological internalization of human rights (Section 6). The chapter concludes with highlighting the critical role freedom of religion or belief can take against sacralizing human rights (Section 7).

2. Substantial Affinities

Human rights language abounds with religious ideas, terms, metaphors, and concepts. The 1776 Declaration of Independence of the United States of America invokes God as the ultimate guarantor of everyone's fundamental rights: "We hold these truths to be self-evident, that all men are created equal, that they are endowed by their Creator with certain unalienable Rights."[1] The French Revolution's Declaration de droits de l'homme et du citoyen (1789), while not explicitly relating to a divine authority, contains the notion of sacredness, which occurs twice in the text. According to the preamble, the authors "have resolved to set forth in a solemn declaration the natural, unalienable and sacred rights of man." Article 17 qualifies the right to property as "inviolable and sacred."[2] Kant, otherwise the intellectual epitome of Prussian sobriety, venerates human rights as the "apple of God's eye."[3] In his essay on enlightenment, he points to the moral duty of enlightenment and warns: "to renounce enlightenment, whether for his own person or even more so for posterity, is to violate the sacred right of humanity and trample it underfoot."[4] A century later, Émile Durkheim declares human rights to be part of a sacralization of the individual person, which he thinks represents the most important moral achievement of the modern era.[5] Drawing on Durkheim's thoughts, Hans Joas recently published a book titled *The Sacredness of the Person.*[6]

The peculiar closeness to religious language is no coincidence. Notions like "inalienability" or "inviolability" illustrate that human rights exceed the usual pragmatic functions of law. They touch upon existential questions: the inherent dignity of all human beings, the unconditioned conditions of any normative interaction, the self-understanding of individuals as responsible agents, the ultimate foundations of morality and law, that is, issues which have also been a traditional domain of various religions. What is at stake in human rights is no less than the humanness of the human being. Some human rights standards, like the ban on torture or the prohibition of any coercive infringements into the person's inner nucleus of faith-formation, command an apodictic respect, which does not allow any exceptions or limitations, even in situations of public emergency. These and other prohibitions demarcate the "red lines" which a state must never cross, regardless of the political circumstances. It is no coincidence that these prohibitions have been qualified as "absolute" norms, thus again carrying a predicate that seems to stem from the religious sphere.

One can also describe the affinities between human rights and religion from the viewpoint of religion. The basic principles and concepts that define the human rights approach—human dignity, justice, liberation, and equality—resonate profoundly within many religious traditions.[7] The frequently cited biblical metaphor accounting for the special rank of human beings is man's and woman's creation in the image and likeness of God (Genesis 1:26–27). The Bible stresses that shedding human blood is taboo (Genesis 9:6). In Psalm 8, the singer admires the sublime beauty of the nightly sky, which makes him simultaneously aware of his frailty and his special calling within the whole of creation. He turns to God wondering: "What is man, that thou art mindful of him?" (Psalm 8:4). In a way, Psalm 8 anticipates Kant's observation that "the starry heavens above me" and "the moral law within me" jointly "fill the mind with ever new and increasing admiration and reverence."[8] Another eminent biblical reference is Israel's escape from slavery. The "exodus" provides a powerful narrative, which inspired abolitionists in their fight against slave trade and slavery. "Let my people go"—this refrain of a famous gospel song has become the banner of liberation movements to the present day.

Such motives are not a monopoly of the biblical tradition. The Qur'an acknowledges man's role as God's vicegerent (*khalifa*) on earth (Sura 2:30), which is the reason why even the angels have to bow before Adam (Sura 2:34). According to Sura 33, the human being has accepted a trust (*amana*), which the mountains and the heavens, representing the most powerful cosmic elements, had previously rejected (Sura 33:72). This Qur'anic verse describes the simultaneous awareness of human frailty and human calling, roughly analogous to Psalm 8. The Qur'an furthermore warns that whoever kills a human being acts as if he killed the whole of humanity (Sura 5:32), thus ascribing to each individual person a worth above any utilitarian calculation. Such biblical and Qur'anic ideas, Jeremy Waldron writes, "convey a profound sense of the sanctity of the human person—each of us unimaginably and incomparably sacred because of this relation to the Most Holy."[9]

The possibilities to invoke substantial affinities between human rights and religions are manifold and accommodate a broad variety of religious traditions, theistic as well as nontheistic traditions.[10] From this observation, it may seem only a small step toward postulating that human rights and religions share their basic normative aspirations. People who assume that the ethical principles underlying human rights stem from the biblical tradition often point to substantial overlaps between human rights and "Jewish-Christian values."[11] The drafters of the Universal Islamic Declaration of Human Rights of 1981, in turn, contend that human rights stem from the Qur'an.[12] Others take a more ecumenical approach by pointing to substantive overlaps between all the major religions and modern ideas of human dignity and human rights.[13] For example, the authors of the 2017 Beirut Declaration use various religious and philosophical quotes to support the eighteen commitments on "Faith for Rights," stressing their "deep conviction that our respective religions and beliefs share a common commitment to upholding the dignity and the equal worth of all human beings" and that "shared human values and equal dignity are therefore common roots of our cultures."[14] It is not only religiously interested people who wish to demonstrate similarities between the ethos of various religions and modern standards of human rights; many human rights advocates, too, strive to further solidify human rights norms by invoking a broad normative consensus traceable to the authoritative scriptures and traditions of the world religions.[15]

3. Areas of Conflicts

Those who postulate a generally harmonious relationship between human rights and religious traditions have to face a number of serious challenges, however. Gender-related rights are the most salient arena of contestation, where numerous complicated conflicts have arisen. The equality of men and women is anchored in numerous human rights documents, starting with the UN Charter and not ending with the 1979 Convention on the Elimination of All Forms of Discrimination Against Women (CEDAW). This standard of equality obviously collides with traditional gender roles, which to the present day have often been justified in the name of religion. The potential for conflicts increases steeply once we add the more recent claims of nondiscrimination based on one's sexual orientation and gender identity.

Freedom of religion or belief is another contentious issue.[16] Owing to its universal nature, freedom of religion or belief provides space for critics, dissenters, converts, members of schismatic movements, skeptics, agnostics, and various minorities. For some believers this is difficult to accept. Especially the right to change one's religion remains a provocation. Does this not mean to place the individual and his or her personal preferences above divine laws? If so, does this not illustrate the "Promethean" spirit of human rights, in the name of which man rebels against his creator? The significance of such fundamental objections for understanding ongoing reservations against human rights can hardly be overemphasized. Beyond the more specific areas of contestation, in particular gender rights, it is ultimately *the human rights approach as such* that has frequently caused anxiety, suspicion, and opposition, given its emancipatory thrust epitomized in notions of empowerment, liberation, and equal respect for all.

In the case of the Catholic Church,[17] the history of open resistance started as early as in 1791, when Pope Pius VI in his breve *Quod aliquantum* condemned the French Revolution's human rights declaration as "scandalous," "senseless," and an offense to reason.[18] Papal polemics culminated in the notorious *Syllabus Errorum* (1864), in which Pius IX castigated human rights among other grave errors of modernity.[19] The conflict gradually ebbed away around the turn of the century and came to an official end in the encyclical *Pacem in terris* (1963) through which John XXIII acknowledged human rights as hope-inspiring "signs of the time."[20] Shortly afterwards, the Second Vatican Council endorsed religious freedom in its Declaration *Dignitatis humanae* (1965).[21] The Protestant churches, too, had their complicated historical encounters with human rights. At the beginning of the twentieth century, church historian Ernst Troeltsch deconstructed the once popular idea that human rights directly stem from the

Protestant Reformation. He pointed out that, unlike some of the marginalized "step children" of the Reformation, for example, mystics, sectarians,
and free-churches, the mainstream Protestant churches only gradually
overcame their initial reluctance toward the idea of equal rights of freedom
for all.[22] Reservations against human rights continue to be strong within
the family of Orthodox churches. Representatives of the Russian Orthodox
Church have associated human rights with "Western" ideas, which they
think should not take root on Russian soil.[23] Obviously, there are also
numerous human rights conflicts in Islamic societies. Some Islamist intellectuals construe an antagonism between "rights of man" and "rights of
God." Others oppose human rights as part of what they consider a "Wes-
toxication," that is, an alleged Western subversion aimed at undermining
collective Islamic identities.[24] Those holding such antagonistic views frequently call for authoritarian policies against civil society organizations,
which they stigmatize as fifth columns operating in the service of alien and
hostile forces. Such anti-human-rights movements exist under the auspices
of most different religions.

    In the view of conservative and traditionalist critics, human rights
reflect an anthropocentric ideology centered on the idea that "man is the
measure of all things."[25] In addition to this come concerns that the freedoms of individuals could erode communitarian loyalty. Others lament a
one-sided emphasis on legal entitlements, to the detriment of social duties
and responsibilities. Such reservation often assumes the language of "traditional religious values," which some pit against the emancipatory spirit of
modern human rights. An example is the discussion within the United
Nations on traditional values, which culminated in the adoption of several
resolutions on this topic by the UN Human Rights Council with the title
"Promoting human rights and fundamental freedoms through a better
understanding of traditional values of humankind."[26] One of the problems
of these resolutions, which enjoyed the support of the Russian Federation
as well as the Russian Orthodox Church, was that they failed to define the
nebulous term "traditional values." This gave rise to fears that the amalgamation of human rights standards with undefined "traditional values"
would ultimately erode normative clarity, thus weakening the force and
prospects of human rights.

    In 2008, the Moscow Patriarchate issued a position paper on human
dignity and human rights. While cautiously endorsing the notion of human
rights, the document contains a number of far-reaching reservations. As

Peter Petkoff observes, the document represents, to say the least, a "sceptical approach to human rights protection."[27] Even the idea of human dignity receives a surprising anti-egalitarian turn. While the Moscow Patriarchate generally acknowledges everyone's dignity as a divine gift bestowed on all human beings, the document at the same time stresses the need for "restoring a person to his appropriate dignity."[28] Drawing on a terminological distinction established by the Christian church fathers in their interpretation of the book of Genesis, the Moscow Patriarchate differentiates between being created "in the image of God," which includes all human beings equally, and the "likeness of God," which was lost through man's fall and thus requires active efforts for restoration: "In Orthodoxy the dignity and ultimate worth of every human person are derived from the image of God, while dignified life is related to the notion of God's likeness achieved through God's grace by efforts to overcome sin and to seek moral purity and *virtue*."[29] This formulation suggests that the dignity of the individual exists in different measures, depending on the degree of living in accordance with the moral teachings of the Church.

The Cairo Declaration on Human Rights in Islam, adopted by the OIC in 1990, displays a similar ambiguity, to say the least. After proclaiming that all humans are equal in terms of basic human dignity, the document adds that "true faith is the guarantee for enhancing such dignity along the path to human perfection."[30] Here again, dignity appears to be an attribute which can be increased by acts of piety and religious compliance. Instead of providing the normative basis for everyone's equal dignity and equal rights, the term dignity thus assumes an anti-egalitarian, meritocratic meaning. The Cairo Declaration furthermore fails to recognize equal rights of men and women.[31] Another striking feature is the absence of freedom of religion or belief, which the Cairo Declaration replaces by a prohibition to exploit the "poverty and ignorance" of people in order to convert them to any religion other than Islam or to become an atheist.[32] This formulation does not merely fall short of Article 18 of the UDHR and Article 18 of the ICCPR; it actually turns their meaning upside down. Finally, the Cairo Declaration stipulates that all the rights enumerated in the document remain subject to the Islamic Sharia.[33] In short, the Cairo Declaration is even further remote from the UN human rights standards than the 2008 document of the Moscow Patriarchate. Yet what both have in common is a tendency to counter the emancipatory spirit of human rights by stipulating the primacy of traditional religious values and religious laws.

In the face of nebulous positions and ongoing conservative religious opposition, skeptics have wondered whether human rights and religions could ever be fully and unequivocally reconciled. Such skepticism, which historically often came from religious traditionalists, has also become popular in humanist circles. Some humanists consider the continued influence of religious communities as a main obstacle to a consistent implementation of human rights. The analysis of concrete conflicts, for example around gender-related emancipation, leads to the diagnosis of an abstract antagonism, that is, an allegedly unbridgeable gulf between human rights and religion(s) in general. It is worth noting in this context that the term "humanism" carries very different connotations. In the German context, "*Humanismus*" traditionally includes Christian intellectuals like Erasmus of Rotterdam or Thomas Moore, who strove for a new synthesis of Christian theology and philanthropic classical philosophy. From this angle, there is no inherent tension between religious and humanistic positions.[34] In English, by contrast, it seems to us that the term "humanism" usually represents a much more critical attitude toward religion. Humanists in this understanding often subscribe to anti- or postreligious belief systems, at times based on a thoroughly scientific worldview. For example, Julian Huxley, first president of the British Humanist Association and one of the founders of the International Humanist and Ethical Union, promoted an atheistic worldview, to which he contributed from his scientific background as an evolutionary biologist. Richard Dawkins, author of the best seller *The God Delusion*,[35] likewise comes from evolutionary biology. Through his books, Dawkins exercises a strong influence among humanist and atheistic circles worldwide.

Now, it is obviously tempting to associate "human rights" with "humanism." Both terms have a common linguistic root, which furthermore points to a common interest to acknowledge the central place human beings occupy in ethical theory and practice. Yet this common linguistic root can also cause confusion when backing up exclusively humanistic ownership claims through which the concept of human rights itself would assume a postreligious or anti-religious flavor. Some humanists actually claim that their own human rights commitment is from the outset more consistent than that of faith-based organizations, because the latter constantly struggle with possible contradictions between their holy scriptures, on the one hand, and modern human rights documents, on the other. Obviously, nonreligious humanists do not have this problem. However, to conclude that postreligious humanists are generally better suited for promoting human rights than religious believers would amount to a particularly "humanistic" superiority claim, which would be no less corrosive for a broad acceptance of human rights than exclusive Christian or other religious ownership claims on human rights.

4. Shaping Pluralism Through Respect for Human Dignity

The two perspectives on the relationship between human rights and religions—the emphasis on affinities and the stress on differences—rest on prima facie correct observations from which they each draw one-sided and thus problematic consequences. With regard to possible affinities, one can certainly say that some of the basic ideas underlying human rights have existed in the ethical teaching of various religions, possibly for millennia. Human dignity may be the most obvious example. Another example is the significance attached to justice in many manifestations of traditional religious ethos. Moreover, countless religious believers show strong commitment to the cause of human rights while at the same time remaining faithful to their traditions, without in the least feeling schizophrenic.[36] They thus bear testimony to the fact that religiosity and human rights commitment can well come together. Religious human rights activists may furthermore find positive inspiration and motivation in their faith tradition when working for dignity, justice, and freedom. Still, the problem remains that the harmonizing viewpoint fails to take conceptual differences and thematic controversies seriously enough, as mentioned above. The all too harmonious vision of the relationship between human rights and religion may not survive the test of serious conflicts or crises once they arise.

By contrast, those who mainly stress normative tensions between human rights and religions likewise capture certain aspects of that complicated relationship. They may base their interpretation on religiously colorized political conflicts concerning gender issues as well as diverging attitudes toward emancipation and equality. What they often neglect, however, is that those conflicts do not necessarily display a zero-sum logic such that one side could only win what the other side loses. Turning concrete tensions into an abstract either-or dichotomy would amount to rejecting, from the outset, any possibility of a meaningful normative rapprochement between the ethos of various religions and the modern idea of human rights. As a result of such a dichotomized view, human rights commitment would remain reserved to a comparatively small circle of religiously distanced humanists. This in turn would seriously hamper the prospect of building a sustainable global human rights culture.[37]

In order to overcome both easy harmonization and abstract dichotomization, it is useful to reflect on the specific function that human rights have in facilitating fair coexistence among people living in religiously and otherwise pluralistic societies. To be able to fulfill this function, human rights must claim independence—and in this sense "secularity"—with regard to the various religious ideas and traditions, without pretending to supersede or replace religions. In other words, human rights claim a specific normative authority, which is at the same time limited and accommodating. It is a space-providing authority, as it were, which for this reason requires modesty and self-restraint.

Historically, human rights developed in response to experiences of structural injustice, often linked to conflict-driven pluralization processes. In Europe,[38] much of this happened in the wake of the Protestant Reformation, which had led to an irredeemable schism within occidental Christendom and concomitant warfare. Instead of continuing futile efforts to restore confessional homogeneity of the territorial state, which had caused bloodshed for more than a century, the idea of human rights represented a paradigm shift toward an explicit recognition of pluralism. Such recognition goes far beyond the early modern politics of "tolerance," because it no longer takes one predominant confession—Catholicism, Lutheran or Reformed Protestantism—as the standard against which to merely condone or "tolerate" others. Rather, human rights appreciate the pluralism of religions and beliefs as something inherently valuable. This is the important innovative insight. As repeatedly emphasized throughout this book, the appreciation of pluralism merely indirectly relates to the various religions or beliefs themselves, because at the end of the day, it is *human beings* who receive legal recognition in the context of human rights. To put it in a nutshell, the guiding idea underpinning the human rights approach is to empower human beings so that they can find their own ways freely, including in the area of religion and belief, as long as their acts are compatible with the equal freedom of others.

The empowerment function of human rights is more than just a procedural device for managing the plurality of convictions, positions, beliefs, and concomitant practices that happen to exist in society. Human rights rest on a basic normative commitment, namely, respect for everyone's *potential of responsible agency.* This potential of responsible agency defines the nucleus of a modern, secular concept of human dignity. It is secular not in the sense of being anti-religious or postreligious, but in the sense of remaining independent of particular religious viewpoints, in order to give space for a broad diversity. Moreover, by emphasizing the word "potential" in the context of responsible agency, we want to highlight that human dignity, thus understood, goes much deeper than the appreciation of a person's actual performance. It precedes any concrete normative actions, efforts, or accomplishments as their implicit sine qua non. Normative claims and obligations of any kind, ranging from personal promises or civil law contracts to constitutional norms and international conventions, necessarily presuppose that human beings, at least in principle, have the capacity of responsible agency. Even those individuals who actually fail to live up to the expectation of responsible conduct are usually held "responsible" for their shortcomings.[39] Moreover, the recognition of the potential of responsible agency cannot depend on empirical qualities or skills of this or that individual. Rather, it defines a *fundamental status position,* which is to be respected in all human beings strictly equally, simply because they are "members of the human family," to cite again from the preamble of the UDHR. Human dignity, thus conceptualized, can only be a universal and egalitarian status position—or it fails to make any sense.[40]

Let us dwell a moment on this idea. We have repeatedly cited the first sentence of Article 1 of the UDHR, which proclaims that "All human beings are born free and equal in dignity and rights." The article goes on to declare that all human beings "are endowed with reason and conscience."[41] While the first sentence of Article 1 is probably the most frequently quoted part of the UDHR, the subsequent sentence has attracted comparatively little attention. The reason may be that the formulation is vulnerable to possible misunderstandings. One could worry that the wording used here—"reason and conscience"—could invite moral perfectionism, which at the end of the day could create a hierarchy between different degrees of dignity, in conjunction to different degrees of moral skills, merits, and performances. Even worse, some individuals might end up being excluded from the realm of human rights, owing to their lack of elementary mental capacities, or so one may worry. Obviously, this interpretation would stand in flagrant discrepancy with the universalistic and egalitarian spirit of the UDHR.

So, what is the point in declaring human beings to be "endowed with reason and conscience"? Reading this proposition as an empirical description does not get us very far. After all, Article 1 of the UDHR makes an all-inclusive universalistic claim by covering no less than "all human beings." If this is to make any sense, the endowment with reason and conscience cannot depend on particular empirical qualities, skills, and performances of this or that individual person. Thus, interpreting the article as an empirically *descriptive* proposition does not seem to work. Now, if we read the formulation as a *prescriptive* proposition—for example, as a kind of "moral appeal"—we end up with even bigger problems of interpretation, because any moral appeal implicitly presupposes that the addressee already possesses something like reason and conscience. A moral appeal would be pointless without the assumption that the addressed individual is generally receptive to moral pleas, emotions, and arguments. However, this very receptiveness is captured in the words "reason and conscience." A moral appeal that first of all aims to "create" the moral receptiveness, without which such appeal cannot function, would be circular. Hence, it looks as if we are again stuck in an impasse. Yet there may be a third possibility of understanding the sentence, which is the only position we find plausible. Instead of entertaining a descriptive or prescriptive interpretation, we propose to read the second sentence of Article 1 in an *ascriptive way*, as it were. The point is that we have to *ascribe* to all human beings a basic potential of responsible agency, without which meaningful normative interaction would be unthinkable. Given the significance of responsible agency for any meaningful normative interaction whatsoever, this basic potential must be attributed to all humans equally. It is not an empirical skill or quality which individuals have in different degrees (or in some cases seemingly do not have at all). Rather, it defines a *fundamental status position*, in relation to which all human beings are to be considered as strictly equal. This status position fully includes individuals whose basic mental skills have not yet developed, or are in a situation of gradual decline, or will most likely never (again) fully function.[42] In other words, no individual has to "prove" through particular moral actions, efforts, or merits that he or she is actually capable of responsible conduct. In the context of universal and egalitarian human rights, dignity cannot become a meritocratic or perfectionist concept, and it should never be turned into a pretext for excluding certain people, such as individuals with grave mental disabilities. No one has to demonstrate their "worthiness" as a precondition for claiming human dignity. It is exactly the other way around in that the international community commits itself in Article 1 of the UDHR to treating all members of the human family as responsible subjects, which is tantamount to respecting everyone's equal human dignity. This is a necessary "ascription" following from the insight into the unconditioned preconditions of any meaningful moral interaction whatsoever. Human rights institutionalize the required respect through a series of basic legal entitlements, which all human beings can equally lay claim to. This justifies their specific authority as "inalienable rights."[43]

5. Authority Linked to Modesty: The Nondoctrinal Primacy of Human Rights

What follows from these observations for understanding the relationship between human rights and religions? The answer is complex. Three interconnected aspects warrant highlighting: (a) the practical primacy that human rights claim, also vis-à-vis religions; (b) the nondoctrinal nature of that primacy, which is tantamount to an awareness of the inherent limitedness of the human rights approach; and (c) the openness for having human rights and their underlying principles appreciated from the standpoint of various religions or beliefs.[44]

(a) Practical Primacy of Human Rights

By enshrining, through means of legal enforcement, respect for the equal dignity of all human beings, human rights embody a specific normative authority, as manifested in their qualification as "inalienable rights." Human rights enjoy a special rank in many constitutions, and they certainly have an outstanding rank in international law. Human rights are not just another set of norms, prescriptions, and entitlements. In the words of the UDHR, they define "the foundation of freedom, justice and peace in the world." Indeed, this is a high aspiration and a strong claim. The special authority that human rights epitomize does not stop at the boundaries of religious communities. As we will discuss in the subsequent section of this chapter, there are a few caveats one should take into account when it comes to touching the internal self-understanding of religious communities. Yet as a matter of principle, human rights unfold their authority also with regard to religious communities. Otherwise, they would abdicate their basic function to facilitate fair coexistence in a religiously and otherwise pluralistic world.

Above all, human rights require the systematic elimination of any coercion between or within religious communities, including abstaining from any threats directed against dissidents, internal critics, or converts. Under international human rights law, it falls upon the state to guarantee strict noncoercion in this field. A litmus test of noncoercion is everyone's right to abandon a religious community and turn to another religion or to no religion, which is one of the few absolute guarantees in international human rights law. Apart from direct forms of coercion, freedom of religion or belief also demands the elimination of all forms of structural religious coercion and discrimination. This implies repealing any criminalization of apostasy, proselytism, or public critique of religion, even if deemed "blasphemous" by some. Reforms may furthermore be necessary in the area of family laws, which in quite a number of countries still reflect traditional religious hegemonies as well as traditional gender roles, often with discriminatory implications in the intersection of both sex/gender and religion/belief. School curricula may also need a general overhaul, for example if they fail to reflect the religious and belief pluralism that has emerged in the respective country. Naturally, this enumeration of possible reform measures remains sketchy and inexhaustive.

Reform policies enacted with the intention to overcome all (direct, indirect, and structural) forms of religious coercion or religious discrimination have often caused resistance, which at times even escalated into fully fledged cultural wars.[45] During the nineteenth century, some European countries—France, Spain, Germany—were split along the lines of those defending secular human rights, including religious freedom, versus those opposing human rights in the name of particular religious values. Although in most parts of Europe, this is now a matter of the past, an echo of those bitter conflicts can still be felt today. In other parts of the globe, similar cultural wars are far from over or may even lie ahead. In a polarized political climate, religious traditionalists often suspect that the state uses the rhetoric of human rights to enforce a doctrinal anthropocentric worldview or a comprehensive "humanistic" value system (in the doctrinal sense of the word), to the detriment of religious beliefs and practices. This is a serious accusation, which warrants a careful and comprehensive response—not only in theory, but also in actual practice. In order to find an appropriate answer, we have to look into another important feature of human rights: their nondoctrinal nature.

(b) Limited Authority

The normative task to shape pluralistic coexistence by enshrining respect for everyone's equal freedom implies that the authority which human rights claim in order to fulfill this function, is from the outset limited. It is a *nondoctrinal authority*, which requires human rights practitioners to exercise deliberate self-restraint in a spirit of modesty.[46] Human rights do not intend to replace the religious ethos in society or to remove community-based religious ceremonies, rites, and liturgies, nor do they compete with the Bible, the Qur'an, or any other religious books. They are neither "the new anthropocentric faith," as David Stamos writes,[47] nor "a kind a secular monotheism with aspirations to civilize the world" and with the UN High Commissioner for Human Rights serving "as the highest of high priests," as Stephen Hopgood wants us to believe.[48] Instead their purpose is more specific, and more modest, namely to facilitate peaceful coexistence in our pluralistic societies by institutionalizing respect for the equal dignity and freedom of all. Human rights would not be able to tackle this function adequately without an awareness of their inherent limitedness.

As elaborated in Chapter 2, freedom is one of the pivotal principles defining the human rights approach. Taking freedom seriously requires a combination of commitment and self-restraint. While the commitment implies a specific authority for "inalienable" human rights, as just pointed out in the above section, the attitude of self-restraint is not less important. In respect of everyone's freedom, human rights accommodate diversity in various areas of human life. Freedom of religion or belief, more specifically, opens the space for the articulation of, inter alia, theocentric, cosmocentric, and other nonanthropocentric religious worldviews and related practices. Within the broad range of religious or belief-related manifestations, freedom of religion or belief also covers voluntary acts of surrendering oneself to God—that is, positions that stand in the starkest possible contrast to an anthropocentric worldview or value system. People are likewise free, for instance, to hold that the human self is just an illusion, which one should try to overcome, when embarking on the long path toward spiritual wisdom. Again, this would be a clear example of a nonanthropocentric attitude. This observation harbors systematic implications for the understanding of human rights. While human rights are doubtless an anthropocentric legal category, they should not be turned into an all-encompassing anthropocentric worldview or doctrine, and it is crucial to protect them from the dangers of going too far and claiming too much.

The primacy which human rights claim is *a practical primacy, not a doctrinal or ideological primacy.*[49] Human rights are not based, for instance, on Ludwig Feuerbach's conjecture that God is a mere product of human imagination and the projection of unfulfilled mundane yearnings,[50] a position formulated already a century earlier by David Hume.[51] Nor do human rights aim to establish a quasi-religious "cult of human reason." Their underlying idea is not to eliminate religion as "the opium of the people"[52] or replace it by some kind of postreligious humanist doctrine. Michael Ignatieff is correct when insisting that the idea of human rights "is not a creed; it is not a metaphysics. To make it so is to turn it into a species of idolatry: humanism worshipping itself."[53] Such idolatry would obfuscate the normative profile of human rights. Hence, the importance to exercise vigilance against the ever-lurking danger of human rights exceeding their specific authority when being turned into a comprehensive belief system or doctrine.

Authority and self-restraint are two interrelated postulates in human rights practice, as it were, because they both originate from respect for human freedom.[54] It is only with a clear awareness of their inherent limits that human rights can unfold the specific authority that they need to be able to shape pluralist coexistence normatively, in accordance with basic normative principles of freedom and equality. It is an authority best exercised in a "listening mode"—that is, in tandem with sensitivity to people's freely articulated wishes, needs, and creative potentials. Within the system of human rights, freedom of religion or belief therefore has an important role to play by keeping that system explicitly open for accommodating the broad range of freely articulated religious or nonreligious convictions, thereby reminding us that human rights themselves are neither a postreligious doctrine nor a modern salvation ideology. They are secular, not sacred. Without such constant self-restraint, human rights politics could inadvertently erode the very authority human rights can reasonably claim.

(c) Openness for Religious Appreciations

The idea of inalienable human rights ultimately rests on respect for everyone's human dignity. Given its roots in the foundational documents of many religions and beliefs, the concept of dignity can help to build bridges between religious traditions and modern human rights. An example is the Vatican II declaration *Dignitatis humanae* (1965), in which the Catholic Church finally endorsed religious freedom: "The declaration of this Vatican Council on the right of man to religious freedom has its foundation in the dignity of the person, whose exigencies . . . are fully known to human reason through centuries of experience."[55] This declaration illustrates that the concept of human dignity can actually facilitate a broad theological appreciation of a human right, which the Catholic Church had previously rejected.

One might object that the semantics of human dignity, just because of the echo it finds in religious traditions, could invite particularistic religious ownership claims, at the expense of normative universalism. Indeed, this danger exists. During the discussions on an advanced draft version of the UDHR, the representative of Brazil proposed to insert a reference to the biblical idea of the human person as being created in the "image of God."[56] He argued that such a theological foundation would lend more legitimacy to the Declaration. Peng Chun Chang, a Confucian philosopher and delegate of the Chinese government,[57] responded that by linking human dignity to a particular Jewish-Christian heritage the Declaration would forfeit its aspiration to represent a normative consensus across religious and cultural divides.[58] In the end, a clear majority sided with Chang's position. When referring to human dignity, the text of the UDHR thus remains silent on religious concepts or metaphors and sticks to a religiously "neutral"—and in this sense "secular"—language.

The secular terminology used in international human rights documents, however, does not preclude the possibility for people to positively relate to their more specific religious or philosophical readings of human dignity when appreciating international human rights. In the context of human rights, secularity can only make sense as openness, not emptiness. Jewish or Christian human rights organizations are perfectly free to understand their advocacy work in the light of the book of Genesis. Likewise, Muslim organizations may refer to the Qur'anic idea of the human person acting as God's vicegerent on earth, if they so wish. Other traditions of understanding human dignity can also come into play. While human rights may thus receive a religious backing from different perspectives, the emancipatory and egalitarian principles of modern human rights law in turn can stimulate new interpretations of religious documents. For example, human rights can challenge a hierarchical dignity semantics, which to the present day often permeate and obfuscate the universalistic understanding of human rights.[59] The goal is broad and inclusive "ownerships" (in the plural!) of human rights, which allows for their appreciation from diverse religious and nonreligious standpoints, without compromising the precise normative contours of human rights, as they have been laid down in a deliberately "secular" legal language.[60]

6. Human Rights Within Religious Communities?

Modern ideas of universal rights, empowerment, gender equality, intellectual and religious freedom, and so on, have begun to permeate theological debates and transform religious self-understandings. Quite a number of religious communities have adopted human rights into their teaching, preaching, and charity or advocacy practices. Faith-based organizations of different religious backgrounds—Jewish, Christian, Muslim, Buddhist, Baha'i, and so forth—promote a broad range of human rights, often in connection with religious reform agendas aimed at adapting internal structures to human rights principles. We have seen examples of amicable cooperation between faith-based, secular, and humanist civil society organizations, which work together in a spirit of mutual appreciation. This illustrates the potential of human rights to forge substantial normative agreements among people who at the same time continue to entertain different worldviews, identities, and practices. Indeed, human rights could not flourish without the support they receive from civil society organizations and religious communities. Tore Lindholm makes an important point in this regard when stressing: "Promotion of international human rights should not be left to states alone: not generally, and particularly not in the field of freedom of religion or belief."[61]

At the same time, there are also religious communities—or parts of communities—which remain reserved. Some see the idea of human rights as alien to their religious self-understanding. Others may appreciate human rights as a useful way of handling diversity within the larger society, while insisting that their own internal structures remain exempt from human rights and antidiscrimination stipulations. One obvious example springing to one's mind is the discriminatory reservation of clerical and leadership positions to males, which characterizes the status quo of many religious communities. Do human rights imply a mandate to change this and work for a doctrinal or structural opening up of religious communities from within, from without, or both? Can the state play an active role in such endeavours? If so, how far should this go?

Let us first recall that human rights can be used with liberal and non-liberal, progressive and conservative, feminist and traditionalist, and many other purposes in mind. It all depends on the rights holders themselves, who are free to use their rights in the way they see fit, provided they do not violate the rights of others. This openness for different usages follows from the inherent logic underlying all rights of freedom. It is not a unique feature of freedom of religion or belief, but likewise characterizes freedom of expression, freedom of peaceful assembly, freedom of association, and other rights. To say it with a grain of salt, "liberal rights" (we use this term here in its broadest sense) cannot remain reserved for "liberals" only.

If nonliberal uses of rights to freedom lead to conflicts or tensions, it may at first glance seem tempting to invoke the limitation clauses linked to the various human rights standards and call for state intervention to rectify the situation. However, this warrants a word of caution. While limitation clauses provide the criteria for handling situations of a direct collision with competing fundamental rights of other people or important purposes of public interest, they do not justify measures of ensuring a "liberal spirit" in the exercise of human rights. Grave misunderstandings concerning the function of limitation clauses arise as soon as rights to freedom get confused with "liberal values" or with a particular "liberal lifestyle." Such amalgamation can lead to policies of confining human rights exclusively to those who factually subscribe to liberal convictions, liberal positions, or liberal ways of life. Consequently, the invocation of limitation clauses with the intention of preserving a certain "liberal spirit" in the exercise of human rights could deprive certain people from the full enjoyment of their rights. Take the example of Jehovah's Witnesses. While their theological beliefs and practices apparently differ from some of the prevailing values and predominant lifestyle of liberal societies, the Jehovah's Witnesses unambiguously stick to the principle of nonviolence and noncoercion, for which many of them have actually served prison sentences as conscientious objectors to military service. Confusing the "liberal right" to freedom of religion with a general promotion of liberal values, liberal lifestyles, liberal theologies, or liberal religious practices could hypothetically strip the Jehovah's Witnesses of a protection they urgently need. One should take note in this context that the Jehovah's Witnesses face religious discrimination world-wide. In July 2017, Russia's Supreme Court upheld the liquidation of all organizations belonging to the Jehovah's Witnesses in the country, as a result of finding the group "extremist."[62] Furthermore, Jehovah's Witnesses face grave violations of their religious freedom also in other countries.

Another test case is the treatment of Muslims and other religious minorities in the context of European integration policies. The state agencies in charge of fostering integration into a liberal society may be tempted to back up the promotion of gender equality and other liberal principles by picking selected verses from the Qur'an, which they consider suitable for such educative purposes. Although the promotion of gender equality is a requirement that the state has to fulfill, state interference into the interpretation of religious texts means trespassing into the internal affairs of communities and thus encroaching on their religious freedom. State activities should be based on a clear awareness that human rights represent a limited—that is, nondoctrinal—authority, as elaborated in the previous section. Human rights do not give the state the mandate to enforce inner-religious reforms, for instance with the intention of opening them up for the adoption of human rights principles into their internal teaching and preaching.

This does not mean that the state when acting as guarantor of human rights should remain merely passive toward religions and religious practices. As mentioned before, one of the core functions of the state is ensuring strict noncoercion in all parts of society.[63] If internal dissidents or converts suffer threats or violence from within their own communities, the state has a duty to come to their rescue. The categorical imperative that "no one shall be subject to coercion" when it comes to adopting, changing, modifying, or abandoning a religion or belief, obviously requires active measures of state protection against possible infringements by third parties, including from inside the religious communities themselves. At the very least, the "exit option"—that is, the effective possibility of leaving a community—must be open for everyone. Where this option does not exist, freedom of religion or belief remains a sheer illusion.

The focus on securing exit options has attracted some criticism. For critics this focus displays a typically liberal prejudice that religious communities are just a kind of "clubs," which people can easily leave when wishing to join an alternative "club." Such an approach, however, they say, belittles the significance that religious communities may have for many people, men and women. Alison Stuart challenges the trivializing interpretation of communities as mere "clubs," while at the same time demanding proactive state interventions, beyond the mere guarantee of exit options, in order to ensure the substantial equality of men and women within the internal structures of religious communities.[64] She concludes: "Women often do not wish to leave their religious community to gain equality; they wish to be recognized as fully functioning and equal members of their religious communities."[65] Peter Kirchschläger likewise calls for state interventions into the internal structures of communities, with the goal of pushing them to a comprehensive embrace of human rights principles. He recommends, "the State and the international community should strategically attempt to reconcile religious and belief communities with human rights."[66]

We agree that for numerous believers, including people who express frustration at existing religiously justified gender inequalities, their religious communities are far more than "clubs," which they would easily join or leave, following their changing whims and tastes. Membership in a religion can be deeply interwoven with issues of personal identity, biography, family history, and group loyalty. Even where the legal option of leaving a community effectively exists, many people may feel that it is not a personal option for them to seriously consider. Nevertheless, it would be wrong to underestimate the far-reaching structural consequences that the legal facilitation of exit options has on the internal dynamics of a religious community. The legal guarantee of exit options ipso facto changes the internal power dynamics, because—at least from a legal perspective—no one is any longer forced to remain within the community. Although old established hierarchies, such as the distinction between (usually male) clergy and laity, may remain untouched on the surface, those on top lose much of their previous power, once people are legally free to leave. Even if only a few people eventually take that step—the option as such exists. This is an important point, which in itself already changes the power of community leaders. Instead of being able to resort to mechanisms of direct or structural enforcement, religious authority will more and more depend on the personal, spiritual, intellectual, and pastoral persuasiveness of those holding the relevant positions. This can create incentives for a long-term change of attitudes, possibly accompanied by structural reforms, including in the area of gender equality.

The exit option is furthermore linked to the possibility of entering into a new community or joining reform movements. While many reform movements still operate within the boundaries of mainstream communities, others have led to the formation of independent groups, sometimes stigmatized as "schismatic." Again, not all those frustrated with the status quo of their religious community will likely take such a step and join a new group. What is legally possible is not for everyone a personal option they would seriously consider. Nevertheless, the legal possibility of setting up or joining reform movements harbors in itself the inducement of structural changes within the religious landscape as a whole. It will have long-term implications also for traditional communities, which at least cannot continue to claim an unchallenged monopoly of interpretation over the respective religious traditions. This in itself is already an important change.

The observations just made should also guide state activities in this field. Bearing in mind the nondoctrinal authority that human rights claim, the state when acting as their guarantor, cannot mingle with theological disputes and inner-religious conflicts. Human rights do not bestow upon the state a contemporary version of a *jus reformandi*, which would entitle governments to undertake theological and ecclesiastical reforms. These limits should always be clear. However, by guaranteeing freedom of religion or belief in conjunction with freedom of expression, freedom of peaceful assembly, freedom of association, and other human rights, the state can improve the conditions for free and open discussions between and within religious communities. This can encourage innovative interpretations of religious traditions, including feminist and other reform theologies, against which conservative religious voices may at the same time continue to express their reservations. The state can furthermore promote awareness of inter- and intrareligious diversity, for instance as part of the school curriculum or in the context of outreach activities toward society as a whole. University teachers have their role to play by subjecting religions to critical academic debates, while at the same time deconstructing essentialist stereotypes of religions and their followers. Criticism of religion from outside and self-criticism undertaken within religious communities can mutually reinforce each other. In short, the state can do a lot to encourage human-rights-based inner-religious reforms indirectly without trespassing into the sphere of theology.

7. Authority, Not Idolatry of Human Rights

The interplay between human rights and religions is replete with pitfalls and possible misunderstandings, some of which historically escalated into political conflicts and cultural wars. Up to the present day, the relationship between human rights and religions has been a battlefield and a source of ongoing political and ideological polarizations. What makes the relationship complicated is that both human rights and religions claim the authority to shape people's lives, as individuals and in community with others. Ironically, it is this common aspiration that exacerbates tensions and potential conflicts.

Harmonious postulates, which assume that human rights and religions ultimately strive for identical goals, underestimate important historical and conceptual differences, for instance in the area of gender issues. At the same time, the creation of a simple hierarchy between the two, either with human rights "trumping" religion or the other way around, does not present a viable alternative. Those who reduce human rights to the mere smallest common denominator of all the ethical ideas that happen to exist in various religious traditions would strip human rights of any genuine normative authority. By contrast, the assumption that human rights provide the overarching authority of a global "civil religion," to which traditional religions should simply surrender, would likewise lead to an impasse, because it is unlikely that many religious believers would accept such a subordinated place of their faith under the supreme quasi-religious umbrella of human rights.

To overcome those prima facie dilemmas, we have proposed to define the authority of human rights with a view to their specific function of facilitating the conditions for respectful coexistence in religiously pluralistic societies. Given the thrust on freedom, including in the area of religion or belief, this authority is from the outset a specific one and thus limited—that is, an authority best exercised in a spirit of modesty and in a "listening mode." When being understood and practiced in this sense, human rights have much to offer to religious communities. Their profession of human dignity and justice can resonate strongly in many religious traditions. Human rights can furthermore serve as a stimulus for religious or belief communities to come to terms with complicated aspects of their own histories, such as historical entanglements with cultural hegemonies, national identity politics, and political authoritarianism. Finally, when positively tackling the challenges of human rights, religious communities may rediscover an insight traceable to the foundational documents of many traditions that authentic belief and authentic religious practice presupposes breathing space for all. An indispensable precondition for human rights to unfold this normative transformative potential within religious communities is a clear awareness that human rights themselves do not embody a quasi-religious, all-encompassing authority. Freedom of religion or belief can serve as a critical reminder in this regard.

Hence, the significance of freedom of religion or belief for human rights theory and practice is multifaceted. At the practical level, freedom of religion or belief has an indispensable protective role to play, alongside other human rights, all of which can ultimately mutually complement each other in the never-ending attempt to eradicate repression, humiliation, and discrimination. At the conceptual level, freedom of religion or belief represents the insight that religiosity, faith, beliefs of all sorts, spirituality, and similar orientations are part of human life, mostly connected with manifold life-worldly expressions, ranging from family rituals to charity organizations and communal cemeteries. While not protecting religious convictions and practices for their own sake, freedom of religion or belief opens the horizon for an acknowledgment of that dimension within human life, always depending on the freely articulated wishes and demands of the rights holders themselves. Without such conceptual openness, human rights would cease to do justice to the complexity of the human condition. At the end of this book, we have furthermore seen that this conceptual function of freedom of religion or belief also has a bearing at the metalevel, as it were. Freedom of religion or belief reminds us that the human rights approach as a whole has its inherent limits, and it is good to be clear about this. Human rights are secular, not sacred. Their purpose is to open and structure the adequate space for the diversity of beliefs and practices, not to occupy that space. The specific authority which human rights claim rests on doctrinal modesty, which requires permanent efforts in doctrinal self-restraint. Freedom of religion or belief plays a crucial role in those efforts. It is a custodian right against sacralizing human rights into an object of idolatry.

NOTES

Introduction

1. For a short overview of relevant international and regional human rights mechanisms see Heiner Bielefeldt, Nazila Ghanea, and Michael Wiener, *Freedom of Religion or Belief: An International Law Commentary* (Oxford: Oxford University Press, 2016), 41–51.

2. An international network of parliamentarians supporting freedom of religion or belief started in November 2014; the International Panel of Parliamentarians for Freedom of Religion or Belief (IPPFoRB) was initiated by Baroness Berridge, who is a member of the House of Lords in London.

3. Nongovernmental organizations have for example founded platforms in New York and Geneva to cooperate on behalf of freedom of religion or belief.

4. In a study first published in 1895, the German lawyer and historian Georg Jellinek contended that religious freedom lies at the origins of modern human rights. This thesis sparked a long controversy. See Georg Jellinek, *The Declaration of the Rights of Man and of Citizens: A Contribution to Modern Constitutional History* (New York: Henry Holt, 1901).

5. Manfred Nowak, *U.N. Covenant on Civil and Political Rights: CCPR Commentary* (Kehl: N. P. Engel, 2nd rev. ed., 2005), 408.

6. For more details, see Chapter 1, Section 4, and Chapter 4, Sections 2 and 3.

7. As we will point out in more detail, freedom of religion or belief also protects human beings in their nonreligious convictions or in their freedom not to care about these issues. However, this does not alter the fact that it opens up the space for the articulation of religious interests within the framework of human rights.

8. For further details, see Chapter 8.

9. We here use the adjective "liberal" in the widest understanding of the word.

10. Some of the reservations that states have made when ratifying a human rights treaty are based on religious grounds. See Başak Çalı and Mariana Montoya, *The March of Universality? Religion-Based Reservations to the Core UN Treaties and What They Tell Us About Human Rights and Universality in the 21st Century: Policy Report* (Versoix: Universal Rights Group, 2017).

11. For further details, see Chapter 1.

12. For further details, see Chapter 2.

13. Chapter 6 entails a typology of violations of freedom of religion or belief.

14. Mary Ann Glendon, "Is Religious Freedom an 'Orphaned' Right?," in *The Changing Nature of Religious Rights Under International Law*, ed. Malcolm D. Evans, Peter Petkoff, and Julian Rivers, 1–8 at 2 (Oxford: Oxford University Press, 2015).

15. See Vera Forester, *Lessing und Moses Mendelssohn: Geschichte einer Freundschaft* (Darmstadt: Wissenschaftliche Buchgesellschaft, 2010).

16. Mendelssohn's letter to Kant of 16 October 1785, cited from Immanuel Kant, *Briefwechsel: Auswahl und Anmerkungen von Otto Schöndorfer* (Hamburg: Meiner, 1972), 272 (our translation).

17. Moses Mendelssohn, *Morgenstunden oder über das Dasein Gottes* (Stuttgart: Reclam, 1979), 144 (our translation).

18. Moses Mendelssohn, *Jerusalem, or On Religious Power and Judaism*, trans. Allan Arkush (Waltham, Mass.: Brandeis University Press, 1983), 138.

19. See Max Horkheimer and Theodor W. Adorno, *Dialectic of Enlightenment: Philosophical Fragments*, trans. Edmund Jephcott (Stanford: Stanford University Press, 2002).

20. See Markus Kneer, *Die dunkle Spur im Denken: Rationalismus und Antijudaismus* (Paderborn: Schöningh, 2003).

21. David Hume, *The Natural History of Religion* (Stanford: Stanford University Press, 1956), 50.

22. Benedict de Spinoza, *Theological-Political Treatise*, trans. and ed. Jonathan Israel (Cambridge: Cambridge University Press, 2007), 55.

23. Immanuel Kant, "Religion Within the Boundaries of Mere Reason," in *Religion and Rational Theology*, trans. and ed. Allen W. Wood and George di Giovanni, 39–215, The Cambridge Edition of the Works of Immanuel Kant (Cambridge: Cambridge University Press, 1996), 155.

24. Mendelssohn, *Jerusalem*, 70 (emphasis in the original).

25. Mendelssohn, *Jerusalem*, 137.

26. Michael Ignatieff, *Human Rights as Politics and Idolatry*, ed. and intro. Amy Gutmann (Princeton: Princeton University Press, 2001), 53.

27. The views expressed in this book are those of the coauthors and do not necessarily reflect the views of the United Nations.

28. See Michael Wiener, *Das Mandat des UN-Sonderberichterstatters über Religions- oder Weltanschauungsfreiheit: Institutionelle, prozedurale und materielle Rechtsfragen* (Frankfurt: Peter Lang, 2007); Michael Wiener, "The Mandate of the Special Rapporteur on Freedom of Religion or Belief: Institutional, Procedural and Substantive Legal Issues," *Religion and Human Rights*, Vol. 2, No. 1 (2007), 3–17.

29. See http://asmajahangir.org.

30. See http://newslinemagazine.com/magazine/learned-valuable-lessons-taught/.

Chapter 1

1. See American Anthropological Association, "Statement on Human Rights," *American Anthropologist*, Vol. 49 (1947), 539–543 at 539: "How can the proposed Declaration be applicable to all human beings, and not be a statement of rights conceived only in terms of the values prevalent in the countries of Western Europe and America?"

2. See Claude Lévi-Strauss, *Race et histoire* (Paris: UNESCO, 1952).

3. Adamantia Pollis and Peter Schwab, "Human Rights: A Western Construct with Limited Applicability," in *Human Rights: Cultural and Ideological Perspectives*, ed. Adamantia Pollis and Peter Schwab, 1–18 (New York: Praeger, 1979).

4. See Samuel P. Huntington, *The Clash of Civilizations and the Remaking of World Order* (New York: Simon and Schuster, 1996), 70–72.

5. See Makau Mutua, "Savages, Victims, and Saviors: The Metaphor of Human Rights," *Harvard International Law Journal*, Vol. 42 (2001), 201–245.

6. See Carl Schmitt, *Der Begriff des Politischen* (Berlin: Duncker and Humblot, 1932; repr., 1963), 55 (our translation). Schmitt here cites Proudhon.

7. See UN Doc. A/C.3/SR.127, pp. 392 and 404. This position did not meet with general approval on the side of Islamic states. In particular, Pakistan voiced a very different position, also in the name of Islam.

8. Winnifred Fallers Sullivan, Elizabeth Shakman Hurd, Saba Mahmood, and Peter G. Danchin, eds., *Politics of Religious Freedom* (Chicago: University of Chicago Press, 2015).

9. Lori G. Beaman, "Beyond Establishment," in Sullivan et al., *Politics of Religious Freedom*, 207–219 at 212.

10. For more details, see Section 4 of the present chapter.

11. Michael Lambek, "Is Religion Free?," in Sullivan et al., *Politics of Religious Freedom*, 289–300 at 299.

12. See UN Doc. A/C.3/SR.92. Notably, the initial title of a draft "*international* declaration of human rights" was changed to "*universal* declaration of human rights" (emphasis added) just before its adoption; see the suggested French amendment of 15 November 1948 (UN Doc. A/C.3/339) and the summary records of the voting in the Third Committee on 30 November 1948 (with 17 in favor, 11 against, and 10 abstentions, see UN Doc. A/C.3/SR.167).

13. James Griffin, *On Human Rights* (Oxford: Oxford University Press, 2008), 2.

14. See Heiner Bielefeldt, *Philosophie der Menschenrechte: Grundlagen eines weltweiten Freiheitsethos* (Darmstadt: Wissenschaftliche Buchgesellschaft, 1998); Michael Wiener, "Universal Freedom of Religion or Belief: A Reality Check Through the Lens of the EU Guidelines," in *Religion and European Society: A Primer*, ed. Ben Schewel and Erin K. Wilson, 179–182 (Chichester: Wiley-Blackwell, 2019).

15. Even this may be debatable.

16. See Ute Gerhard, Mechthild Jansen, Andrea Maihofer, Pia Schmid, and Irmgard Schulz, eds., *Differenz und Gleichheit: Menschenrechte haben (k)ein Geschlecht* (Frankfurt: Ulrich Helmer Verlag, 1990).

17. See Mutua, "Savages, Victims, and Saviors," 205.

18. For a critical discussion see Heiner Bielefeldt, *Menschenrechte in der Einwanderungsgesellschaft: Plädoyer für einen aufgeklärten Multikulturalismus* (Bielefeld: transcript Verlag, 2007), 43–55. See also Hans Joas, *Sind die Menschenrechte westlich?* (Munich: Kösel, 2016).

19. Georg Wilhelm Friedrich Hegel, *Vorlesungen über die Philosophie der Geschichte*, vol. 12 of *Werke* (Frankfurt: Suhrkamp, 1986), 496 (emphasis in the original, our translation).

20. See Georg Jellinek, *The Declaration of the Rights of Man and of Citizens: A Contribution to Modern Constitutional History* (New York: Henry Holt, 1901).

21. Winnifred Fallers Sullivan, *The Impossibility of Religious Freedom* (Princeton: Princeton University Press, 2005), 154.

22. Elizabeth Shakman Hurd, *Beyond Religious Freedom: The New Global Politics of Religion* (Princeton: Princeton University Press, 2015).

23. See Schmitt, *Der Begriff des Politischen*, 67 (our translation).

24. Ibid., 54 (our translation).

25. Max Weber, "Wissenschaft als Beruf," in *Werke*, vol. 1, *Studienausgabe*, ed. Wolfgang J. Mommsen and Wolfgang Schluchter, 1–25 at 17 (Tübingen: Mohr Siebeck, 1994) (our translation).

26. See Helmuth Plessner, "Die Frage nach der Conditio humana (1961)," in *Gesammelte Schriften*, vol. 8, 136–217 (Frankfurt: Suhrkamp, 1980).

27. With regard to Germany, see Richard Traunmüller, *Religiöse Vielfalt, Sozialkapital und gesellschaftlicher Zusammenhalt: Religionsmonitor* (Gütersloh: Bertelsmann-Stiftung, 2014), 30–45 and 89.

28. Jürgen Habermas, "The Concept of Human Dignity and the Realistic Utopia of Human Rights," *Metaphilosophy*, Vol. 41, No. 4 (2010), 464–480 at 478.

29. Michael Ignatieff, *Human Rights as Politics and Idolatry*, ed. and intro. Amy Gutmann (Princeton: Princeton University Press, 2001), 53.

30. Article 1 of the UDHR. See also the beginning of the preamble of the American Declaration of the Rights and Duties of Man (adopted by the Ninth International Conference of American States on 2 May 1948): "All men are born free and equal, in dignity and in rights, and, being endowed by nature with reason and conscience, they should conduct themselves as brothers one to another." In this context, see Kathryn Sikkink, "Latin American Countries as Norm Protagonists of the Idea of International Human Rights," *Global Governance*, Vol. 20 (2014), 389–404.

31. For further discussion, see also Chapter 9, Section 4.

32. See Mutua, "Savages, Victims, and Saviors," 201–245 at 208: "Human rights bestow naturalness, transhistoricity and universality to rights." While we do not subscribe to Mutua's assessment that human rights per se presuppose such an idea of transhistoricity, there can be no doubt that such notions exist.

33. See Malcolm D. Evans, "Historical Analysis of Freedom of Religion or Belief as a Technique for Resolving Religious Conflict," in *Facilitating Freedom of Religion or Belief: A Deskbook*, ed. Tore Lindholm, W. Cole Durham Jr., and Bahia G. Tahzib-Lie, 1–17 (Leiden: Martinus Nijhoff, 2004).

34. See Ernst Cassirer, *Die Philosophie der Aufklärung* (Hamburg: Meiner, 1998), 219.

35. The fact that in the previous paragraph we have alluded to certain features of early modern European history, does not mean that in our view Europe provides the binding model for the rest of the world to follow. Coming ourselves from a European country, we are just much more familiar with European history than with historical developments in other parts of the world. Experiences made in Europe can only be examples of the vast variety of experiences of injustice which people face across the globe. See Heiner Bielefeldt, "Historical and Philosophical Foundations of Human Rights," in *International Protection of Human Rights: A Textbook*, ed. Martin Scheinin and Catarina Krause, 3–18 (Turku: Åbo Akademi University, 2009).

36. This is missing in Lorenzo Zucca, "Freedom of Religion in a Secular World," in *Philosophical Foundations of Human Rights*, ed. Rowan Cruft, S. Matthew Liao, and Massimo Renzo, 388–406 (Oxford: Oxford University Press, 2015). When asking the question "whether religion deserves special protection" (p. 389), Zucca obviously ignores the human rights logic underneath freedom of religion or belief.

37. Sullivan, *Impossibility*, 151.

38. For example, some Arabic states merely recognize the followers of "divinely revealed religions." In addition, Article 13, paragraph 2, first sentence, of the Constitution of Greece provides: "All known religions shall be free and their rites of worship shall be performed unhindered and under the protection of the law." The term "known religions" remains undefined.

39. See Michael Wiener, *Das Mandat des UN-Sonderberichterstatters über Religions- oder Weltanschauungsfreiheit—Institutionelle, prozedurale und materielle Rechtsfragen* (Frankfurt: Peter Lang, 2007), 4–6.

40. Human Rights Committee, General Comment No. 22, UN Doc. CCPR/C/21/Rev.1/Add.4, para. 2.

41. Arcot Krishnaswami, *Study of Discrimination in the Matter of Religious Rights and Practices* (New York: United Nations, 1960), E/CN.4/Sub.2/200/Rev.1, p. 1. See Wiener, *Das Mandat des UN-Sonderberichterstatters*, 260–261.

42. See Chapter 2, Section 3.

43. See Roger Trigg, *Equality, Freedom and Religion* (Oxford: Oxford University Press, 2012), 103–106.

44. See Office for National Statistics, *Census 2001 Summary Theme Figures and Rankings—390,000 Jedi There Are*, 13 February 2003 (http://www.ons.gov.uk/ons/dcp171780_225970.pdf). At the next census in 2011, the number of "Jedi Knights" in England and Wales decreased by more than 50 percent to 176,632 people; however, it still constituted the most popular group in the category "No religion" (https://webarchive.nationalarchives.gov.uk/20160130011015/http://www.ons.gov.uk/ons/rel/census/2011-census/key-statistics-for-local-authorities-in-england-and-wales/rft-table-qs210ew.xls).

45. See http://www.venganza.org/about/.

46. Ronald Dworkin, *Religion Without God* (Cambridge, Mass.: Harvard University Press, 2013), 24.

47. See T. Jeremy Gunn, "The Complexity of Religion and the Definition of 'Religion' in International Law," *Harvard Human Rights Journal*, Vol. 16 (2003), 189–214.

48. European Court of Human Rights, *Campbell and Cosans v. United Kingdom* (appl. 7511/76 and 7743/76) of 25 February 1982. This formulation has since been regularly repeated in the Court's jurisprudence on Article 9 of the European Convention on Human Rights (ECHR).

49. It may still be a position protected by freedom of opinion and expression.

50. See Jocelyn Maclure and Charles Taylor, *Secularism and Freedom of Conscience*, trans. Jane Marie Todd (Cambridge, Mass.: Harvard University Press, 2011), 75–80.

51. See W. Cole Durham Jr. and Brett G. Scharffs, *Law and Religion: National, International, and Comparative Perspectives* (New York: Aspen, 2010), 46.

52. Dworkin, *Religion Without God*, 11.

53. Robert Yelle, "Imagining the Hebrew Republic: Christian Genealogies of Religious Freedom," in Sullivan et al., *Politics of Religious Freedom*, 17–28 at 18.

54. Elizabeth Shakman Hurd, "Believing in Religious Freedom," in Sullivan et al., *Politics of Religious Freedom*, 45–56 at 50.

55. Ronan McCrea, "Religion, Law and State in Contemporary Europe: Key Trends and Dilemmas," in *Belief, Law and Politics: What Future for a Secular Europe?*, ed. Marie-Claire Foblets, Katayoun Alidadi, Jørgen S. Nielsen, and Zeynep Yanasmayan, 91–98 at 92 (Farnham: Ashgate, 2014).

56. See, e.g., Cécile Laborde, "Protecting Freedom of Religion in the Secular Age," in Sullivan et al., *Politics of Religious Freedom*, 269–279 at 278: "Yet the emphasis on conscience tends to favor a Protestant understanding of what a religion is, and it also relies on an implicit, unarticulated theory of the good."

57. See Arvind Sharma, *Problematizing Religious Freedom* (Dordrecht: Springer, 2012).

58. See Friedrich Wilhelm Graf, *Götter Global: Wie die Welt zum Supermarkt der Religionen wird* (Munich: C. H. Beck, 2014), 141–142.

59. Concerning conscientious objection to military service see Chapter 7, Section 7.

60. For more details see Chapter 2, Section 3.

61. For more detailed discussion see Heiner Bielefeldt, Nazila Ghanea, and Michael Wiener, *Freedom of Religion or Belief: An International Law Commentary* (Oxford: Oxford University Press, 2016), 92–305.

62. The underlying idea is that in order for limitation on human rights to be justified it must be conceivable to defend them plausibly toward those human beings who are potentially affected. This does not mean that the affected individuals have actually to agree and endorse the limitations imposed on their freedom (which would be an unrealistic demand). Instead, what is at stake is a hypothetical thought experiment whether it at least appears conceivable to defend such limitations in a plausible—that is, not self-contradictory—way vis-à-vis those individuals who have to bear the negative consequences.

63. For a more detailed discussion see Chapter 2, Section 3.

64. See Saba Mahmood, *Religious Difference in a Secular Age: A Minority Report* (Princeton: Princeton University Press, 2016), 155–157.

65. See Joseph de Maistre, *Considerations on France*, trans. Richard Lebrun (Cambridge: Cambridge University Press, 1994).

66. See Friedrich Wilhelm Georg Hegel, *Vorlesungen über die Philosophie der Geschichte*, vol. 12 of *Werke* (Frankfurt: Suhrkamp, 1986), 534 (our translation).

67. See Karl Marx, *Zur Judenfrage*, vol. 1 of *Marx-Engels Werke* (Berlin: Dietz Verlag, 1976), 347–377 at 364 (our translation).

68. For a critical discussion of the notion of "Asian values," see Amartya Sen, *Human Rights and Asian Values* (New York: Carnegie Council on Ethics and International Affairs, 1997), 7–32.

69. See Article 18 UDHR and Article 18(1) of the ICCPR.

70. Mahmood, *Religious Difference in a Secular Age*, 51.

71. Peter G. Danchin, "Religious Freedom in the Panopticon of Enlightenment Rationality," in Sullivan et al., *Politics of Religious Freedom*, 240–252 at 251 (Chicago: University of Chicago Press, 2015).

72. In her criticism of proselytism, Saba Mahmood wonders how this might "infringe upon the rights of the proselytized to maintain *his or her* beliefs without being subject to another person's convictions" (Mahmood, *Religious Difference in a Secular Age*, 178). She seems to ignore that the right to convert others only covers noncoercive forms of persuasion.

73. See Makau wa Mutua, "Limitations on Religious Rights: Problematizing Religious Freedom in the African Context," in *Religious Human Rights in Global Perspective: Legal Perspectives*, ed. Johan David van der Vyver and John Witte Jr., 417–440 (The Hague: Martinus Nijhoff, 1996).

74. See Sharma, *Problematizing Religious Freedom*, 89.

75. Human Rights Committee, General Comment No. 22, UN Doc. CCPR/C/21/Rev.1/Add.4, para. 5.

76. This issue comes up clearly in the country report on Paraguay by the UN Special Rapporteur on freedom of religion or belief, Heiner Bielefeldt. See UN Doc. A/HRC/19/60/Add.1, paras. 45–53.

77. For a detailed discussion on religious minority rights see Bielefeldt, Ghanea, and Wiener, *Freedom of Religion or Belief*, 439–465.

78. Talal Asad, *Formations of the Secular: Christianity, Islam, Modernity* (Stanford: Stanford University Press, 2003), 147.

79. Hurd, "Believing in Religious Freedom," 45–56 at 52.

80. See ibid., 49. Hurd sees a particular psychology in operation according to which the individual "chooses and enacts beliefs."

81. This formulation implies the right to change. See also Human Rights Committee, General Comment No. 22, UN Doc. CCPR/C/21/Rev.1/Add.4, para. 5.

82. Trigg, *Equality, Freedom and Religion*, 106.

83. Patrick Riordan, "Which Dignity? Which Religious Freedom?," in *Understanding Human Dignity*, ed. Christopher McCrudden, 420–434 at 429 (Oxford: Oxford University Press, 2013).

84. Julian Rivers, "Justifying Freedom of Religion: Does Dignity Help?" in *Understanding Human Dignity*, ed. Christopher McCrudden, 405–419 at 415 (Oxford: Oxford University Press, 2013).

85. See Grégor Puppinck, "Conscientious Objection and Human Rights: A Systematic Analysis," *Brill Research Perspectives in Law and Religion*, Vol. 1, No. 1 (2017), 1–75 at 5–7.

86. Hurd, "Believing in Religious Freedom," 52.

87. Incidentally, the conceptualization of other human rights can lead to similar complications. Take the example of the right to privacy. It gives rise to questions like, who defines privacy, which concepts of privacy should apply, how to accommodate intercultural diversity in the understanding of privacy, what role should gender aspects play, and so on? Still, there are good reasons to stick to the idea of a right to privacy.

88. Stephen Hopgood, *The Endtimes of Human Rights* (Ithaca, N.Y.: Cornell University Press, 2013), 2.

89. Marc O. DeGirolami, *The Tragedy of Religious Freedom* (Cambridge, Mass.: Harvard University Press, 2013), 219.

90. Ibid., 40.

91. Incidentally, critics who aim to unmask hidden agendas and concealed power dynamics underlying freedom of religion or belief, usually fail to discuss the consequences we would have to face if we were to rid ourselves of the normative matrix provided by human rights standards and the case law attached to courts and monitoring bodies. While it may be true that human rights politics, including the politics of religious freedom, always show elements of "realpolitik" under the normative surface, it would be naïve to assume that the deconstruction of normative standards would redeem us from those ambiguities.

92. For more evidence, one may also look into the country-specific reports submitted by the mandate of the Special Rapporteur on freedom of religion or belief, available under: http://www.ohchr.org/EN/Issues/FreedomReligion/Pages/FreedomReligionIndex.aspx.

93. One source of confusion is that many of these people call themselves "non-believers." That the component of "belief," which is supposed also to cover nonreligious convictions, should include nonbelievers actually sounds strange. The French version of freedom of religion or belief may be more adequate, as it uses the term "conviction" instead of belief. In Norway, associations of nonreligious humanists choose the term "livssyn," translated to English as "life-stance." This has the advantage that it also addressed practical—that is, ethical

and ceremonial—consequences of a profound conviction on the way people shape their lives. See Ingvill Thorson Plesner, *Religionspolitikk* (Oslo: Universitetsforlaget, 2016), 24–27.

94. See mission report on Lebanon, UN Doc. A/HRC/31/18/Add.1, paras. 81–83.

95. Makau Mutua, "Proselytism and Cultural Integrity," in *Facilitating Freedom of Religion or Belief: A Deskbook*, ed. Tore Lindholm, W. Cole Durham Jr., and Bahia G. Tahzib-Lie, 651–668 at 661 (Leiden: Martinus Nijhoff, 2004).

96. See mission report on Bangladesh, UN Doc. A/HRC/31/18/Add.2, paras. 89–92.

Chapter 2

1. See http://www.ewtn.com/library/PAPALDOC/P9SYLL.HTM.

2. See http://www.vatican.va/archive/hist_councils/ii_vatican_council/documents/vat-ii_decl_19651207_dignitatis-humanae_en.html.

3. This is the title (our translation) of Beck's article published on 20 December 2007, https://www.zeit.de/2007/52/Essay-Religion.

4. Winnifred Fallers Sullivan, *The Impossibility of Religious Freedom* (Princeton: Princeton University Press, 2005), 155.

5. Ibid., 156.

6. Michael Lambek, "Is Religion Free?," in *Politics of Religious Freedom*, ed. Winnifred Fallers Sullivan, Elizabeth Shakman Hurd, Saba Mahmood, and Peter G. Danchin, 289–300 at 298 (Chicago: University of Chicago Press, 2015).

7. Immanuel Kant, "On the Common Saying: This May Be Correct in Theory, but It Is of No Use in Practice," in *Practical Philosophy*, 277–309 (Cambridge: Cambridge University Press, 1996), 302.

8. Moses Mendelssohn, *Jerusalem, or On Religious Power and Judaism*, trans. Allan Arkush (Waltham, Mass.: Brandeis University Press, 1983), 70.

9. The first sentence of the preamble of the UDHR qualifies human rights as "equal and inalienable rights of all members of the human family."

10. As elaborated in Chapter 1, recognition strictly speaking always refers to human beings, not to their religious convictions and practices as such.

11. See UN Human Rights Committee, General Comment No. 22, UN Doc. CCPR/C/21/Rev.1/Add.4, para. 5.

12. Article 18 of the ICCPR does not repeat the controversial term "change."

13. This is a sentence ascribed to Luther when standing before the Emperor Charles V at the Imperial Diet in the city of Worms.

14. See Paul M. Taylor, *Freedom of Religion: UN and European Human Rights Law and Practice* (Cambridge: Cambridge University Press, 2005), 203–222.

15. For a criticism of the European Court of Human Rights, see ibid., 343.

16. Saba Mahmood misses the logic of Article 18(3) of the ICCPR when contending that "the state has a legitimate right to regulate and limit" manifestations of freedom of religion or belief. See Saba Mahmood, *Religious Difference in a Secular Age: A Minority Report* (Princeton: Princeton University Press, 2016), 156.

17. UN Human Rights Committee, General Comment No. 22, UN Doc. CCPR/C/21/Rev.1/Add.4, para. 8.

18. See, e.g., the article by Manfred Nowak and Tanja Vorspernik, "Permissible Restrictions on Freedom of Religion or Belief," in *Facilitating Freedom of Religion or Belief: A Deskbook*, ed. Tore Lindholm, W. Cole Durham Jr., and Bahia G. Tahzib-Lie, 147–172 (Leiden: Martinus Nijhoff, 2004).

19. Guglielmo Verdirame, "Rescuing Human Rights from Proportionality," in *Philosophical Foundations of Human Rights*, ed. Rowan Cruft, S. Matthew Liao, and Massimo Renzo, 341–357 at 354 (Oxford: Oxford University Press, 2015).

20. On the following see also Heiner Bielefeldt, Nazila Ghanea, and Michael Wiener, *Freedom of Religion or Belief: An International Law Commentary* (Oxford: Oxford University Press, 2016), 551–570.

21. See, e.g., Lorenzo Zucca, "Freedom of Religion in a Secular World," in *Philosophical Foundations of Human Rights*, ed. Rowan Cruft, S. Matthew Liao, and Massimo Renzo, 388–406 at 398 (Oxford: Oxford University Press, 2015): "The strength of the interest protected by freedom of religion can be limited on the basis of interests of public safety, for the protection of public order, health or morals, and finally—last but not least—for the protection of the rights and freedoms of others." Zucca here refers to Article 9 of the European Convention on Human Rights. The limitation clause in that article is almost identical to Article 18 of the ICCPR and follows the same logic. It is remarkable and indeed revealing that Zucca ignores the crucial word "only" when paraphrasing the limitation clause.

22. T. Jeremy Gunn, "Permissible Limitations on the Freedom of Religion or Belief," in *Religion and Human Rights: An Introduction*, ed. John Witte Jr. and M. Christian Green, 254–268 at 265 (Oxford: Oxford University Press, 2012).

23. For further details and examples, see Chapter 4, which deals with possible conflicts between freedom of religion or belief and other human rights concerns, in particular freedom of expression and gender-related human rights issues.

24. The term "change," which made it into Article 18 of the UDHR is not repeated in Article 18 of the ICCPR. However, the wording employed there serves as an equivalent to the right to change.

25. Quoted from Martha C. Nussbaum, *Liberty of Conscience: In Defense of America's Tradition of Religious Equality* (New York: Basic Books, 2008), 37.

26. See Bielefeldt, Ghanea, and Wiener, *Freedom of Religion or Belief*, 75–91. Manfred Nowak and Tanja Vospernik trivialize the *forum internum* of freedom of religion or belief by confusing this with the "private" application of this right. See Nowak and Vospernik, "Permissible Restrictions on Freedom of Religion or Belief," 148. When these authors (on p. 149) wonder how to "balance the right to teach religious views and to convince others with the 'absolute' right of others not to suffer violation of their *forum internum*" they ignore the important fact that the right to convert others only covers noncoercive forms of communicative persuasion. Leaving aside the relativistic language of "balancing," there is not even a conflict that would possibly permit invoking the limitation clause.

27. This section is by and large modelled on Heiner Bielefeldt, "Misperceptions of Freedom of Religion or Belief," *Human Rights Quarterly*, Vol. 35 (2013), 33–68 at 40–50.

28. The OIC's previous name "Organization of the Islamic Conference" was changed in June 2011 to "Organization of Islamic Cooperation." For an analysis of the OIC, in particular with regard to human rights, see Ioana Cismas, *Religious Actors and International Law* (Oxford: Oxford University Press, 2014), 239–305.

29. See Commission on Human Rights resolutions 1999/82, 2000/84, 2001/4, 2002/9, 2003/4, 2004/6, and 2005/3; General Assembly resolutions 60/150, 61/164, 62/154, 63/171, 64/156, and 65/224; Human Rights Council resolutions 4/9, 7/19, 10/22, and 13/16. For a critical assessment, see Robert C. Blitt, "The Bottom Up Journey of 'Defamation of Religions' from

Muslim States to the United Nations: A Case Study of the Migration of Anti-Constitutional Ideas," *Studies in Law, Politics and Society*, Vol. 56 (2011), 121–211.

30. See Jeroen Temperman, "Blasphemy, Defamation of Religions and Human Rights Law," *Netherlands Quarterly of Human Rights*, Vol. 26, No. 4 (2008), 485–516.

31. See Jo-Anne Prud'homme, *Policing Belief: The Impact of Blasphemy Laws on Human Rights* (Washington, D.C.: Freedom House, 2010), 69–76.

32. For more details see, Chapter 4, Section 2.

33. See Report of the Special Rapporteur on freedom of religion or belief, Asma Jahangir, and the Special Rapporteur on contemporary forms of racism, racial discrimination, xenophobia and related intolerance, Doudou Diène, further to Human Rights Council decision 1/107 on incitement to racial and religious hatred and the promotion of tolerance, UN Doc. A/HRC/2/3, para. 36.

34. See UN Doc. A/67/357.

35. See UN Doc. A/HRC/31/18.

36. See UN Docs. A/HRC/34/50, para. 18; A/72/365, paras. 28 and 76; A/73/362, para. 46; A/HRC/40/58.

37. See UN Doc. A/HRC/RES/16/18.

38. See the comprehensive study undertaken by Jeroen Temperman, *Religious Hatred and International Law: The Prohibition of Incitement to Violence or Discrimination* (Cambridge: Cambridge University Press, 2016), 192–203.

39. See David Nash, *Blasphemy in the Christian World: A History* (Oxford: Oxford University Press, 2007).

40. See European Commission for Democracy Through Law (Venice Commission), Report on the Relationship Between Freedom of Expression and Freedom of Religion: The Issue of Regulation and Prosecution of Blasphemy, Religious Insult and Incitement to Religious Hatred, Council of Europe Doc. CDL-AD(2008)026.

41. See European Court of Human Rights, *Otto-Preminger-Institut v. Austria* (appl. 13470/87) of 20 September 1994. For more details see Chapter 4, Section 2 of this book.

42. Heiner Bielefeldt participated in the Jeddah conference in his capacity as UN Special Rapporteur on freedom of religion or belief.

43. See Jürgen Habermas, "Struggles for Recognition in the Democratic Constitutional State," in *Multiculturalism: Examining the Politics of Recognition*, ed. Amy Gutmann, 148–197 (Princeton: Princeton University Press, 1994).

44. See UN Doc. A/HRC/AC.1/2/2.

45. This does not per se mean that it should be treated as a criminal offence. For good reasons, the threshold for criminalizing even hate speech is very high and should remain at a very high level.

46. Emphasis added.

47. See Immanuel Kant, "Toward Perpetual Peace: A Philosophical Project," in *Practical Philosophy*, 317–351 (Cambridge: Cambridge University Press, 1996), 317.

48. See Ziya Meral, *No Place to Call Home: Experiences of Apostates from Islam; Failures of the International Community* (New Malden: Christian Solidarity Worldwide, 2008).

49. See Amos N. Guiora, *Freedom from Religion: Rights and National Security*, 2nd ed. (Oxford: Oxford University Press, 2013). The author is mainly concerned with religious extremism; see p. 20: "To protect civil democratic society, religious rights need to be curtailed."

50. For a more detailed discussion on the various meanings of secularism or secularity, see Chapter 5.

51. Anti-religious sentiments came to the fore in a very emotional public discussion in Germany, triggered by a lower court in May 2012, which had ruled religiously motivated male circumcision of a child to be in violation of the child's right to physical integrity. See Heiner Bielefeldt, "Kulturkampf um Beschneidung? Zum diskursiven Umfeld des Kölner Urteils," *Blätter für deutsche und internationale Politik*, September 2012, 63–71.

Chapter 3

1. See https://ccla.org/cclanewsite/wp-content/uploads/2015/09/INCLO-Report-Drawing-the-Line-EQ-vs-FoR.pdf.

2. Emphasis added.

3. Emphasis added.

4. See Chapter 4, Section 3.

5. Winnifred Fallers Sullivan, Elizabeth Shakman Hurd, Saba Mahmood, and Peter G. Danchin, "Introduction," in *Politics of Religious Freedom*, ed. Winnifred Fallers Sullivan, Elizabeth Shakman Hurd, Saba Mahmood, and Peter G. Danchin, 1–9 at 7 (Chicago: University of Chicago Press, 2015).

6. See "Politics on the School Dinner Menu in France," BBC News of 21 October 2015, www.bbc.com/news/world-europe-34570187.

7. See Aristotle, *The Nicomachean Ethics*, trans. J. E. C. Welldon (Buffalo, N.Y.: Prometheus Press, 1987), section 5.6.

8. See Aristotle, *Politics*, trans. H. Rackham (Cambridge, Mass.: Harvard University Press, 1932), sections 1.2.5, 1.2.7.

9. See for example Cécile Laborde, "Religious Accommodation and Inclusive Even-Handedness," in *Belief, Law and Politics: What Future for a Secular Europe?*, ed. Marie-Claire Foblets, Katayoun Alidadi, Jørgen S. Nielsen, and Zeynep Yanasmayan, 167–169 at 167 (Farnham: Ashgate, 2014).

10. On the following, see Heiner Bielefeldt, *Symbolic Representation in Kant's Practical Philosophy* (Cambridge: Cambridge University Press, 2003), 104–107.

11. See Immanuel Kant, "Metaphysics of Morals," in *Practical Philosophy*, 363–603 (Cambridge: Cambridge University Press, 1996), 393–394: "This principle of innate freedom already involves the following authorizations, which are not really distinct from it. . . : innate *equality*, that is, independence from being bound by others to more than one can in turn bind them." (emphasis in the original)

12. For an interpretation of human dignity, see Chapter 1, Section 3, and Chapter 9, Section 3.

13. See https://www.coe.int/en/web/portal/campaigns.

14. See Margaret Davies, "Pluralism in Law and Religion," in *Law and Religion in Theoretical and Historical Contexts*, ed. Peter Cane, Carolyn Evans, and Zoe Robinson, 72–99 at 79 (Cambridge: Cambridge University Press, 2008): "It is inadequate, even hypocritical, for our political leaders to protest that we live in a secular state without critically reflecting on the multitude of ways in which Christianity remains embedded in our law."

15. For a critical discussion on assumptions of neutrality see Roland Pierik and Wibren van der Burg, "What Is Neutrality?," *Ratio Juris*, Vol. 27 (2014), 496–515.

16. See Supreme Court of the United States, *Sherbert v. Verner*, 374 U.S. 398 (1963).

17. See W. Cole Durham Jr. and Brett G. Scharffs, *Law and Religion: National, International, and Comparative Perspectives* (New York: Aspen, 2010), 210–223; Martha C. Nussbaum, *Liberty of Conscience: In Defense of America's Tradition of Religious Equality* (New York: Basic Books, 2008), 115–174.

18. See Supreme Court of Canada, *Multani v. Commission scolaire Marguerite-Bourgeoys and Attorney General of Quebec*, 1 S.C.R. 256, 2006 SCC 6 (2006).

19. Gérard Bouchard and Charles Taylor, *Building the Future: A Time for Reconciliation; Abridged Report* (Quebec: Government of Quebec, 2008), 25.

20. Ibid., 25.

21. Ibid., 38.

22. Gabrielle Caceres, "Reasonable Accommodation as a Tool to Manage Religious Diversity in the Workplace: What About the 'Transposability' of an American Concept in the French Secular Context?," in *A Test of Faith? Religious Diversity and Accommodation in the European Workplace*, ed. Katayoun Alidadi, Marie-Claire Foblets, and Jogchum Vrielink, 283–316 at 284 (London: Ashgate, 2012).

23. W. Cole Durham Jr., "Religion and Equality: Reconcilable Differences?," in *Religion and Equality: Law in Conflict*, ed. W. Cole Durham Jr. and Donlu D. Thayer, 185–202 at 190 (London: Routledge, 2016).

24. In her book on "deep equality," Lori Beaman criticizes the concept of accommodation as still remaining within the traditional paradigm of tolerance. Her own alternative, while possibly going deeper, however, strips equality of any precise legal contours. See Lori G. Beaman, *Deep Equality in an Era of Religious Diversity* (Oxford: Oxford University Press, 2017), 197: "Deep equality may include cooperation, agonistic respect, generosity, negotiation, forgiveness, contaminated diversity, immanence, similarity, humour, discomfort, neighbourliness, and love."

25. Dworkin misses this point, namely, the presupposition of a predicament, when stating: "If the Native American Church is entitled to an exemption from drug-control laws, then Huxley followers would also be entitled to an exemption." See Ronald Dworkin, *Religion Without God* (Cambridge, Mass.: Harvard University Press, 2013), 135.

26. See Marie-Claire Foblets and Katayoun Alidadi, "The RELIGARE Report: Religion in the Context of the European Union; Engaging the Interplay Between Religious Diversity and Secular Models," in *Belief, Law and Politics: What Future for a Secular Europe?*, ed. Marie-Claire Foblets, Katayoun Alidadi, Jørgen S. Nielsen, and Zeynep Yanasmayan, 11–50 (Farnham: Ashgate, 2014).

27. Katayoun Alidadi, *Religion, Equality and Employment in Europe: The Case for Reasonable Accommodation* (Oxford: Hart Publishing, 2017), 250.

28. See European Court of Human Rights, *Sessa v. Italy* (appl. 28790/08) of 3 April 2012.

29. See European Court of Human Rights, *Jakóbski v. Poland* (appl. 18429/06) of 7 December 2010.

30. See European Court of Human Rights, *Eweida and Others v. the United Kingdom* (appl. 48420/10, 36516/10, 51671/10, 59842/10) of 15 January 2015.

31. Article 2, which defines the crucial concepts employed in the CRPD, inter alia provides that "'Discrimination on the basis of disability' means any distinction, exclusion or restriction on the basis of disability which has the purpose or effect of impairing or nullifying the recognition, enjoyment or exercise, on an equal basis with others, of all human rights and

fundamental freedoms in the political, economic, social, cultural, civil or any other field. It includes all forms of discrimination, including denial of reasonable accommodation."

32. Critics have objected that, unlike disability, religion is not an immutable personal characteristic. However, religion can define the identity of a person to such a degree that noncompliance with certain religious rules would amount to an act of self-betrayal in the understanding of the concerned person. This problem once again illustrates that the term choice, indispensable though it is in international human rights law, can lead to confusion. See the discussions in Chapter 1, Section 5, and Chapter 2, Section 2.

33. Martha C. Nussbaum, *The New Religious Intolerance: Overcoming the Politics of Fear in an Anxious Age* (Cambridge, Mass: Harvard University Press, 2012), 93.

Chapter 4

1. Peter Cumper, "Freedom of Religion and Human Rights Laws—Awkward Bedfellows," in *Equality and Human Rights: Nothing but Trouble? Liber amicorum Titia Loenen*, ed. Marjolein van den Brink, Susanne Burri, and Jenny Goldschmidt, 283–304 (Utrecht: Netherlands Institute of Human Rights, 2015). The article mainly deals with issues in the intersection of freedom of religion or belief and gender-related rights.

2. This is the general tone in the book by Elizabeth Shakman Hurd, *Beyond Religious Freedom: The New Global Politics of Religion* (Princeton: Princeton University Press, 2015).

3. Vienna Declaration and Programme of Action, UN Doc. A/CONF.157/24 (Part 1), chapter 3, section 1, para. 5.

4. For more details, see Heiner Bielefeldt, Nazila Ghanea, and Michael Wiener, *Freedom of Religion or Belief: An International Law Commentary* (Oxford: Oxford University Press, 2016), 481–506.

5. Article 19 of the ICCPR provides an absolute protection to the inner sphere of freedom of opinion.

6. See Déclaration des droits de l'homme et du citoyen, Article 10: "Nul ne doit être inquiété pour ses opinions, même religieuses, pourvu que leur manifestation ne trouble pas l'ordre public établi par la Loi." (English translation from https://www.conseil-constitution nel.fr/sites/default/files/as/root/bank_mm/anglais/cst2.pdf).

7. Patrick Loobuyck, "Critical Remarks on the Pro-Religion Apriority of the RELIGARE Project," in *Belief, Law and Politics: What Future for a Secular Europe?*, ed. Marie-Claire Foblets, Katayoun Alidadi, Jørgen S. Nielsen, and Zeynep Yanasmayan, 227–236 at 236 (Farnham: Ashgate, 2014).

8. See also the discussion in Chapter 2.

9. European Court of Human Rights, *Otto-Preminger-Institut v. Austria* (appl. 13470/87) judgment of 20 September 1994, para. 55.

10. *Otto-Preminger-Institut v. Austria*, Joint Dissenting Opinion of the Judges Palm, Pekkanen, and Makardzyk, Section 6. For a critical analysis see also Paul M. Taylor, *Freedom of Religion: UN and European Human Rights Law and Practice* (Cambridge: Cambridge University Press, 2005), 84–102.

11. European Court of Human Rights, *E. S. v. Austria* (appl. 38450/12) judgment of 25 October 2018, para. 57.

12. UN Doc. A/62/280, para. 80.

13. It should be noted in passing that Asma Jahangir herself was from Pakistan.

14. UN Doc. A/HRC/2/3, para. 41.

15. UN Doc. A/HRC/2/3, para. 37.

16. See for example UN Docs. A/HRC/31/18, paras. 59–61; A/71/269, paras. 45–46; A/HRC/34/50, para. 40; A/72/365, paras. 26–31.

17. See Malcolm D. Evans, "The Freedom of Religion or Belief and the Freedom of Expression," *Religion and Human Rights*, Vol. 4 (2009), 197–235.

18. See UN Doc. A/HRC/22/17/Add.4, appendix.

19. Natan Lerner, "Incitement to Hatred and the 1981 United Nations Declaration on Religion or Belief," in *The Changing Nature of Religious Rights Under International Law*, ed. Malcolm D. Evans, Peter Petkoff, and Julian Rivers, 80–100 at 89 (Oxford: Oxford University Press, 2015).

20. See Agnès Callamard, "Towards an Interpretation of Article 20 of the ICCPR: Thresholds for the Prohibition of Incitement to Hatred—Work in Progress," www.ohchr.org/Documents/Issues/Expression/ICCPR/Vienna/CRP7Callamard.pdf.

21. See Rabat Plan of Action, UN Doc. A/HRC/22/17/Add.4, appendix, para. 29.

22. See Rabat Plan of Action, UN Doc. A/HRC/22/17/Add.4, appendix, para. 25; Beirut Declaration and its eighteen commitments on "Faith for Rights," UN Doc. A/HRC/40/58, annex II, commitment 11; Plan of Action for Religious Leaders and Actors to Prevent Incitement to Violence that could lead to Atrocity Crimes, www.un.org/en/genocideprevention/documents/Plan%20of%20Action%20Advanced%20Copy.pdf, p. 9.

23. Rabat Plan of Action, UN Doc. A/HRC/22/17/Add.4, appendix, para. 37.

24. Entscheidungen des Bundesverfassungsgerichts, vol. 7, p. 198 (our translation, emphasis in the original).

25. See Michael O'Flaherty, "Freedom of Expression: Article 19 of the International Covenant on Civil and Political Rights and the Human Rights Committee's General Comment No. 34," *Human Rights Law Review*, Vol. 12 (2012), 627–654.

26. For more details, see Bielefeldt, Ghanea, and Wiener, *Freedom of Religion or Belief*, 363–389; Michael Wiener, "Freedom of Religion or Belief and Sexuality: Tracing the Evolution of the Special Rapporteur's Mandate Practice over Thirty Years," *Oxford Journal of Law and Religion*, Vol. 6, No. 2 (2017), 253–267.

27. Michael O'Flaherty, "Sexual Orientation and Gender Identity," in *International Human Rights Law*, 2nd ed., ed. Daniel Moeckli, Sangeeta Shah, and Sandesh Sivakumaran, 331–344 (Oxford: Oxford University Press, 2014).

28. See Yogyakarta Principles on the Application of International Human Rights Law in Relation to Sexual Orientation and Gender Identity, www.yogyakartaprinciples.org.

29. Ritual male circumcision, albeit a complicated issue, does not obviously fall under the category of harmful practices. See Heiner Bielefeldt, "Menschenrecht, kein Sonderrecht," in *Beschneidung: Das Zeichen des Bundes in der Kritik; Zur Debatte um das Kölner Urteil*, ed. Johannes Heil and Stephan J. Kramer, 71–82 (Berlin: Metropol, 2012).

30. See Mathias Rohe, *Das Islamische Recht: Geschichte und Gegenwart*, 3rd enlarged ed. (Munich: C. H. Beck, 2011), 79–99.

31. PACE resolution 1763 (2010), para. 1. The resolution goes beyond the issue of conscientious objection by also including hospitals and other institutions. However, freedom of conscience—as well as the right to conscientious objection as its necessary implication—applies to individuals only.

32. It should be noted in passing that an individual's conscientious objection and an institution's claim to respect for its internal autonomy, albeit both falling within freedom of

religion or belief, are very different phenomena, which would also warrant a different normative assessment. The fact that the PACE resolution addressed both in one breath, as it were, is certainly a weak point.

33. See www.astra.org.pl/pdf/bulletin/biuletyn_97pdf. Sweden does not accommodate any conscientious objection by health professionals when requested to perform abortions.

34. See European Court of Human Rights, *Eweida and Others v. the United Kingdom* (appl. 48420/10, 36516/10, 51671/10, 59842/10) of 15 January 2013.

35. See Entscheidung des Bundesverfassungsgerichts, 1 BvR 471/10 (27 January 2015); Saba Mahmood, *Religious Difference in a Secular Age: A Minority Report* (Princeton: Princeton University Press, 2016), 176, gives a wrong account of the juridical situation in Germany. She writes that the Federal Constitutional Court of Germany "upheld the Baden-Württemberg legislation which bans teachers from wearing Islamic symbols in schools, while allowing Christian and Jewish ones." The truth is that the Federal Constitutional Court in 2015 explicitly rejected the law in North Rhine-Westphalia, which was directly modeled after the law of Baden-Württemberg. Citing the German jurisprudence as an example of a court, which "consecrate[d] majoritarian sensibilities" (ibid.), is thus unfounded.

36. See Konrad Hesse, *Grundzüge des Verfassungsrechts der Bundesrepublik Deutschland*, 20th ed. (repr., Heidelberg: C. F. Müller, 1999), para. 70; Bielefeldt, Ghanea, and Wiener, *Freedom of Religion or Belief*, 190.

37. See also our critical remarks on "balances" in Chapter 2, Section 3.

38. See the observations on reasonable accommodation in Chapter 3, Section 5.

39. See Holger Zaborowski, "Wohlwollen, Dialog und die Anerkennung des Anderen: Zur Hermeneutik von Religionsfreiheit," in *Umstrittene Religionsfreiheit: Zur Diskussion um ein Menschenrecht*, ed. Thomas Brose and Philipp W. Hildmann, 23–42 at 40–42 (Frankfurt: Peter Lang, 2016).

40. This misunderstanding sometimes occurs.

41. The Vatican continues to be a bastion of men only, and Orthodox, old Oriental and other churches likewise reserve clerical positions to males. Orthodox Judaism merely acknowledges male rabbis, and imams within mainstream Islam are mostly men as well. Similar structures can also be found within religious communities outside of the circle of monotheistic religions of revelation. It thus may seem that religions by and large are the last fortresses of male prevalence over modern claims of gender-based emancipation and nondiscrimination.

42. Their worldwide center is in Bonn, Germany.

43. See www.alt-katholisch.de/information/frauenordination.html.

44. See www.svenskakyrkan.se/om-arkebiskop-antje-jackelen.

45. See www.asianews.it/news-en/West-Java,-Muslim-women-conference-rejects-poly gamy-40592.html.

46. Ayelet Shachar, "Entangled: Family, Religion and Human Rights," in *Human Rights: The Hard Questions*, ed. Cindy Holder and David Reidy, 115–135 at 127 (Cambridge: Cambridge University Press, 2013). See also the overview provided by Katharina Ceming, *Ernstfall Menschenrechte: Die Würde des Menschen und die Weltreligionen* (Munich: Kösel, 2010).

47. Zainah Anwar, "From Local to Global: Sisters in Islam and the Making of Musawah," in *Gender and Equality in Muslim Family Law: Justice and Ethics in the Islamic Legal Tradition*, ed. Ziba Mir-Hosseini, Kari Vogt, Lena Larsen, and Christian Moe, 107–124 at 108–109 (London: Tauris, 2013).

48. Beirut Declaration and its eighteen commitments on "Faith for Rights," UN Doc. A/HRC/40/58, annex II, commitment 3.

49. See https://www.ohchr.org/EN/NewsEvents/Pages/DisplayNews.aspx?NewsID = 22 504&LangID = E.

50. See http://mccchurch.org/overview/ourchurches.

51. See www.bbc.com/news/world-europe-18363157; www.reuters.com/article/us-nor way-gaymarriage-idUSKBN15E1O2.

52. See www.queertheology.com/sodom-gomorrah-homosexuality-bible.

53. See Javaid Rehman and Eleni Polymenopoulou, "Is Green a Part of the Rainbow? Sharia, Homosexuality and LGBT Rights in the Muslim World," *Fordham International Law Journal*, Vol. 37 (2013), 1–52 at 50.

54. See http://www.mpvusa.org/who-we-are.

55. For more details see Chapter 5.

56. See Erica Howard, "Religious Rights Versus Sexual Orientation Discrimination: A Fair Deal for Everyone," *Religion and Human Rights*, Vol. 10 (2015), 128–159.

57. See UN Doc. A/HRC/31/18/Add.2, paras. 92–95.

58. Deputy High Commissioner Kate Gilmore moderated the penal discussion toward the end of the conference "Religious Freedom and Human Sexuality," which was organized by the UN Special Rapporteur on freedom of religion or belief in cooperation with Muslims for Progressive Values, Palais des Nations, Geneva, 10 June 2016, www.ohchr.org/Documents/Issues/Religion/FORBAndSexuality.pdf.

59. See Sherene H. Razack, "Imperilled Muslim Women, Dangerous Muslim Men and Civilised Europeans: Legal and Social Responses to Forced Marriages," *Feminist Legal Studies*, Vol. 12 (2004), 129–174.

60. For a discussion of such a shift from "invisibility" to "indivisibility" see Wiener, "Freedom of Religion or Belief and Sexuality, 253–267.

61. Immanuel Kant, "On the Common Saying: This May Be Correct in Theory, but It Is of No Use in Practice," in *Practical Philosophy*, 277–309 (Cambridge: Cambridge University Press, 1996), 302.

Chapter 5

1. The following observations are based on UN Doc. A/HRC/28/66/Add.1.

2. Secularism already figures as one of the defining principles in Article 1 of the Constitution: "The Republic of Kazakhstan proclaims itself a democratic, secular, legal and social state whose highest values are an individual, his life, rights and freedoms."

3. The following observations are based on UN Doc. A/HRC/31/18/Add.2.

4. See Constitution of the People's Republic of Bangladesh, Article 2A: "The state religion of the Republic is Islam, but the State shall ensure equal status and equal right in the practice of the Hindu, Buddhist, Christian and other religions."

5. The following observations are based on UN Doc. A/HRC/34/50/Add.1.

6. See § 4 of the Danish Constitution: "The Evangelical Lutheran Church shall be the Established Church of Denmark, and as such shall be supported by the State."

7. See the information provided by the Danish Grundtvig Forum: www.grundtvig.dk.

8. See www.bbc.com/news/world-europe-18363157.

9. Rosemarie van den Breemer, José Casanova, and Trygve Wyller, "Introduction," in *Secular and Sacred? The Scandinavian Case of Religion in Human Rights, Law and Public Space*,

ed. Rosemarie van den Breemer, José Casanova, and Trygve Wyller, 9–20 at 10 (Göttingen: Vandenhoek and Ruprecht, 2014).

10. Ibid., 14. For an application of this theological underpinning to the situation in Denmark see Lisbet Christoffersen, "Sacred Spaces in Secular (Post-) Lutheran Contexts," in *Secular and Sacred? The Scandinavian Case of Religion in Human Rights, Law and Public Space*, 102–122.

11. See https://danskfolkeparti.dk/politik/in-another-languages-politics/1757–2/: "Christianity draws a sharp distinction between the temporal world and the world of faith—a distinction of crucial importance for any country's evolution, for freedom, openness and democracy. The Danish People's Party wants the Government to support the National Church. This does not prejudice ordinary religious freedom, of which we are supporters—and protectors."

12. In this chapter, we will focus on concepts of state secularity and accordingly not deal with secularization of the society at large. These phenomena are different and not always related. There are examples of highly religious societies with a secular state and vice versa.

13. See José Casanova, *Public Religions in the Modern World* (Chicago: University of Chicago Press, 1994).

14. See Gerhard Robbers, ed., *State and Church in the European Union* (Baden-Baden: Nomos, 2005).

15. See T. Jeremy Gunn and John Witte Jr., eds., *No Establishment of Religion: America's Original Contribution to Religious Liberty* (Oxford: Oxford University Press, 2012).

16. See Alberto Patiño Reyes, "Religion and the Secular State in Mexico," in *Religion and the Secular State: Interim National Reports, Issued for the Occasion of the XVIIIth International Congress of Comparative Law, Washington, D.C., 2010*, ed. Javier Martínez-Torrón and W. Cole Durham Jr., 505–516 (Provo: International Center for Law and Religious Studies at Brigham Young University, 2010).

17. Veit Bader, "Constitutionalizing Secularism, Alternative Secularisms or Liberal Democratic Constitutionalism? A Critical Reading of Some Turkish, ECtHR and Indian Supreme Court Cases on 'Secularism,'" *Utrecht Law Review*, Vol. 6 (2010), 8–35 at 8.

18. Some authors distinguish between "secularism" and "secularity." For instance, Cole Durham defines secularism as a postreligious ideology, while using the term secularity to describe constitutional arrangements that are not driven by ideological interests. See W. Cole Durham Jr., "Patterns of Religion State Relations," in *Religion and Human Rights: An Introduction*, ed. John Witte Jr. and M. Christian Green, 360–378 (Oxford: Oxford University Press, 2012). While we agree that the conceptual differentiation is important, we are afraid that the proposed terminological distinction is not self-explanatory and may not suffice to avoid confusion—unless one adds further adjectives. For this reason, we have decided to focus in this book on the clarifying adjectives without using the distinction between "secularism" and "secularity."

19. See T. Jeremy Gunn, "Secularism, the Secular, and Secularization," in *Trends of Secularism in a Pluralistic World*, ed. Jaime Contreras and Rosa María Martínez de Codes, 59–105, especially 65–69 (Madrid: Iberoamericana, 2013).

20. See Istar Gözaydin, "Management of Religion in Turkey: The *Diyanet* and Beyond," in *Freedom of Religion or Belief in Turkey*, ed. Özgür Heval Cinar and Mine Yildirim, 10–35 (Newcastle upon Tyne: Cambridge Scholars Publishing, 2014).

21. See the Special Rapporteur's mission reports (UN Docs. A/HRC/7/10/Add.2; A/HRC/10/8/Add.4; and A/HRC/37/49/Add.2) as well as the regular information provided by Forum 18, an NGO specialized on freedom of religion or belief in Central Asia, www.forum18.org.

22. See David Little, "Roger Williams and the Puritan Background of the Establishment Clause," in *Essays on Religion and Human Rights: Ground to Stand On*, ed. David Little, 243–271 (Cambridge: Cambridge University Press, 2015).

23. See Jefferson's letter to the Danbury Baptists, www.billofrightsinstitute.org/founding-documents/primary-source-documents/danburybaptists.

24. See José Casanova, "The Religious Situation in Europe," in *Secularization and the World Religions*, ed. Hans Joas and Klaus Wiegand, 206–228 (Liverpool: Liverpool University Press, 2009).

25. See Jean Baubérot, *La laïcité, quel héritage? De 1789 à nos jours* (Geneva: Labor et Fides, 1990).

26. On the features of secularism in India and its various sources, see Triloki Nath Madan, "Indian Secularism: A Religio-Secular Ideal," in *Comparative Secularisms in a Global Age*, ed. Linell E. Cady and Elizabeth Shakman Hurd, 181–196 at 187–192 (New York: Palgrave Macmillan, 2010).

27. George J. Holyoake, *English Secularism: A Confession of Belief* (Chicago: Open Publishing, 1896), 35.

28. See Hermann Lübbe, *Säkularisierung: Geschichte eines ideenpolitischen Begriffs* (Freiburg: Alber, 1965), 42.

29. Ibid., 51.

30. See Ernst Haeckel, *Die Welträtsel: Gemeinverständliche Studien über monistische Philosophie* (repr., Stuttgart: Kröner, 1984), 425–427.

31. Ibid., 427–428 (our translation, emphasis in the original).

32. Ibid., 20 (our translation, emphasis in the original).

33. This slogan has made it into the official flag of Brazil.

34. See August Comte, *Système de politique positive, ou Traité de sociologie, instituant la religion de l'humanité*, vol. 3 (Paris: Les presses universitaires de France, 1853), 605.

35. See Charles Taylor, *A Secular Age* (Cambridge, Mass.: Harvard University Press, 2007), 13: "But the presumption of unbelief has become dominant in more and more of these milieux; and has achieved hegemony in certain crucial ones, in the academic and intellectual life, for instance; whence it can more easily extend itself to others."

36. See Johannes Heil and Stephan J. Kramer, eds., *Beschneidung: Das Zeichen des Bundes in der Kritik; Zur Debatte um das Kölner Urteil* (Berlin: Metropol Verlag, 2012).

37. See Jürgen Habermas, "Religion in der Öffentlichkeit: Kognitive Voraussetzungen für den 'öffentlichen Vernunftgebrauch' religiöser und säkularer Bürger," in *Zwischen Naturalismus und Religion: Philosophische Aufsätze*, ed. Jürgen Habermas, 119–154 at 145 (Frankfurt: Suhrkamp, 2005).

38. Jocelyn Maclure and Charles Taylor, *Secularism and Freedom of Conscience*, trans. Jane Marie Todd (Cambridge, Mass.: Harvard University Press, 2011), 13. See also David Little, "The Global Challenge of Secularism to Religious Freedom," in *Trends of Secularism in a Pluralistic World*, ed. Jaime Contreras and Rosa María Martínez de Codes, 31–58 (Madrid: Iberoamericana, 2013).

39. For a detailed criticism of the German *Leitkultur*, see Heiner Bielefeldt, *Menschenrechte in der Einwanderungsgesellschaft: Plädoyer für einen aufgeklärten Multikulturalismus* (Bielefeld: transcript Verlag, 2007).

40. Matthew 22:21 (Authorized King James Version by Zondervan Bible Publishers, Michigan, 1962).

41. Beirut Declaration and its eighteen commitments on "Faith for Rights," Un Doc. A/HRC/40/58, annex II, commitment 4. See also UN Doc. A/HRC/37/49, para. 89.

42. Human Rights Committee General Comment No. 22 (1993), UN Doc. CCPR/C/21/ Rev.1/Add.4, para. 9. The subsequent para. 10 applies these considerations to states with a nonreligious official state ideology.

43. See also David Little, "Religion, Human Rights, and the Secular State: Clarification and Some Islamic, Jewish and Christian Responses," in *Essays on Religion and Human Rights: Ground to Stand On*, ed. David Little, 83–111 at 105 (Cambridge: Cambridge University Press, 2015).

44. See the reports of the UN Special Rapporteur on freedom of religion or belief, UN Docs. A/HRC/19/60, para. 62; A/67/303, para. 47; A/HRC/34/50, para. 32; A/HRC/37/49, para. 81.

45. Un Doc. A/HRC/37/49, para. 89.

46. Martha C. Nussbaum, *Liberty of Conscience: In Defense of America's Tradition of Religious Equality* (New York: Basic Books, 2008), 20–21.

47. Nussbaum, *Liberty of Conscience*, 11–12 (emphasis in the original).

48. Inclusive secularism has sometimes been termed "moderate" as opposed to "radical" secularism. This terminology suggests that inclusive secularism is less consistent than exclusive secularism, which thus somehow seems to provide the yardstick of what secularism is all about. For example, some constitutional lawyers have described the German system as a "limping separation" ("*hinkende Trennung*"). We do not deny that the German way of handling the relationship of state and religious communities is characterized by a number of inconsistencies and thus calls for reformist adaptations. However, this does not mean that the French "*laïcité*" should serve as the binding model.

49. See Udo di Fabio, *Gewissen, Glaube, Religion: Wandelt sich die Religionsfreiheit?* (Freiburg: Herder, 2012), 31.

50. See Maclure and Taylor, *Secularism and Freedom of Conscience*, 16: "The state's neutrality is, therefore, not complete."

51. See Rex Tauati Ahdar, "Why Secularism Is Not Neutral," in *Trends of Secularism in a Pluralistic World*, ed. Jaime Contreras and Rosa María Martínez de Codes, 107–144 at 115 (Madrid: Iberoamericana, 2013).

52. The Court of Justice of the European Union, in two judgments of 14 March 2017, applies the concept of neutrality to companies, which as part of their economic freedom should have the option to declare policies of religious neutrality with implications for their staff (*Samira Achbita and Centrum voor gelijkheid van kansen en voor racismebestrijding v. G4S Secure Solutions NV*, Case C-157/15; *Asma Bougnaoui and Association de défense des droits de l'homme (ADDH) v. Micropole SA*, Case C-188/15). However, this may lead to undue restrictions of freedom of religion or belief, in particular manifestations in the area of dress codes and religious symbols.

Chapter 6

1. The "we" is not necessarily identical with both coauthors of this book. The following examples stem from reports of fact-finding missions of the UN Special Rapporteur on

freedom of religion or belief between 2010 and 2016. The reports are available on the website of the Office of the United Nations High Commissioner for Human Rights at www.ohchr.org/EN/Issues/FreedomReligion/Pages/FreedomReligionIndex.aspx. The following typological observations on patterns of violations of religious freedom have also been summarized in German in Heiner Bielefeldt, "Verletzungen der Religionsfreiheit weltweit: Ursachen und Erscheinungsformen im Überblick," in *Religionsfreiheit im säkularen Staat: Aktuelle Auslegungsfragen in der Schweiz, in Deutschland und weltweit*, ed. Julia Hänni, Sebastian Heselhaus, and Adrian Loretan, 193–210 (Zurich: Dike, 2019).

2. Owing to the typological structure, we will not add many country-specific sources, except concerning specific acts of legislation, court decisions, or similar institutional responses.

3. See also Ani Sarkissian, *The Varieties of Religious Repression: Why Governments Restrict Religion* (Oxford: Oxford University Press, 2015). The author focuses attention on frequently neglected lower-intensity forms of state coercion; see p. 182: "Because these types of restrictions tend to operate under the cover of the rule of law, they are often overlooked in studies on religion and politics in favor of higher intensity forms of religious persecution."

4. See Bitola Court of First Instance, as quoted by the European Court of Human Rights in its decision of 26 May 2009, *Vraniskoski v. the former Yugoslav Republic of Macedonia* (appl. 37973/05). See also related statements by state representatives, as quoted by the European Court of Human Rights in its judgment of 16 November 2017, *Orthodox Ohrid Archdiocese (Greek-Orthodox Ohrid Archdiocese of the Peć Patriarchy) v. the former Yugoslav Republic of Macedonia* (appl. 3532/07), paras. 8 and 37–41.

5. See mission report on Lebanon, UN Doc. A/HRC/31/18/Add.1, paras. 68–74.

6. See UN Doc. A/HRC/16/53.

7. See UN Doc. CRC/C/MMR/CO/3–4, para. 45.

8. See European Court of Human Rights, *Folgerø and Others v. Norway* (appl. 15472/02) of 29 June 2007. For details see Chapter 7, section 5.

9. See European Court of Human Rights, *Zengin v. Turkey* (appl. 1448/04) of 9 October 2007.

10. See Article 298-B of the Pakistan Penal Code, which specifically targets "Qadianis"—a negative term used to define Ahmadis.

11. See Asma Jahangir's mission report on India, UN Doc. A/HRC/10/8/Add.3, paras. 27–28.

12. See European Court of Human Rights, *Metropolitan Church of Bessarabia and Others v. Moldova* (appl. 45701/99) of 13 December 2001.

13. See UN Docs. A/HRC/7/10/Add.1, para. 61; A/HRC/18/51, p. 92 (case number CHN 9/2011); A/HRC/22/67, p. 68 (case number CHN 8/2012).

14. See also the discussion in Chapter 8, section 4.

15. See UN Doc. A/HRC/31/18/Add.2, para. 50.

16. An influential example is the organization "Open Doors," which in their annual reports regularly provide a ranking of countries where Christians suffer persecution. In its 2017 report, Open Doors estimates the number of persecuted Christians as about 200 million. The methodology chapter in the report does not give any clear account as to how this figure has come about. See www.opendoorsusa.org/christian-persecution/stories/announcing-2017-world-watch-list.

17. See Pew Research Center, "Global Uptick in Government Restrictions on Religion in 2016," 21 June 2018, http://www.pewforum.org/wp-content/uploads/sites/7/2018/06/Restrictions-IX-FULL-REPORT-WITH-APPENDIXES.pdf, which also includes the following caveat on pp. 17–18: "It is important to note, however, that these restrictions and hostilities do not necessarily affect the religious groups and citizens of these countries equally, as certain groups or individuals—especially religious minorities—may be targeted more frequently by these policies and actions than others. Thus, the actual proportion of the world's population that is affected by high levels of religious restrictions may be considerably lower than 85%." However, this important caveat tends to get lost in media reports, see for example, https://www.christianitytoday.com/news/2018/june/global-religious-freedom-christian-persecution-pew-research.html.

18. For a critical analysis see Anja Nicole Hoffmann, "Measuring Freedom of Religion: An Analysis of Religious Freedom Indexes" (master's thesis, Vienna, 2017). The author, inter alia, criticizes the vague notion of restrictions which lacks a solid human rights basis.

19. Guest workers from a Hindu background in Qatar may outnumber the Muslim population of this Islamic country by far. Furthermore, the number of Buddhists in Cyprus is apparently much higher than the number of the three traditionally recognized religious minorities—Maronites, Armenians, and Latins—taken together (see UN Doc. A/HRC/22/51/Add.1, para. 29).

20. See UN Doc. A/HRC/7/10/Add.1, para. 94.

Chapter 7

1. Human Rights Committee, General Comment No. 33, The Obligations of States Parties under the Optional Protocol to the International Covenant on Civil and Political Rights, UN Doc. CCPR/C/GC/33, paras. 11 and 13; Heiner Bielefeldt, Nazila Ghanea, and Michael Wiener, *Freedom of Religion or Belief: An International Law Commentary* (Oxford: Oxford University Press, 2016), 160–161.

2. While the International Criminal Court (ICC), based in The Hague, has significance for human rights protection through prosecuting individuals who are accused or suspected of serious international crimes such as genocide, war crimes, or crimes against humanity, it is not a human rights court. Similarly, the Court of Justice of the European Union (CJEU), based in Luxembourg, can annul EU legal acts if they violate EU treaties or fundamental rights; however, it is not a human rights court as such (see Opinion of Advocate General Sharpston, delivered on 30 September 2010, Case C-34/09, *Gerardo Ruiz Zambrano v. Office national de l'emploi (ONEM)*, para. 155).

3. Stephen Hopgood, *The Endtimes of Human Rights* (Ithaca, N.Y.: Cornell University Press, 2013), 2.

4. Ibid., 6 (emphasis in the original).

5. César Rodríguez-Garavito, "Towards a Human Rights Ecosystem," in *Debating the Endtimes of Human Rights: Activism and Institutions in a Neo-Westphalian World*, ed. Doutje Lettinga and Lars van Troost, 39–45 (Amsterdam: Amnesty International Netherlands, 2014).

6. Michael O'Boyle, "*Ne bis in idem* for the Benefit of States?," in *Liber Amicorum Luzius Wildhaber: Human Rights—Strasbourg Views, Droits de l'homme—Regards de Strasbourg*, ed. Lucius Caflisch, Johan Callewaert, Roderick Liddell, Paul Mahoney, and Mark Villiger, 329–346 at 329 (Kehl: N. P. Engel, 2007).

7. Article 35(2)(b) of the European Convention on Human Rights (emphasis added).

8. Article 5(2)(a) of the Optional Protocol to the International Covenant on Civil and Political Rights (emphasis added).

9. For a list of these states see https://treaties.un.org/Pages/ViewDetails.aspx?src = TREATY&mtdsg _no = IV-5&chapter = 4&clang = _en.

10. See http://juris.ohchr.org/search/documents.

11. See United Kingdom Supreme Court judgment of 25 July 2012, *RT (Zimbabwe) and others v. Secretary of State for the Home Department*, [2012] UKSC 38, para. 33; Kasey L. McCall-Smith, "Interpreting International Human Rights Standards: Treaty Body General Comments as a Chisel or a Hammer," in *Tracing the Roles of Soft Law in Human Rights*, ed. Stéphanie Lagoutte, Thomas Gammeltoft-Hansen, and John Cerone, 27–46 at 36–37 (Oxford: Oxford University Press, 2016).

12. See for example European Court of Human Rights, *İzzettin Doğan and Others v. Turkey* (appl. 62649/10) of 26 April 2016, paras. 58–59. The European Court of Human Rights has no mandate to issue thematic general comments, as the UN Human Rights Committee does.

13. European Court of Human Rights, *Cyprus v. Turkey* (appl. 25781/94) of 10 May 2001, paras. 245–246. Following the measures adopted by the authorities, the Committee of Ministers decided in 2007 to close the examination of the living conditions of Greek Cypriots in northern Cyprus as regards freedom of religion (see Interim Resolution CM/Res DH(2007)25, adopted on 4 April 2007).

14. European Court of Human Rights, *Cyprus v. Turkey* (appl. 25781/94), judgment (just satisfaction) of 12 May 2014. On the same day, however, the Ministry of Foreign Affairs of Turkey observed that the judgment was "deprived of a legal basis" and lacked "the capacity of being implemented under the conditions in which the Cyprus question continues to be unsettled" (see UN Doc. A/HRC/28/20, para. 17).

15. See Inter-American Court of Human Rights, *Nadege Dorzema et al. v. Dominican Republic*, judgment of 24 October 2012, footnote 283; African Court on Human and Peoples' Rights, *African Commission on Human and Peoples' Rights v. Republic of Kenya* (appl. 006/12), judgment of 26 May 2017, footnotes 42 and 43.

16. See European Court of Human Rights, *Lautsi and Others v. Italy* (appl. 30814/06), Grand Chamber judgment of 18 March 2011; UN Doc. E/CN.4/2006/5, para. 36 (with references to national legal judgments in endnote 1).

17. Human Rights Committee, *Bikramjit Singh v. France*, Views of 1 November 2012, UN Doc. CCPR/C/106/D/1852/2008, para. 8.7.

18. European Court of Human Rights, *Jasvir Singh v. France* (appl. 25463/08) decision of 30 June 2009; and *Ranjit Singh v. France* (appl. 27561/08), decision of 30 June 2009.

19. Therefore France's reservation to Article 5(2)(a) of the Optional Protocol to the ICCPR (specifying "that the Human Rights Committee shall not have competence to consider a communication from an individual if the same matter is being examined or has already been considered under another procedure of international investigation or settlement") did not have an impact on the admissibility of the case in Geneva.

20. European Court of Human Rights, *Mann Singh v. France* (appl. 24479/07), decision of 13 November 2008.

21. Human Rights Committee, *Shingara Mann Singh v. France*, Views of 19 July 2013, UN Doc. CCPR/C/108/D/1928/2010, para. 9.5. See also the same argument by the Human

Rights Committee in the previous case of *Ranjit Singh v. France*, Views of 22 July 2011, UN Doc. CCPR/C/102/D/1876/2009, para. 8.4.

22. UN Doc. CCPR/C/112/3, p. 15.

23. Articles 26 and 27 of the 1969 Vienna Convention on the law of treaties.

24. See Bielefeldt, Ghanea, and Wiener, *Freedom of Religion or Belief*, 161.

25. European Court of Human Rights, *S.A.S. v. France* (appl. 43835/11), Grand Chamber judgment of 1 July 2014, paras. 153–157.

26. Human Rights Committee, *Yaker v. France*, Views of 17 July 2018, UN Doc. CCPR/C/123/D/2747/2016, para. 8.17; *Hebbadj v. France*, Views of 17 July 2018, UN Doc. CCPR/C/123/D/2807/2016, para. 7.17.

27. See UN Doc. CCPR/C/123/D/2747/2016, para. 8.15 and CCPR/C/123/D/2807/2016, para. 7.15, in which the Human Rights Committee explicitly quoted the gender-related reasoning of the European Court of Human Rights that "a State Party cannot invoke gender equality in order to ban a practice that is defended by women—such as the applicant—in the context of the exercise of the rights enshrined in those provisions, unless it were to be understood that individuals could be protected on that basis from the exercise of their own fundamental rights and freedoms" (see *S.A.S. v. France*, para. 119).

28. See CCPR/C/123/D/2807/2016, para. 6.4 and the similar wording in UN Doc. CCPR/C/123/D/2747/2016, para. 6.2.

29. See Human Rights Committee, *Leirvåg and Others v. Norway*, Views of 3 November 2004, UN Doc. CCPR/C/82/D/1155/2003, para. 8.2.

30. Ibid., para. 10.3.

31. European Court of Human Rights, *Folgerø and Others v. Norway* (appl. 15472/02), Third Section decision of 26 October 2004.

32. Human Rights Committee, *Leirvåg and Others v. Norway*, Views of 3 November 2004, UN Doc. CCPR/C/82/D/1155/2003, paras. 14.6 and 14.7.

33. European Court of Human Rights, *Folgerø and Others v. Norway* (appl. 15472/02), Grand Chamber judgment of 29 June 2007, para. 100.

34. Ibid., Separate Opinion of judges Zupančič and Borrego Borrego.

35. Human Rights Committee, *Muhonen v. Finland*, decision of 6 April 1984, UN Doc. CCPR/C/24/D/89/1981; *L. T. K. v. Finland*, decision of 9 July 1985, UN Doc. CCPR/C/25/D/185/1984; *Järvinen v. Finland*, Views of 25 July 1990, UN Doc. CCPR/C/39/D/295/1988.

36. Human Rights Committee, *Yoon and Choi v. Republic of Korea*, Views of 3 November 2006, UN Doc. CCPR/C/88/D/1321–1322/2004; *Jung et al. v. Republic of Korea*, Views of 23 March 2010, UN Doc. CCPR/C/98/D/1593–1603/2007.

37. Human Rights Committee, *Jeong et al. v. Republic of Korea*, Views of 24 March 2011, UN Doc. CCPR/C/101/D/1642–1741/2007; *Jong-Nam Kim et al. v. Republic of Korea*, Views of 25 October 2012, UN Doc. CCPR/C/106/D/1786/2008; *Atasoy and Sarkut v. Turkey*, Views of 29 March 2012, UN Doc. CCPR/C/104/D/1853–1854/2008; *Young-Kwan Kim et al. v. Republic of Korea*, Views of 15 October 2014, UN Doc. CCPR/C/112/D/2179/2012; *Abdullayev v. Turkmenistan*, Views of 25 March 2015, UN Doc. CCPR/C/113/D/2218/2012; *Mahmud Hudaybergenov v. Turkmenistan*, Views of 29 October 2015, UN Doc. CCPR/C/115/D/2221/2012; *Ahmet Hudaybergenov v. Turkmenistan*, Views of 29 October 2015, UN Doc. CCPR/C/115/D/2222/2012; *Japparow v. Turkmenistan*, Views of 29 October 2015, UN Doc. CCPR/C/115/D/2223/2012; *Aminov v. Turkmenistan*, Views of 14 July 2016, UN Doc. CCPR/C/117/D/

2220/2012; *Matyakubov v. Turkmenistan*, Views of 14 July 2016, UN Doc. CCPR/C/117/D/ 2224/2012; *Yegendurdyyew v. Turkmenistan*, Views of 14 July 2016, UN Doc. CCPR/C/117/D/ 2227/2012; *Nasyrlayev v. Turkmenistan*, Views of 15 July 2016, UN Doc. CCPR/C/117/D/ 2219/2012; *Nurjanov v. Turkmenistan*, Views of 15 July 2016, UN Doc. CCPR/C/117/D/2225/ 2012; *Uchetov v. Turkmenistan*, Views of 15 July 2016, UN Doc. CCPR/C/117/D/2226/2012.

38. See European Commission of Human Rights, *Grandrath v. Germany* (appl. 2299/64), report of 12 December 1966; *G. Z. v. Austria* (appl. 5591/72), decision of 2 April 1973; *X v. Germany* (appl. 7705/76), decision of 5 July 1977; *A. v. Switzerland* (appl. 10640/83), decision of 9 May 1984; European Court of Human Rights, *Bayatyan v. Armenia* (appl. 23459/03), chamber judgment of 27 October 2009.

39. European Court of Human Rights, *Bayatyan v. Armenia* (appl. 23459/03), Grand Chamber judgment of 7 July 2011, paras. 59–64 and 105.

40. European Court of Human Rights, *Bayatyan v. Armenia* (appl. 23459/03), Grand Chamber judgment of 7 July 2011, para. 112; *Erçep v. Turkey* (appl. 43965/04), judgment of 22 November 2011, para. 49.

41. Human Rights Committee, *Atasoy and Sarkut v. Turkey*, Views of 29 March 2012, CCPR/C/104/D/1853–1854/2008, Individual opinion of Committee member Sir Nigel Rodley, jointly with members Mr. Krister Thelin and Mr. Cornelis Flinterman (concurring).

42. See Bielefeldt, Ghanea, and Wiener, *Freedom of Religion or Belief*, 289.

43. Ibid., 269–275.

44. Saïla Ouald Chaib, "Ranjit Singh v. France: The UN Committee asks the questions the Strasbourg Court didn't ask in turban case" (6 March 2012), available online at https:// strasbourgobservers.com/2012/03/06/ranjit-singh-v-france-the-un-committee-asks-the-ques tions-the-strasbourg-court-didnt-ask-in-turban-case/. Please note that this article refers to the UN Human Rights Committee's Views of 22 July 2011 in the case of *Ranjit Singh v. France* (UN Doc. CCPR/C/102/D/1876/2009) and not to the different case decided on 30 June 2009 by the European Court of Human Rights in *Ranjit Singh v. France* (appl. 27561/08).

45. Rosalyn Higgins, "A Babel of Judicial Voices? Ruminations from the Bench," *International and Comparative Law Quarterly*, Vol. 55, No. 4 (2006), 791–804 at 804.

Chapter 8

1. This chapter is in parts based on the annual report submitted by Heiner Bielefeldt as the UN Special Rapporteur on freedom of religion or belief in 2014: see UN Doc. A/HRC/ 28/66.

2. An earlier and shorter draft version of Sections 2, 3, 4, 5, and 7 of this chapter has been published in German: see Heiner Bielefeldt, "Kein unabänderliches Schicksal: Gewalt im Namen der Religion," in *Gewalt—Herrschaft—Religion: Beiträge zur Hermeneutik von Gewalttexten*, ed. Birgit Jeggle-Merz and Michael Durst, 49–71 (Einsiedeln, Switzerland: Paulus Verlag, 2018).

3. See UN Doc. A/HRC/31/18, para. 3. The workshop took place in October 2015 and was jointly organized by the "Religious Track of the Cyprus Peace Project" and the mandate of the UN Special Rapporteur on freedom of religion or belief. It brought together parliamentarians, religious leaders, politicians, human rights defenders, and others from the Middle East and North Africa region.

4. See R. Scott Appleby, *The Ambivalence of the Sacred: Religion, Violence, and Reconciliation* (New York: Rowman and Littlefield, 2000), 30: "To interpret acts of violence and terrorism committed in the name of religion as necessarily motivated by other concerns and lacking in religious qualities is therefore an error."

5. See, for instance, www.theguardian.com/uk-news/2017/jun/07/anti-muslim-hate-crimes-increase-fivefold-since-london-bridge-attacks.

6. See Deana Heath, and Chandana Mathur, eds., *Communalism and Globalization in South Asia and Its Diaspora* (London: Routledge, 2013).

7. UN Doc. A/HRC/39/64, para. 73. See also Azeem Ibrahim, *The Rohingyas: Inside Myanmar's Hidden Genocide* (London: C. Hurst, 2016), 79–98.

8. See Ruth Margalit, "Israel's Jewish-Terrorist Problem," *New Yorker*, 4 August 2015, www.newyorker.com/news/news-desk/israels-jewish-terrorist-problem.

9. See Gay Clark Jennings, "Homophobia in Christian Africa: How the Church Affects LGBT Repression," 27 January 2014, www.huffingtonpost.com/2014/01/27/homophobia-christian-africa_n_4675618.html.

10. An example of militant Christian Islamophobic conspiracies is the book by Joel Richardson, *The Islamic Antichrist: The Shocking Truth About the Real Nature of the Beast* (Los Angeles: WND Books, 2009).

11. See Markus A. Weingardt, *Religion, Macht, Frieden: Das Friedenspotential von Religionen in politischen Gewaltkonflikten* (Stuttgart: Kohlhammer, 2007).

12. See Reinhold Mokrosch, Thomas Held, and Roland Czada, eds., *Religionen und Weltfrieden: Friedens- und Konfliktlösungspotenzial von Religionsgemeinschaften* (Stuttgart: Kohlhammer, 2013).

13. Appleby, *Ambivalence of the Sacred*.

14. See https://derwille.wordpress.com/beitrage/das-interview-mit-hans-peter-raddatz (emphasis added). The interview was conducted in German. Here is the original wording: "Vereinfacht lässt sich sagen, ein Christ missbraucht seine Religion, wenn er Gewalt anwendet, und ein Muslim missbraucht seine Religion ebenso, wenn er Gewalt nicht anwendet."

15. See Tim Allen and Koen Vassenroot, eds., *The Lord's Resistance Army: Myth and Reality* (London: Zed Books, 2010).

16. David Hume, *The Natural History of Religion* (Stanford: Stanford University Press, 1956), 50.

17. See Jan Assmann, *The Price of Monotheism* (Stanford: Stanford University Press, 2010). For a discussion of Assmann's thesis, see the contributions in Rolf Schieder, ed., *Die Gewalt des einen Gottes* (Darmstadt: Wissenschaftliche Buchgesellschaft, 2014).

18. See Peter Sloterdijk, "Im Schatten des Sinai: Fußnote über Ursprünge und Wandlungen totaler Mitgliedschaft," in *Die Gewalt des einen Gottes: Die Monotheismus-Debatte zwischen Jan Assmann, Micha Brumlik, Rolf Schieder, Peter Sloterdijk und anderen*, ed. Rolf Schieder, 124–149 at 131 (Berlin: Berlin University Press, 2014; our translation).

19. Nelson Mandela, *Long Walk to Freedom: The Autobiography of Nelson Mandela* (Boston: Little, Brown, 1994), 542. See also Laurel Wamsley, "Quoting Mandela, Obama's Tweet After Charlottesville Is the Most-Liked Ever," https://www.npr.org/sections/thetwo-way/2017/08/16/543882516/obama-s-tweet-after-charlottesville-is-the-most-liked-tweet-ever.

20. Norani Othman, "The Sociopolitical Dimensions of Islamisation in Malaysia: A Cultural Accommodation of Social Change?," in *Shari'a Law and the Modern Nation-State: A*

Malaysian Symposium, ed. Norani Othman, 123–143 at 128 (Kuala Lumpur: Sisters in Islam Forum, 1994; emphasis in the original).

21. 1 Corinthians 14:34.

22. See Appleby, *Ambivalence of the Sacred*, 30.

23. This is the element of truth in the analysis provided by Assmann, *Price of Monotheism*.

24. See also Chapter 6, Section 3.

25. Markus A. Weingardt, "Religion als politischer Faktor zur Gewaltüberwindung," in *Gewaltfreiheit und Gewalt in den Religionen: Politische und theologische Herausforderungen*, ed. Fernando Enns and Wolfram Weiße, 95–104 at 101 (Münster: Waxmann, 2016).

26. Rabat Plan of Action, UN Doc. A/HRC/22/17/Add.4, appendix, para. 36.

27. See http://www.ohchr.org/Documents/Press/Faith4Rights.pdf.

28. High Commissioner Zeid Ra'ad Al Hussein referred to "the soft law standards emerging from Rabat and Beirut" (see http://www.ohchr.org/EN/NewsEvents/Pages/DisplayNews.aspx?NewsID;eq22504&LangID = E); and Special Rapporteur Ahmed Shaheed quoted the Beirut Declaration in his 2018 report to the Human Rights Council (A/HRC/37/49, para. 29) under the chapter "C. International legal standards; 1. Hard and soft law." In general see John Cerone, "A Taxonomy of Soft Law: Stipulating a Definition," in *Tracing the Roles of Soft Law in Human Rights*, ed. Stéphanie Lagoutte, Thomas Gammeltoft-Hansen, and John Cerone, 15–26 (Oxford: Oxford University Press, 2016).

29. Human Rights Council resolution 34/22, Situation of human rights in Myanmar, adopted on 24 March 2017; and resolution 37/32, adopted on 23 March 2018.

30. Human Rights Council resolution 30/15, Human rights and preventing and countering violent extremism, adopted on 2 October 2015.

31. European Court of Human Rights, *Mariya Alekhina and Others v. Russia* (appl. 38004/12) of 17 July 2018, paras. 110, 187, 190–191, and 223; as well as in the partly dissenting opinion of Judge Elósegui, para. 14.

32. For reports of the Secretary-General see UN Docs. S/2018/25, para. 27; A/72/219, para. 26; A/72/381, para. 94; A/73/1, para. 93; A/73/153, paras. 16 and 51; A/73/371, para. 64; A/73/391, para. 28. For reports of the High Commissioner or OHCHR see UN Docs. A/HRC/34/35, para. 91; A/HRC/37/3, para. 69; A/HRC/37/22, para. 38; A/HRC/37/26, paras. 27–29; A/HRC/37/44, paras. 28 and 80; A/HRC/38/CRP.2, para. 49; A/HRC/39/24, para. 31; A/HRC/39/33, para. 77; A/HRC/40/30, paras. 45 and 83; A/HRC/WG.6/31/NGA/2, para. 13. For reports of the Special Rapporteur on freedom of religion or belief see UN Docs. A/72/365, paras. 28, 60, 78, and 83; A/73/362, paras. 63, 67–68, and 79–80; A/HRC/37/49, paras. 29 and 89; A/HRC/40/58, paras. 21 and 66, and annexes I and II.

33. See UN Doc. CEDAW/C/NGA/CO/7–8, para. 12; and with explicit references to "Faith for Rights" in UN Doc. CEDAW/C/SR.1518, para. 16 concerning Nigeria. See also UN Docs. CEDAW/C/SR.1516, para. 28 concerning Niger; CEDAW/C/SR.1508, para. 20; and CEDAW/C/CRI/CO/7, para. 15 concerning Costa Rica; CEDAW/C/SR.1578, para. 62 concerning Fiji; and CEDAW/C/SR.1678; para. 24 concerning Botswana.

34. See http://www.ohchr.org/EN/NewsEvents/Pages/DisplayNews.aspx?NewsID;eq22 125&LangID = E.

35. See Andreas Hasenclever, "Zwischen Himmel und Hölle: Überlegungen zur Politisierung von Religion in bewaffneten Konflikten," in *Gewaltfreiheit und Gewalt in den Religionen:*

Politische und theologische Herausforderungen, ed. Fernando Enns and Wolfram Weiße, 53–74 (Münster: Waxmann, 2016).

36. The purpose cannot be to end up with yet another version of fatalism, owing to the multiplicity of complicated structural factors, but an increased awareness of the challenges that lie ahead.

37. For more details, see also Section 8(a) of this chapter.

38. See Wilfried Buchta, *Terror vor Europas Toren: Der Islamische Staat, Iraks Zerfall und Amerikas Ohnmacht* (Frankfurt: Campus, 2015).

39. Martha C. Nussbaum, *The New Religious Intolerance: Overcoming the Politics of Fear in an Anxious Age* (Cambridge, Mass.: Harvard University Press, 2012). On pp. 20–58 Nussbaum analyses fear as a particularly "narcissistic" emotion that hinders the development of empathy.

40. For example, the conflict between Protestants and Catholics in Northern Ireland in the late twentieth century had little or nothing to do with theological issues, such as the understanding of the sacraments, but all the more displayed main features of militant rivalry between inimical "tribes." See Rüdiger Noll, "The Role of Religion and Religious Freedom in Contemporary Conflict Situations," in *Facilitating Freedom of Religion or Belief: A Deskbook*, ed. Tore Lindholm, W. Cole Durham Jr., and Bahia G. Tahzib-Lie, 747–760 at 752–753 (Leiden: Martinus Nijhoff, 2004).

41. Mark Juergensmeyer, *Terror in the Mind of God: The Global Rise of Religious Violence*, updated ed. (Berkeley: University of California Press, 2000), 123.

42. See http://www.ohchr.org/EN/NewsEvents/Pages/DisplayNews.aspx?LangID;eqE& NewsID = 16966; and http://www.ohchr.org/EN/NewsEvents/Pages/DisplayNews.aspx?News ID;eq22165&LangID = E.

43. See UN Doc. A/HRC/34/30, para. 56.

44. For more details, see the discussion on limitations in Chapter 2, Section 3.

45. See UN Doc. A/73/362, para. 8.

46. See http://english.conseil-etat.fr/Activities/Press-releases/The-Council-of-State-or ders-a-decision-banning-clothes-demonstrating-an-obvious-religious-affiliation-to-be-sus pended.

47. See UN Doc. A/HRC/22/17/Add.4, appendix.

48. For more details, see the discussion in Chapter 4, Section 2.

49. See Rabat Plan of Action, UN Doc. A/HRC/22/17/Add.4, appendix, para. 29; as well as Beirut Declaration on "Faith for Rights," Un Doc. A/HRC/40/58, annex I, para. 20.

50. See Hannah Arendt, "Truth and Politics," *New Yorker*, 25 February 1967, 49–88.

51. See Rabat Plan of Action, UN Doc. A/HRC/22/17/Add.4, appendix, para. 25; as well as eighteen commitments on "Faith for Rights," UN Doc. A/HRC/40/58, annex II, commitment 11.

52. Appleby, *Ambivalence of the Sacred*, 17.

53. Hasenclever, "Zwischen Himmel und Hölle," 70 (our translation).

54. Appleby, *Ambivalence of the Sacred*, 16 (emphasis in the original).

55. It should be noted that this is not always the case. Religious peace activities can be traced far back in history; they historically precede the establishment of modern human rights standards.

56. It is in this spirit that the preamble of the UDHR proclaims that "recognition of the inherent dignity and of the equal and inalienable rights of all members of the human family is the foundation of freedom, justice and peace in the world."

57. Depending on the interpretation of "liberalism," one may well term freedom of religion or belief a "liberal right." Yet it does not privilege liberal over conservative theologies. The assessment of theologies on their merits remains outside of the remit of human rights.

58. For more details, see Chapter 5, Sections 3–4.

59. Some reformers may claim that their "innovation" is actually only a rediscovery of original insights, which had been overshadowed or fallen into oblivion.

60. See Gordon W. Allport, *The Nature of Prejudice* (Cambridge, Mass.: Addison Wesley, 1954).

61. For more details see UN Doc. A/66/156.

62. See UN Doc. A/HRC/19/60/Add.2, para. 44.

63. For the following see UN Doc. A/HRC/31/18/Add.1, paras. 28–32.

64. For the following see UN Doc. A/HRC/25/58/Add.1, paras. 12–19, 26 and 30–32.

65. See the mural in Freetown by the street artist Vhils, celebrating Sierra Leone's inter- and intra-religious tolerance, https://www.instagram.com/p/BqLF5tvAT-6/: "This special project culminated in the depiction of two local children, Paul and Alfreda, who belong to the same family—the boy being a Christian and the girl a Muslim. A country where it is common to have members of the same family belonging to different religions can teach us a lot about tolerance."

66. See www.religionsforpeace.org.

67. Noll, "The Role of Religion and Religious Freedom in Contemporary Conflict Situations," 757.

68. Monica Duffy Toft, Daniel Philpott, and Timothy Samuel Shah, *God's Century: Resurgent Religion and Global Politics* (New York: W. W. Norton, 2011), 205.

69. Mary Robinson, "Foreword," in *Facilitating Freedom of Religion or Belief: A Deskbook*, ed. Tore Lindholm, W. Cole Durham Jr., and Bahia G. Tahzib-Lie, xix–xx at xix (Leiden: Martinus Nijhoff, 2004).

Chapter 9

1. See https://www.archives.gov/founding-docs/declaration-transcript.

2. See https://www.conseil-constitutionnel.fr/sites/default/files/as/root/bank_mm/anglais/cst2.pdf.

3. Immanuel Kant, "Toward Perpetual Peace: A Philosophical Project," in *Practical Philosophy*, 316–351 (Cambridge: Cambridge University Press, 1996), 325.

4. Immanuel Kant, "What Is Enlightenment?," in *Practical Philosophy*, 16–22 (Cambridge: Cambridge University Press, 1996), 20.

5. See Émile Durkheim, *Les formes élémentaires de la vie religieuse* (Paris: Félix Alcan, 1912).

6. Hans Joas, *The Sacredness of the Person: A New Genealogy of Human Rights* (Washington, D.C.: Georgetown University Press, 2013).

7. For an overview, see Arlene Swidler, ed., *Human Rights in Religious Traditions* (New York: Pilgrim Press, 1982).

8. Immanuel Kant, "Critique of Practical Reason," in *Practical Philosophy*, 137–271 at 269. This dictum, which sums up Kant's practical philosophy, has been carved in his tombstone.

9. Jeremy Waldron, *One Another's Equals: The Basis of Human Equality* (Cambridge, Mass.: Harvard University Press, 2017), 196.

10. We have limited ourselves to a few examples from the Bible and the Qur'an for the simple reason that we know these religious texts better than other scriptures or traditions.

11. See Wolfgang Fikentscher, "Die heutige Bedeutung des nicht-säkularen Ursprungs der Grundrechte," in *Menschenrechte und Menschenwürde: Historische Voraussetzungen— säkulare Gestalt—christliches Verständnis*, ed. Ernst-Wolfgang Böckenförde and Robert Spaemann, 43–73 (Stuttgart: Klett-Cotta, 1987).

12. The Universal Islamic Declaration of Human Rights (1981) proclaims in its foreword: "Islam gave to mankind an ideal code of human rights fourteen centuries ago." Cited from http://hrlibrary.umn.edu/instree/islamic_declaration_HR.html. See also Heiner Bielefeldt, " 'Western' Versus 'Islamic' Human Rights Conceptions? A Critique of Cultural Essentialism in the Discussion on Human Rights," *Political Theory*, Vol. 28 (2000), 90–121.

13. See David Little, Abdulaziz A. Sachedina, and John Kelsay, "Human Rights and World's Religions: Christianity, Islam and Religious Liberty," in *Religion and Human Rights: Why Protect Freedom of Religion or Belief and Models for Protection of Freedom of Religion or Belief?*, ed. Nazila Ghanea, 57–83 (New York: Routledge, 2010).

14. See OHCHR, *The Beirut Declaration and Its 18 Commitments on "Faith for Rights,"* UN Doc. A/HRC/40/58, annex I, para. 1 and annex II.

15. See Johannes Morsink, *The Universal Declaration of Human Rights and the Challenge of Religion* (Columbia: University of Missouri Press, 2017).

16. See Christoph Engel, "Law as a Precondition for Religious Freedom," in "Secularism and Religious Freedom," *Fides et Libertas: The Journal of the International Religious Liberty Association*, 2011, 18–35 at 26: "The attitude of most religions towards freedom of religion as a constitutional guarantee is ambivalent at best."

17. For an overview see Konrad Hilpert, *Menschenrechte und Theologie: Forschungsbeiträge zur ethischen Dimension der Menschenrechte* (Freiburg: Herder, 2001), 390–397.

18. See www.papalencyclicals.net/pius06/quod-aliquantum.htm.

19. See http://www.ewtn.com/library/PAPALDOC/P9SYLL.HTM.

20. See www.cctwincities.org/wp-content/uploads/2015/10/Pacem-in-Terris.pdf.

21. See http://www.vatican.va/archive/hist_councils/ii_vatican_council/documents/vat -ii_decl_19651207_dignitatis-humanae_en.html.

22. See Ernst Troeltsch, *Die Soziallehren der christlichen Kirchen und Gruppen* (Tübingen: J. C. B Mohr, 1912).

23. See Joachim Willems, "Die Russisch-Orthodoxe Kirche und die Menschenrechte," in *Schwerpunkt: Religionsfreiheit*, ed. Heiner Bielefeldt, Volkmar Deile, Brigitte Hamm, Franz-Josef Hutter, Sabine Kurtenbach, and Hanne Tretter, Jahrbuch Menschenrechte 2009, 152–165 (Vienna: Böhlau, 2008).

24. See Ann E. Mayer, *Islam and Human Rights: Tradition and Politics*, 5th ed. (Boulder, Colo.: Westview, 2012).

25. This motto has been ascribed to the ancient Greek sophist Protagoras.

26. See UN Human Rights Council resolutions 12/21, 16/3, and 21/3.

27. Peter Petkoff, "Religious Exceptionalism, Religious Rights, and Public International Law," in *The Changing Nature of Religious Rights Under International Law*, ed. Malcolm D. Evans, Peter Petkoff, and Julian Rivers, 211–234 at 224 (Oxford: Oxford University Press, 2015).

28. See Moscow Patriarchate 2008, *The Russian Orthodox Church's Basic Teachings on Human Dignity, Freedom and Rights*, I.5, http://www.mospat.ru/en/documents/dignity-free dom-rights/i/.

29. Ibid., I.2 (emphasis in the original).

30. Article 1 of the Cairo Declaration of Human Rights in Islam, UN Doc. A/CONF.157/ PC/62/Add.18. For an analysis of the Cairo Declaration see Ioana Cismas, *Religious Actors and International Law* (Oxford: Oxford University Press, 2014), 255–285.

31. See Article 6 of the Cairo Declaration.

32. See Article 10 of the Cairo Declaration.

33. See Articles 24 and 25 of the Cairo Declaration.

34. Many of the "humanistic gymnasiums" in Germany are actually run by the Catholic Church. While in German this observation holds no surprise, in English it may come close to an oxymoron.

35. Richard Dawkins, *The God Delusion* (London: Bantam Press, 2006).

36. See Mahmoud Bassiouni, *Menschenrechte zwischen Universalität und islamischer Legitimität* (Frankfurt: Suhrkamp, 2014), 234–241.

37. See Stephen Hopgood's prognosis of an imminent end of the human rights era, which he bases on a postreligious conceptualization of human rights, thus concluding that with the recent reemergence of religiosity in international politics, human rights are per definition doomed to collapse. See Stephen Hopgood, "The Endtimes of Human Rights," in *Debating the Endtimes of Human Rights: Activism and Institutions in a Neo-Westphalian World*, ed. Doutje Lettinga and Lars van Troost, 11–18 at 17 (Amsterdam: Amnesty International Netherlands, 2014): "The new salience of religion globally . . . means that the foundations on which secular human rights were based are not available universally."

38. The reference to a particular history, namely, European history, does not imply that Europe provides the binding model which people from other parts of the world should merely emulate. Our reason to focus on European experiences stems from our higher degree of familiarity with that region.

39. Within the limits of this chapter, we cannot engage in a discussion of difficult cases, where the potential of responsible agency may appear questionable. The axiomatic status of the ascription of human dignity requires that even such cases must be covered by respect for human dignity. See Heiner Bielefeldt, *Auslaufmodell Menschenwürde? Warum sie in Frage steht und warum wir sie verteidigen müssen* (Freiburg: Herder, 2011).

40. See Jeremy Waldron, *Dignity, Rank, and Rights*, with comments by Wai Chee Dimock, Don Herzog, and Michael Rosen, ed. Meir Dan-Cohen, paperback (Oxford: Oxford University Press, 2015), 33: "So that is my hypothesis: the modern notion of *human* dignity involves an upwards equalization of rank, so that we now try to accord to every human being something of the dignity, rank, and expectation of respect that was formerly accorded to nobility." (emphasis in the original)

41. The sentence culminates in the admonition that all human beings "should act towards one another in a spirit of brotherhood." The obvious androcentric bias may be one of the reasons accounting for the lack of popularity of the whole sentence.

42. See Waldron, *One Another's Equals*, 215–256.

43. We cannot embark here on a discussion about nonhuman animals and their normative status. In short, our position is the following: while nonhuman animals have moral claims to decent treatment by humans, they are not partners, with whom to share normative responsibility. It is for this reason that we reserve the language of rights to human beings.

44. Our reflection draws on John Rawls, who in his *Political Liberalism* (New York: Columbia University Press, 1993), proposes a distinction between the legally binding concept

of "political justice," on the one hand, and a multiplicity of "comprehensive doctrines," on the other. This differentiation is supposed to facilitate a broad endorsement of the guiding idea of political justice within a pluralistic society, which is characterized by a rich diversity of religious or nonreligious worldviews, philosophies, and so on. Rawls's main point is that the guiding idea of political justice is inherently limited in its scope by having its focus on basic normative issues of fair coexistence and cooperation. Only on the understanding of such inherent limitedness can the idea of political justice claim a practical priority over the various existing worldviews ("comprehensive doctrines"). Whereas the idea of political justice claims a clear priority at the level of politics and law, the various comprehensive doctrines may in many ways exceed the realm of political justice. Rawls's purpose is the facilitation of an "overlapping consensus" which accommodates a broad variety of religions, philosophies, and worldviews, whose holders may nonetheless be able to endorse the main principles of political justice that normatively govern societal coexistence and cooperation.

45. On the German "Kulturkampf" between the newly erected modern state and the Catholic Church, which culminated during the 1870s, see Thomas Nipperdey, *Religion im Umbruch: Deutschland 1870–1918* (Munich: C. H. Beck, 1988), 9–62; Johannes Wallmann, *Kirchengeschichte Deutschlands seit der Reformation*, 6th ed. (Tübingen: Mohr Siebeck, 2006), 235–257.

46. See also James Griffin, *On Human Rights* (Oxford: Oxford University Press, 2008), 41: "Human rights do not exhaust the whole moral domain; they do not exhaust even the whole domain of justice and fairness."

47. David N. Stamos, *The Myth of Universal Human Rights: Its Origin, History, and Explanation; Along with a More Humane Way* (Abingdon: Routledge, 2016), 255.

48. See Stephen Hopgood, *The Endtimes of Human Rights* (Ithaca, N.Y.: Cornell University Press, 2013), ix. When writing about the High Commissioner, Hopgood refers to Mary Robinson.

49. This is not to say that human rights are "neutral" concerning doctrinal issues. However, the trust of their authorities rests on the establishment of normative standards, which themselves aim to accommodate the unfolding of diverse convictions and related practices.

50. See Ludwig Feuerbach, *Vorlesungen über das Wesen der Religion* (Leipzig: Otto Wigand, 1851), 241.

51. See David Hume, *The Natural History of Religion* (Stanford: Stanford University Press, 1956), 29: "There is a universal tendency among mankind to conceive all beings like themselves."

52. See Karl Marx, "Contribution to the Critique of Hegel's Philosophy of Law: Introduction," in Karl Marx and Friedrich Engels, *Collected Works*, vol. 3 (New York: International Publishers, 1976).

53. Michael Ignatieff, *Human Rights as Politics and Idolatry*, ed. and intro. Amy Gutmann (Princeton: Princeton University Press, 2001), 53.

54. In the wake of Michael Walzer it has become fashionable to distinguish between "thick" and "thin" moral arguments. While "thick" arguments presuppose comprehensive moral values, a "thin" position is limited in its claim in order to accommodate a variety of more substantial positions. For an understanding of human rights, however, this juxtaposition is misleading, because their focus on fostering human freedom simultaneously accounts for both their "thickness" (i.e., their specific authority) and their "thinness" (i.e., their nondoctrinal character). See Michael Walzer, *Thick and Thin: Moral Argument at Home and Abroad* (Notre Dame, Ind.: University of Notre Dame Press, 1994).

55. www.vatican.va/archive/hist_councils/ii_vatican_council/documents/vat-ii_decl_19651207_dignitatis-humanae_en.html, para. 1. For an in-depth interpretation of the encyclical see Marianne Heimbach-Steins, *Religionsfreiheit: Ein Menschenrecht unter Druck* (Paderborn: Schöningh, 2012), 53–101.

56. See the proposed amendment to draft Article 1 submitted by Brazil in the Third Committee of the General Assembly, UN Doc. A/C.3/215.

57. The Chinese government was not yet Communist at this time.

58. See Wolfgang Vögele, "Christliche Elemente in der Begründung von Menschenrechten und Menschenwürde im Kontext der Entstehung der Vereinten Nationen," in *Ethik der Menschenrechte: Zum Streit um die Universalität einer Idee*, vol. 1, ed. Hans-Richard Reuter, 103–133 at 122. (Tübingen: Mohr Siebeck, 1999).

59. See the above examples (in Section 3 of this chapter) from the Cairo Declaration and the Russian Orthodox Church's Basic Teachings on Human Dignity, Freedom and Rights.

60. Sheila Benhabib has proposed a "dual track approach" in the understanding of human dignity and human rights. The dual track approach accommodates specific readings of the basic principles of human rights, including religious or philosophical in-depth interpretations of human dignity and other principles, while at the same time upholding the established consensus around the existing normative standards. Both tracks are equally important, but should be kept distinct. See Sheila Benhabib, *The Claims of Culture: Equality and Diversity in the Global Era* (Princeton: Princeton University Press, 2002).

61. Tore Lindholm, "Philosophical and Religious Justifications of Freedom of Religion or Belief," in *Facilitating Freedom of Religion or Belief: A Deskbook*, ed. Tore Lindholm, W. Cole Durham Jr., and Bahia G. Tahzib-Lie, 19–61 at 60 (Leiden: Martinus Nijhoff, 2004).

62. See the reports by Forum 18, including www.forum18.org/archive.php?article_id = 2297.

63. The autonomy which religious communities can claim under freedom of religion or belief does not exempt them from all forms of state interference.

64. See Alison Stuart, "Freedom of Religion and Gender Equality: Inclusive or Exclusive?," *Human Rights Law Review*, Vol. 10 (2010), 429–459 at 447: "If religious institutions or beliefs are internally discriminating against or causing discrimination against women, then States are obliged to take action to prevent any such discrimination."

65. Ibid., 444.

66. Peter G. Kirchschläger, *Menschenrechte und Religionen: Nicht-staatliche Akteure und ihr Verhältnis zu den Menschenrechten* (Paderborn: Schöningh, 2016), 138 (our translation).

BIBLIOGRAPHY

Monographs, Books, and Chapters

Alidadi, Katayoun. *Religion, Equality and Employment in Europe: The Case for Reasonable Accommodation.* Oxford: Hart Publishing, 2017.

Allen, Tim, and Koen Vassenroot, eds. *The Lord's Resistance Army: Myth and Reality.* London: Zed Books, 2010.

Allport, Gordon W. *The Nature of Prejudice.* Cambridge, Mass.: Addison Wesley, 1954.

An-Na'im, Abdullahi Ahmed. *Islam and the Secular State: Negotiating the Future of Shari'a.* Cambridge, Mass.: Harvard University Press, 2010.

Anwar, Zainah. "From Local to Global: Sisters in Islam and the Making of Musawah." In *Gender and Equality in Muslim Family Law: Justice and Ethics in the Islamic Legal Tradition,* ed. Ziba Mir-Hosseini, Kari Vogt, Lena Larsen, and Christian Moe, 107–124. London: Tauris, 2013.

Appleby, R. Scott. *The Ambivalence of the Sacred: Religion, Violence, and Reconciliation.* New York: Rowman and Littlefield, 2000.

Aristotle. *The Nicomachean Ethics,* trans. J. E. C. Welldon. Buffalo: Prometheus Press, 1987.

Aristotle. *Politics,* trans. H. Rackham. Cambridge, Mass.: Harvard University Press, 1932.

Asad, Talal. *Formations of the Secular: Christianity, Islam, Modernity.* Stanford: Stanford University Press, 2003.

Assmann, Jan. *The Price of Monotheism.* Stanford: Stanford University Press, 2010.

Bassiouni, Mahmoud. *Menschenrechte zwischen Universalität und islamischer Legitimität.* Frankfurt: Suhrkamp, 2014.

Baubérot, Jean. *La laïcité, quel héritage? De 1789 à nos jours.* Geneva: Labor et Fides, 1990.

Beaman, Lori G. "Beyond Establishment." In *Politics of Religious Freedom,* ed. Winnifred Fallers Sullivan, Elizabeth Shakman Hurd, Saba Mahmood, and Peter G. Danchin, 207–219. Chicago: University of Chicago Press, 2015.

Beaman, Lori G. *Deep Equality in an Era of Religious Diversity.* Oxford: Oxford University Press, 2017.

Benhabib, Sheila. *The Claims of Culture: Equality and Diversity in the Global Era.* Princeton: Princeton University Press, 2002.

Bielefeldt, Heiner. *Auslaufmodell Menschenwürde? Warum sie in Frage steht und warum wir sie verteidigen müssen.* Freiburg: Herder, 2011.

Bielefeldt, Heiner. "Historical and Philosophical Foundations of Human Rights." In *International Protection of Human Rights: A Textbook,* ed. Martin Scheinin and Catarina Krause, 3–18. Turku: Åbo Akademi University, 2009.

Bielefeldt, Heiner. "Kein unabänderliches Schicksal: Gewalt im Namen der Religion." In *Gewalt—Herrschaft—Religion: Beiträge zur Hermeneutik von Gewalttexten*, ed. Birgit Jeggle-Merz and Michael Durst, 49–71. Einsiedeln, Switzerland: Paulus Verlag, 2018.

Bielefeldt, Heiner. "Menschenrecht, kein Sonderrecht." In *Beschneidung: Das Zeichen des Bundes in der Kritik; Zur Debatte um das Kölner Urteil*, ed. Johannes Heil and Stephan J. Kramer, 71–82. Berlin: Metropol, 2012.

Bielefeldt, Heiner. *Menschenrechte in der Einwanderungsgesellschaft: Plädoyer für einen aufgeklärten Multikulturalismus*. Bielefeld: transcript Verlag, 2007.

Bielefeldt, Heiner. *Philosophie der Menschenrechte: Grundlagen eines weltweiten Freiheitsethos*. Darmstadt: Wissenschaftliche Buchgesellschaft, 1998.

Bielefeldt, Heiner. *Symbolic Representation in Kant's Practical Philosophy*. Cambridge: Cambridge University Press, 2003.

Bielefeldt, Heiner. "Verletzungen der Religionsfreiheit weltweit: Ursachen und Erscheinungsformen im Überblick." In *Religionsfreiheit im säkularen Staat: Aktuelle Auslegungsfragen in der Schweiz, in Deutschland und weltweit*, ed. Julia Hänni, Sebastian Heselhaus, and Adrian Loretan, 193–210. Zurich: Dike, 2019.

Bielefeldt, Heiner, Nazila Ghanea, and Michael Wiener. *Freedom of Religion or Belief: An International Law Commentary*. Oxford: Oxford University Press, 2016.

Bouchard, Gérard, and Charles Taylor. *Building the Future: A Time for Reconciliation; Abridged Report*. Quebec: Government of Quebec, 2008.

Buchta, Wilfried. *Terror vor Europas Toren: Der Islamische Staat, Iraks Zerfall und Amerikas Ohnmacht*. Frankfurt: Campus, 2015.

Caceres, Gabrielle. "Reasonable Accommodation as a Tool to Manage Religious Diversity in the Workplace: What About the 'Transposability' of an American Concept in the French Secular Context?" In *A Test of Faith? Religious Diversity and Accommodation in the European Workplace*, ed. Katayoun Alidadi, Marie-Claire Foblets, and Jogchum Vrielink, 283–316. London: Ashgate, 2012.

Çalı, Başak, and Mariana Montoya. *The March of Universality? Religion-Based Reservations to the Core UN Treaties and What They Tell Us About Human Rights and Universality in the 21st Century: Policy Report*. Versoix: Universal Rights Group, 2017.

Casanova, José. *Public Religions in the Modern World*. Chicago: University of Chicago Press, 1994.

Casanova, José. "The Religious Situation in Europe." In *Secularization and the World Religions*, ed. Hans Joas and Klaus Wiegand, 206–228. Liverpool: Liverpool University Press, 2009.

Cassirer, Ernst. *Die Philosophie der Aufklärung*. Hamburg: Meiner, 1998.

Ceming, Katharina. *Ernstfall Menschenrechte: Die Würde des Menschen und die Weltreligionen*. Munich: Kösel, 2010.

Cerone, John. "A Taxonomy of Soft Law: Stipulating a Definition." In *Tracing the Roles of Soft Law in Human Rights*, ed. Stéphanie Lagoutte, Thomas Gammeltoft-Hansen, and John Cerone, 15–26. Oxford: Oxford University Press, 2016.

Christoffersen, Lisbet. "Sacred Spaces in Secular (Post-) Lutheran Contexts." In *Secular and Sacred? The Scandinavian Case of Religion in Human Rights, Law and Public Space*, ed. Rosemarie van den Breemer, José Casanova, and Trygve Wyller, 102–122. Göttingen: Vandenhoek and Ruprecht, 2014.

Cismas, Ioana. *Religious Actors and International Law*. Oxford: Oxford University Press, 2014.

Comte, August. *Système de politique positive, ou Traité de sociologie, instituant la religion de l'humanité.* Vol. 3. Paris: Les presses universitaires de France, 1853.

Cumper, Peter. "Freedom of Religion and Human Rights Laws—Awkward Bedfellows." In *Equality and Human Rights: Nothing but Trouble? Liber amicorum Titia Loenen,* ed. Marjolein van den Brink, Susanne Burri, and Jenny Goldschmidt, 283–304. Utrecht: Netherlands Institute of Human Rights, 2015.

Danchin, Peter G. "Religious Freedom in the Panopticon of Enlightenment Rationality." In *Politics of Religious Freedom,* ed. Winnifred Fallers Sullivan, Elizabeth Shakman Hurd, Saba Mahmood, and Peter G. Danchin, 240–252. Chicago: University of Chicago Press, 2015.

Davie, Grace. *Religion in Britain: A Persistent Paradox.* 2nd ed. Chichester: Wiley-Blackwell, 2015.

Davies, Margaret. "Pluralism in Law and Religion." In *Law and Religion in Theoretical and Historical Contexts,* ed. Peter Cane, Carolyn Evans, and Zoe Robinson, 72–99. Cambridge: Cambridge University Press, 2008.

Dawkins, Richard. *The God Delusion.* London: Bantam Press, 2006.

DeGirolami, Marc O. *The Tragedy of Religious Freedom.* Cambridge, Mass.: Harvard University Press, 2013.

Di Fabio, Udo. *Gewissen, Glaube, Religion: Wandelt sich die Religionsfreiheit?* Freiburg: Herder, 2012.

Durham, W. Cole, Jr. "Patterns of Religion State Relations." In *Religion and Human Rights: An Introduction,* ed. John Witte Jr. and M. Christian Green, 360–378. Oxford: Oxford University Press, 2012.

Durham, W. Cole, Jr. "Religion and Equality: Reconcilable Differences?" In *Religion and Equality: Law in Conflict,* ed. W. Cole Durham Jr. and Donlu D. Thayer, 185–202. London: Routledge, 2016.

Durham, W. Cole, Jr., and Brett G. Scharffs. *Law and Religion: National, International, and Comparative Perspectives.* New York: Aspen, 2010.

Durkheim, Émile. *Les formes élémentaires de la vie religieuse.* Paris: Félix Alcan, 1912.

Dworkin, Ronald. *Religion Without God.* Cambridge, Mass.: Harvard University Press, 2013.

Dworkin, Ronald. "Rights as Trumps." In *Theory of Rights,* ed. Jeremy Waldron, 153–167. Oxford: Oxford University Press, 1984.

Evans, Malcolm D. "Historical Analysis of Freedom of Religion or Belief as a Technique for Resolving Religious Conflict." In *Facilitating Freedom of Religion or Belief: A Deskbook,* ed. Tore Lindholm, W. Cole Durham Jr., and Bahia G. Tahzib-Lie, 1–17. Leiden: Martinus Nijhoff, 2004.

Feuerbach, Ludwig. *Vorlesungen über das Wesen der Religion.* Leipzig: Otto Wigand, 1851.

Fikentscher, Wolfgang. "Die heutige Bedeutung des nicht-säkularen Ursprungs der Grundrechte." In *Menschenrechte und Menschenwürde: Historische Voraussetzungen—säkulare Gestalt—christliches Verständnis,* ed. Ernst-Wolfgang Böckenförde and Robert Spaemann, 43–73. Stuttgart: Klett-Cotta, 1987.

Foblets, Marie-Claire, and Katayoun Alidadi. "The RELIGARE Report: Religion in the Context of the European Union; Engaging the Interplay Between Religious Diversity and Secular Models." In *Belief, Law and Politics: What Future for a Secular Europe?,* ed. Marie-Claire Foblets, Katayoun Alidadi, Jørgen S. Nielsen, and Zeynep Yanasmayan, 11–50. Farnham: Ashgate, 2014.

Fokas, Effie. "Greece: Religion, Nation and European Identity." In *Citizenship and Ethnic Conflict: Challenging the Nation State*, ed. H. Gulalp, 39–60. London: Routledge, 2006.

Forester, Vera. *Lessing und Moses Mendelssohn: Geschichte einer Freundschaft.* Darmstadt: Wissenschaftliche Buchgesellschaft, 2010.

Gerhard, Ute, Mechthild Jansen, Andrea Maihofer, Pia Schmid, and Irmgard Schulz, eds. *Differenz und Gleichheit: Menschenrechte haben (k)ein Geschlecht.* Frankfurt: Ulrich Helmer Verlag, 1990.

Glendon, Mary Ann. "Is Religious Freedom an 'Orphaned' Right?" In *The Changing Nature of Religious Rights Under International Law*, ed. Malcolm D. Evans, Peter Petkoff, and Julian Rivers, 1–8. Oxford: Oxford University Press, 2015.

Gözaydin, Istar. "Management of Religion in Turkey: The *Diyanet* and Beyond." In *Freedom of Religion or Belief in Turkey*, ed. Özgür Heval Cinar and Mine Yilderim, 10–35. Newcastle upon Tyne: Cambridge Scholars Publishing, 2014.

Graf, Friedrich Wilhelm. *Götter Global: Wie die Welt zum Supermarkt der Religionen wird.* Munich: C. H. Beck, 2014.

Griffin, James. *On Human Rights.* Oxford: Oxford University Press, 2008.

Guiora, Amos N. *Freedom from Religion: Rights and National Security.* 2nd ed. Oxford: Oxford University Press, 2013.

Gunn, T. Jeremy. "Permissible Limitations on the Freedom of Religion or Belief." In *Religion and Human Rights: An Introduction*, ed. John Witte Jr. and M. Christian Green, 254–268. Oxford: Oxford University Press, 2012.

Gunn, T. Jeremy. "Secularism, the Secular, and Secularization." In *Trends of Secularism in a Pluralistic World*, ed. Jaime Contreras and Rosa María Martínez de Codes, 59–105. Madrid: Iberoamericana, 2013.

Gunn, T. Jeremy, and John Witte Jr., eds. *No Establishment of Religion: America's Original Contribution to Religious Liberty.* Oxford: Oxford University Press, 2012.

Habermas, Jürgen. "Religion in der Öffentlichkeit: Kognitive Voraussetzungen für den 'öffentlichen Vernunftgebrauch' religiöser und säkularer Bürger." In *Zwischen Naturalismus und Religion: Philosophische Aufsätze*, ed. Jürgen Habermas, 119–154. Frankfurt: Suhrkamp, 2005.

Habermas, Jürgen. "Struggles for Recognition in the Democratic Constitutional State." In *Multiculturalism: Examining the Politics of Recognition*, ed. Amy Gutmann, 148–197. Princeton: Princeton University Press, 1994.

Haeckel, Ernst. *Die Welträtsel: Gemeinverständliche Studien über monistische Philosophie.* Reprint, Stuttgart: Kröner, 1984.

Hasenclever, Andreas. "Zwischen Himmel und Hölle: Überlegungen zur Politisierung von Religion in bewaffneten Konflikten." In *Gewaltfreiheit und Gewalt in den Religionen: Politische und theologische Herausforderungen*, ed. Fernando Enns and Wolfram Weiße, 53–74. Münster: Waxmann, 2016.

Heath, Deana, and Chandana Mathur, eds. *Communalism and Globalization in South Asia and Its Diaspora.* London: Routledge, 2013.

Hegel, Georg Wilhelm Friedrich. *Vorlesungen über die Philosophie der Geschichte.* Vol. 12 of *Werke.* Frankfurt: Suhrkamp, 1986.

Heil, Johannes, and Stephan J. Kramer, eds. *Beschneidung: Das Zeichen des Bundes in der Kritik; Zur Debatte um das Kölner Urteil.* Berlin: Metropol Verlag, 2012.

Heimbach-Steins, Marianne. *Religionsfreiheit: Ein Menschenrecht unter Druck.* Paderborn: Schöningh, 2012.

Hesse, Konrad. *Grundzüge des Verfassungsrechts der Bundesrepublik Deutschland.* 20th ed. Reprint, Heidelberg: C. F. Müller, 1999.

Hilpert, Konrad. *Menschenrechte und Theologie: Forschungsbeiträge zur ethischen Dimension der Menschenrechte.* Freiburg: Herder, 2001.

Hoffmann, Anja Nicole. "Measuring Freedom of Religion: An Analysis of Religious Freedom Indexes." Master's thesis, Vienna, 2017.

Holyoake, George J. *English Secularism: A Confession of Belief.* Chicago: Open Publishing, 1896.

Hopgood, Stephen. *The Endtimes of Human Rights.* Ithaca, N.Y.: Cornell University Press, 2013.

Horkheimer, Max, and Theodor W. Adorno. *Dialectic of Enlightenment: Philosophical Fragments*, trans. Edmund Jephcott. Stanford: Stanford University Press, 2002.

Hume, David. *The Natural History of Religion.* Stanford: Stanford University Press, 1956.

Huntington, Samuel P. *The Clash of Civilizations and the Remaking of World Order.* New York: Simon and Schuster, 1996.

Hurd, Elizabeth Shakman. "Believing in Religious Freedom." In *Politics of Religious Freedom*, ed. Winnifred Fallers Sullivan, Elizabeth Shakman Hurd, Saba Mahmood, and Peter G. Danchin, 45–56. Chicago: University of Chicago Press, 2015.

Hurd, Elizabeth Shakman. *Beyond Religious Freedom: The New Global Politics of Religion.* Princeton: Princeton University Press, 2015.

Ibrahim, Azeem. *The Rohingyas: Inside Myanmar's Hidden Genocide.* London: C. Hurst, 2016.

Ignatieff, Michael. *Human Rights as Politics and Idolatry*, ed. and intro. Amy Gutmann. Princeton: Princeton University Press, 2001.

Jellinek, Georg. *The Declaration of the Rights of Man and of Citizens: A Contribution to Modern Constitutional History.* New York: Henry Holt, 1901.

Joas, Hans. *The Sacredness of the Person: A New Genealogy of Human Rights.* Washington, D.C.: Georgetown University Press, 2013.

Joas, Hans. *Sind die Menschenrechte westlich?* Munich: Kösel, 2016.

Juergensmeyer, Mark. *Terror in the Mind of God: The Global Rise of Religious Violence.* Updated ed. Berkeley: University of California Press, 2000.

Kant, Immanuel. *Briefwechsel: Auswahl und Anmerkungen von Otto Schöndorfer.* Hamburg: Meiner, 1972.

Kant, Immanuel. "Critique of Practical Reason." In *Practical Philosophy*, 137–271. Cambridge: Cambridge University Press, 1996.

Kant, Immanuel. "Metaphysics of Morals." In *Practical Philosophy*, 363–603. Cambridge: Cambridge University Press, 1996.

Kant, Immanuel. "On the Common Saying: This May Be Correct in Theory, but It Is of No Use in Practice." In *Practical Philosophy*, 277–309. Cambridge: Cambridge University Press, 1996.

Kant, Immanuel. "Religion Within the Boundaries of Mere Reason." In *Religion and Rational Theology*, trans. and ed. Allen W. Wood and George di Giovanni, 39–215. The Cambridge Edition of the Work of Immanuel Kant. Cambridge: Cambridge University Press, 1996.

Kant, Immanuel. "Toward Perpetual Peace: A Philosophical Project." In *Practical Philosophy*, 317–351. Cambridge: Cambridge University Press, 1996.

Kant, Immanuel. "What Is Enlightenment?" In *Practical Philosophy*, 16–22. Cambridge: Cambridge University Press, 1996.

Kirchschläger, Peter G. *Menschenrechte und Religionen: Nicht-staatliche Akteure und ihr Verhältnis zu den Menschenrechten.* Paderborn: Schöningh, 2016.

Kneer, Markus. *Die dunkle Spur im Denken: Rationalismus und Antijudaismus.* Paderborn: Schöningh, 2003.

Krishnaswami, Arcot. *Study of Discrimination in the Matter of Religious Rights and Practices.* New York: United Nations, 1960.

Laborde, Cécile. "Protecting Freedom of Religion in the Secular Age." In *Politics of Religious Freedom*, ed. Winnifred Fallers Sullivan, Elizabeth Shakman Hurd, Saba Mahmood, and Peter G. Danchin, 269–279. Chicago: University of Chicago Press, 2015.

Laborde, Cécile. "Religious Accommodation and Inclusive Even-Handedness." In *Belief, Law and Politics: What Future for a Secular Europe?*, ed. Marie-Claire Foblets, Katayoun Alidadi, Jørgen S. Nielsen, and Zeynep Yanasmayan, 167–169. Farnham: Ashgate, 2014.

Lambek, Michael. "Is Religion Free?" In *Politics of Religious Freedom*, ed. Winnifred Fallers Sullivan, Elizabeth Shakman Hurd, Saba Mahmood, and Peter G. Danchin, 289–300. Chicago: University of Chicago Press, 2015.

Lerner, Natan. "Incitement to Hatred and the 1981 United Nations Declaration on Religion or Belief." In *The Changing Nature of Religious Rights Under International Law*, ed. Malcolm D. Evans, Peter Petkoff, and Julian Rivers, 80–100. Oxford: Oxford University Press, 2015.

Lerner, Natan. "Religion and the Secular State in Israel." In *Religion and the Secular State: Interim National Reports, Issued for the Occasion of the XVIIIth International Congress of Comparative Law, Washington, D.C., 2010*, ed. Javier Martínez-Torrón and W. Cole Durham Jr., 421–430. Provo: International Center for Law and Religious Studies at Brigham Young University, 2010.

Lévi-Strauss, Claude. *Race et histoire.* Paris: UNESCO, 1952.

Lindholm, Tore. "Philosophical and Religious Justifications of Freedom of Religion or Belief." In *Facilitating Freedom of Religion or Belief: A Deskbook*, ed. Tore Lindholm, W. Cole Durham Jr., and Bahia G. Tahzib-Lie, 19–61. Leiden: Martinus Nijhoff, 2004.

Little, David. "The Global Challenge of Secularism to Religious Freedom." In *Trends of Secularism in a Pluralistic World*, ed. Jaime Contreras and Rosa María Martínez de Codes, 31–58. Madrid: Iberoamericana, 2013.

Little, David. "Religion, Human Rights, and the Secular State: Clarification and Some Islamic, Jewish and Christian Responses." In *Essays on Religion and Human Rights: Ground to Stand On*, ed. David Little, 83–111. Cambridge: Cambridge University Press, 2015.

Little, David. "Roger Williams and the Puritan Background of the Establishment Clause." In *Essays on Religion and Human Rights: Ground to Stand On*, ed. David Little, 243–271. Cambridge: Cambridge University Press, 2015.

Little, David, Abdulaziz A. Sachedina, and John Kelsay. "Human Rights and World's Religions: Christianity, Islam and Religious Liberty." In *Religion and Human Rights: Why Protect Freedom of Religion or Belief and Models for Protection of Freedom of Religion or Belief?*, ed. Nazila Ghanea, 57–83. New York: Routledge, 2010.

Loobuyck, Patrick. "Critical Remarks on the Pro-Religion Apriority of the RELIGARE Project." In *Belief, Law and Politics: What Future for a Secular Europe?*, ed. Marie-Claire

Foblets, Katayoun Alidadi, Jørgen S. Nielsen, and Zeynep Yanasmayan, 227–236. Farnham: Ashgate, 2014.

Lübbe, Hermann. *Säkularisierung: Geschichte eines ideenpolitischen Begriffs.* Freiburg: Alber, 1965.

Maclure, Jocelyn, and Charles Taylor. *Secularism and Freedom of Conscience,* trans. Jane Marie Todd. Cambridge, Mass.: Harvard University Press, 2011.

Madan, Triloki Nath. "Indian Secularism: A Religio-Secular Ideal." In *Comparative Secularisms in a Global Age,* ed. Linell E. Cady and Elizabeth Shakman Hurd, 181–196. New York: Palgrave Macmillan, 2010.

Mahmood, Saba. *Religious Difference in a Secular Age: A Minority Report.* Princeton: Princeton University Press, 2016.

Maistre, Joseph de. *Considerations on France,* trans. Richard Lebrun. Cambridge: Cambridge University Press, 1994.

Malinar, Angelika. "Religionsfreiheit im Hinduismus." In *Religionsfreiheit: Positionen— Konflikte—Herausforderungen,* ed. Hans-Georg Ziebertz, 183–209. Würzburg: Echter, 2015.

Mandela, Nelson. *Long Walk to Freedom: The Autobiography of Nelson Mandela.* Boston: Little, Brown, 1994.

Maritain, Jacques. *Man and the State.* Chicago: University of Chicago Press, 1956.

Marx, Karl. "Contribution to the Critique of Hegel's Philosophy of Law: Introduction." In Karl Marx and Friedrich Engels. *Collected Works.* Vol. 3. New York: International Publishers, 1976.

Marx, Karl. *Zur Judenfrage.* Vol. 1 of *Marx-Engels Werke.* Berlin: Dietz Verlag, 1976.

Mayer, Ann E. *Islam and Human Rights: Tradition and Politics.* 5th ed. Boulder, Colo.: Westview, 2012.

McCall-Smith, Kasey L. "Interpreting International Human Rights Standards: Treaty Body General Comments as a Chisel or a Hammer." In *Tracing the Roles of Soft Law in Human Rights,* ed. Stéphanie Lagoutte, Thomas Gammeltoft-Hansen, and John Cerone, 27–46. Oxford: Oxford University Press, 2016.

McCrea, Ronan. "Religion, Law and State in Contemporary Europe: Key Trends and Dilemmas." In *Belief, Law and Politics: What Future for a Secular Europe?,* ed. Marie-Claire Foblets, Katayoun Alidadi, Jørgen S. Nielsen, and Zeynep Yanasmayan, 91–98. Farnham: Ashgate 2014.

Mendelssohn, Moses. *Jerusalem, or On Religious Power and Judaism,* trans. Allan Arkush. Waltham, Mass.: Brandeis University Press, 1983.

Mendelssohn, Moses. *Morgenstunden oder über das Dasein Gottes.* Stuttgart: Reclam, 1979.

Meral, Ziya. *No Place to Call Home: Experiences of Apostates from Islam; Failures of the International Community.* New Malden: Christian Solidarity Worldwide, 2008.

Mokrosch, Reinhold, Thomas Held, and Roland Czada, eds. *Religionen und Weltfrieden: Friedens- und Konfliktlösungspotenzial von Religionsgemeinschaften.* Stuttgart: Kohlhammer, 2013.

Morsink, Johannes. *The Universal Declaration of Human Rights and the Challenge of Religion.* Columbia: University of Missouri Press, 2017.

Mutua, Makau wa. "Limitations on Religious Rights: Problematizing Religious Freedom in the African Context." In *Religious Human Rights in Global Perspective,* ed. Johan David van der Vyver and John Witte, 417–440. The Hague: Martinus Nijhoff, 1996.

Mutua, Makau. "Proselytism and Cultural Integrity." In *Facilitating Freedom of Religion or Belief: A Deskbook*, ed. Tore Lindholm, W. Cole Durham Jr., and Bahia G. Tahzib-Lie, 651–668. Leiden: Martinus Nijhoff, 2004.

Nash, David. *Blasphemy in the Christian World: A History*. Oxford: Oxford University Press, 2007.

Nipperdey, Thomas. *Religion im Umbruch: Deutschland 1870–1918*. Munich: C. H. Beck, 1988.

Noll, Rüdiger. "The Role of Religion and Religious Freedom in Contemporary Conflict Situations." In *Facilitating Freedom of Religion or Belief: A Deskbook*, ed. Tore Lindholm, W. Cole Durham Jr., and Bahia G. Tahzib-Lie, 747–760. Leiden: Martinus Nijhoff, 2004.

Nowak, Manfred. *U.N. Covenant on Civil and Political Rights: CCPR Commentary*. 2nd rev. ed. Kehl: N. P. Engel, 2005.

Nowak, Manfred, and Tanja Vorspernik. "Permissible Restrictions on Freedom of Religion or Belief." In *Facilitating Freedom of Religion or Belief: A Deskbook*, ed. Tore Lindholm, W. Cole Durham Jr., and Bahia G. Tahzib-Lie, 147–172. Leiden: Martinus Nijhoff, 2004.

Nussbaum, Martha C. *Liberty of Conscience: In Defense of America's Tradition of Religious Equality*. New York: Basic Books, 2008.

Nussbaum, Martha C. *The New Religious Intolerance: Overcoming the Politics of Fear in an Anxious Age*. Cambridge, Mass.: Harvard University Press, 2012.

O'Boyle, Michael. "*Ne bis in idem* for the Benefit of States?" In *Liber Amicorum Luzius Wildhaber: Human Rights—Strasbourg Views, Droits de l'homme—Regards de Strasbourg*, ed. Lucius Caflisch, Johan Callewaert, Roderick Liddell, Paul Mahoney, and Mark Villiger, 329–346. Kehl: N. P. Engel, 2007.

O'Flaherty, Michael. "Sexual Orientation and Gender Identity." In *International Human Rights Law*. 2nd ed., ed. Daniel Moeckli, Sangeeta Shah, and Sandesh Sivakumaran, 331–344. Oxford: Oxford University Press, 2014.

Othman, Norani. "The Sociopolitical Dimensions of Islamisation in Malaysia: A Cultural Accommodation of Social Change?" In *Shari'a Law and the Modern Nation-State: A Malaysian Symposium*, ed. Norani Othman, 123–143. Kuala Lumpur: Sisters in Islam Forum, 1994.

Patiño Reyes, Alberto. "Religion and the Secular State in Mexico." In *Religion and the Secular State: Interim National Reports, Issued for the Occasion of the XVIIIth International Congress of Comparative Law, Washington, D.C., 2010*, ed. Javier Martínez-Torrón and W. Cole Durham Jr., 505–516. Provo: International Center for Law and Religious Studies at Brigham Young University, 2010.

Petkoff, Peter. "Religious Exceptionalism, Religious Rights, and Public International Law." In *The Changing Nature of Religious Rights Under International Law*, ed. Malcolm D. Evans, Peter Petkoff, and Julian Rivers, 211–234. Oxford: Oxford University Press, 2015.

Plesner, Ingvill Thorson. *Religionspolitikk*. Oslo: Universitetsforlaget, 2016.

Plessner, Helmuth. "Die Frage nach der Conditio humana (1961)." In *Gesammelte Schriften*. Vol. 8, 136–217. Frankfurt: Suhrkamp, 1980.

Pollis, Adamantia, and Peter Schwab. "Human Rights: A Western Construct with Limited Applicability." In *Human Rights: Cultural and Ideological Perspectives*, ed. Adamantia Pollis and Peter Schwab, 1–18. New York: Praeger, 1979.

Prud'homme, Jo-Anne. *Policing Belief: The Impact of Blasphemy Laws on Human Rights*. Washington, D.C.: Freedom House, 2010.

Puniyani, Ram. *God Politics*. New Delhi: Vitasta Publishing, 2012.

Rawls, John. *Political Liberalism*. New York: Columbia University Press, 1993.

Richardson, Joel. *The Islamic Antichrist: The Shocking Truth About the Real Nature of the Beast.* Los Angeles: WND Books, 2009.

Riordan, Patrick. "Which Dignity? Which Religious Freedom?" In *Understanding Human Dignity*, ed. Christopher McCrudden, 420–434. Oxford: Oxford University Press, 2013.

Rivers, Julian. "Justifying Freedom of Religion: Does Dignity Help?" In *Understanding Human Dignity*, ed. Christopher McCrudden, 405–419. Oxford: Oxford University Press, 2013.

Robbers, Gerhard. *State and Church in the European Union*. Baden-Baden: Nomos, 2005.

Robinson, Mary. "Foreword." In *Facilitating Freedom of Religion or Belief: A Deskbook*, ed. Tore Lindholm, W. Cole Durham Jr., and Bahia G. Tahzib-Lie, xix–xx. Leiden: Martinus Nijhoff, 2004.

Rodríguez-Garavito, César. "Towards a Human Rights Ecosystem." In *Debating the Endtimes of Human Rights: Activism and Institutions in a Neo-Westphalian World*, ed. Doutje Lettinga and Lars van Troost, 39–45. Amsterdam: Amnesty International Netherlands, 2014.

Rohe, Mathias. *Das Islamische Recht: Geschichte und Gegenwart*. 3rd enlarged ed. Munich: C. H. Beck, 2011.

Sarkissian, Ani. *The Varieties of Religious Repression: Why Governments Restrict Religion*. Oxford: Oxford University Press, 2015.

Schieder, Rolf. *Die Gewalt des einen Gottes: Die Monotheismus-Debatte zwischen Jan Assmann, Micha Brumlik, Rolf Schieder, Peter Sloterdijk und anderen*. Berlin: Berlin University Press, 2014.

Schmitt, Carl. *Der Begriff des Politischen*. Berlin: Duncker and Humblot, 1932. Reprint, 1963.

Sen, Amartya. *Human Rights and Asian Values*. New York: Carnegie Council on Ethics and International Affairs, 1997.

Shachar, Ayelet. "Entangled: Family, Religion and Human Rights." In *Human Rights: The Hard Questions*, ed. Cindy Holder and David Reidy, 115–135. Cambridge: Cambridge University Press, 2013.

Sharma, Arvind. *Problematizing Religious Freedom*. Dordrecht: Springer, 2012.

Sloterdijk, Peter. "Im Schatten des Sinai: Fußnote über Ursprünge und Wandlungen totaler Mitgliedschaft." In *Die Gewalt des einen Gottes: Die Monotheismus-Debatte zwischen Jan Assmann, Micha Brumlik, Rolf Schieder, Peter Sloterdijk und anderen*, ed. Rolf Schieder, 124–149. Berlin: Berlin University Press, 2014.

Spinoza, Benedict de. *Theological-Political Treatise*, trans. and ed. Jonathan Israel. Cambridge: Cambridge University Press, 2007.

Stamos, David N. *The Myth of Universal Human Rights: Its Origin, History, and Explanation; Along with a More Humane Way*. Abingdon: Routledge, 2016.

Sullivan, Winnifred Fallers. *The Impossibility of Religious Freedom*. Princeton: Princeton University Press, 2005.

Sullivan, Winnifred Fallers, Elizabeth Shakman Hurd, Saba Mahmood, and Peter G. Danchin. "Introduction." In *Politics of Religious Freedom*, ed. Winnifred Fallers Sullivan, Elizabeth Shakman Hurd, Saba Mahmood, and Peter G. Danchin, 1–9. Chicago: University of Chicago Press, 2015.

Swidler, Arlene. *Human Rights in Religious Traditions*. New York: Pilgrim Press, 1982.

Tauati Ahdar, Rex. "Why Secularism Is Not Neutral." In *Trends of Secularism in a Pluralistic World*, ed. Jaime Contreras and Rosa María Martínez de Codes, 107–144. Madrid: Iberoamericana, 2013.

Taylor, Charles. *A Secular Age*. Cambridge, Mass.: Harvard University Press, 2007.

Taylor, Paul M. *Freedom of Religion: UN and European Human Rights Law and Practice*. Cambridge: Cambridge University Press, 2005.

Temperman, Jeroen. *Religious Hatred and International Law: The Prohibition of Incitement to Violence or Discrimination*. Cambridge: Cambridge University Press, 2016.

Toft, Monica Duffy, Daniel Philpott, and Timothy Samuel Shah. *God's Century: Resurgent Religion and Global Politics*. New York: W. W. Norton, 2011.

Traunmüller, Richard. *Religiöse Vielfalt, Sozialkapital und gesellschaftlicher Zusammenhalt: Religionsmonitor*. Gütersloh: Bertelsmann-Stiftung, 2014.

Trigg, Roger. *Equality, Freedom and Religion*. Oxford: Oxford University Press, 2012.

Troeltsch, Ernst. *Die Soziallehren der christlichen Kirchen und Gruppen*. Tübingen: J. C. B Mohr, 1912.

Valero Estrellas, Maria J. "State Neutrality, Religion, and the Workplace in the Recent Case Law of the European Court of Human Rights." In *Religion and Equality: Law in Conflict*, ed. W. Cole Durham Jr. and Donlu D. Thayer, 35–55. London: Routledge, 2016.

Van den Breemer, Rosemarie, José Casanova, and Trygve Wyller. "Introduction." In *Secular and Sacred? The Scandinavian Case of Religion in Human Rights, Law and Public Space*, ed. Rosemarie van den Breemer, José Casanova, and Trygve Wyller, 9–20. Göttingen: Vandenhoek and Ruprecht, 2014.

Verdirame, Guglielmo. "Rescuing Human Rights from Proportionality." In *Philosophical Foundations of Human Rights*, ed. Rowan Cruft, S. Matthew Liao, and Massimo Renzo, 341–357. Oxford: Oxford University Press, 2015.

Vögele, Wolfgang. "Christliche Elemente in der Begründung von Menschenrechten und Menschenwürde im Kontext der Entstehung der Vereinten Nationen." In *Ethik der Menschenrechte: Zum Streit um die Universalität einer Idee*. Vol. 1, ed. Hans-Richard Reuter, 103–133. Tübingen: Mohr Siebeck, 1999.

Waldron, Jeremy. *Dignity, Rank, and Rights*, with comments by Wai Chee Dimock, Don Herzog, and Michael Rosen, ed. Meir Dan-Cohen. Paperback. Oxford: Oxford University Press, 2015.

Waldron, Jeremy. *One Another's Equals: The Basis of Human Equality*. Cambridge, Mass.: Harvard University Press, 2017.

Wallmann, Johannes. *Kirchengeschichte Deutschlands seit der Reformation*. 6th ed. Tübingen: Mohr Siebeck, 2006.

Walzer, Michael. *Thick and Thin: Moral Argument at Home and Abroad*. Notre Dame, Ind.: University of Notre Dame Press, 1994.

Weber, Max. "Wissenschaft als Beruf." In *Werke*. Vol. 1, *Studienausgabe*, ed. Wolfgang J. Mommsen and Wolfgang Schluchter. Tübingen: Mohr Siebeck, 1994.

Weingardt, Markus A. "Religion als politischer Faktor zur Gewaltüberwindung." In *Gewaltfreiheit und Gewalt in den Religionen: Politische und theologische Herausforderungen*, ed. Fernando Enns and Wolfram Weiße, 95–104. Münster: Waxmann, 2016.

Weingardt, Markus A. *Religion Macht Frieden: Das Friedenspotential von Religionen in politischen Gewaltkonflikten*. Stuttgart: Kohlhammer, 2007.

Wiener, Michael. *Das Mandat des UN-Sonderberichterstatters über Religions- oder Weltanschauungsfreiheit—Institutionelle, prozedurale und materielle Rechtsfragen*. Frankfurt: Peter Lang, 2007.

Wiener, Michael. "Universal Freedom of Religion or Belief: A Reality Check Through the Lens of the EU Guidelines." In *Religion and European Society: A Primer*, ed. Ben Schewel and Erin K. Wilson, 171–182. Chichester: Wiley-Blackwell, 2019.

Willems, Joachim. "Religionsfreiheit im multireligiösen Russland: Historische Entwicklungen und aktuelle Herausforderungen." In *Religionsfreiheit: Positionen—Konflikte—Herausforderungen*, ed. Hans-Georg Ziebertz, 113–131. Würzburg: Echter, 2015.

Willems, Joachim. "Die Russisch-Orthodoxe Kirche und die Menschenrechte." In *Schwerpunkt: Religionsfreiheit*, ed. Heiner Bielefeldt, Volkmar Deile, Brigitte Hamm, Franz-Josef Hutter, Sabine Kurtenbach, and Hanne Tretter, 152–165. Jahrbuch Menschenrechte 2009. Vienna: Böhlau, 2008.

Yelle, Robert. "Imagining the Hebrew Republic: Christian Genealogies of Religious Freedom." In *Politics of Religious Freedom*, ed. Winnifred Fallers Sullivan, Elizabeth Shakman Hurd, Saba Mahmood, and Peter G. Danchin, 17–28. Chicago: University of Chicago Press, 2015.

Zaborowski, Holger. "Wohlwollen, Dialog und die Anerkennung des Anderen: Zur Hermeneutik von Religionsfreiheit." In *Umstrittene Religionsfreiheit: Zur Diskussion um ein Menschenrecht*, ed. Thomas Brose and Philipp W. Hildmann, 23–42. Frankfurt: Peter Lang, 2016.

Zucca, Lorenzo. "Freedom of Religion in a Secular World." In *Philosophical Foundations of Human Rights*, ed. Rowan Cruft, S. Matthew Liao, and Massimo Renzo, 388–406. Oxford: Oxford University Press, 2015.

Journal Articles

American Anthropological Association. "Statement on Human Rights." *American Anthropologist*, Vol. 49 (1947), 539–543.

Anderson, John. "Religion, State and 'Sovereign Democracy' in Putin's Russia." *Journal of Religious and Political Practice*, Vol. 2 (2016), 249–266.

Arendt, Hannah. "Truth and Politics." *New Yorker*, 25 February 1967, 49–88.

Bader, Veit. "Constitutionalizing Secularism, Alternative Secularisms or Liberal Democratic Constitutionalism? A Critical Reading of Some Turkish, ECtHR and Indian Supreme Court Cases on 'Secularism.'" *Utrecht Law Review*, Vol. 6 (2010), 8–35.

Bielefeldt, Heiner. "Kulturkampf um Beschneidung? Zum diskursiven Umfeld des Kölner Urteils." *Blätter für deutsche und internationale Politik*, September 2012, 63–71.

Bielefeldt, Heiner. "Misperceptions of Freedom of Religion or Belief." *Human Rights Quarterly*, Vol. 35 (2013), 33–68.

Bielefeldt, Heiner. "'Western' Versus 'Islamic' Human Rights Conceptions? A Critique of Cultural Essentialism in the Discussion on Human Rights." *Political Theory*, Vol. 28 (2000), 90–121.

Blitt, Robert C. "The Bottom Up Journey of 'Defamation of Religions' from Muslim States to the United Nations: A Case Study of the Migration of Anti-Constitutional Ideas." *Studies in Law, Politics and Society*, Vol. 56 (2011), 121–211.

Engel, Christoph. "Law as a Precondition for Religious Freedom." In "Secularism and Religious Freedom." *Fides et Libertas: The Journal of the International Religious Liberty Association*, 2011, 18–35.

Evans, Malcolm D. "The Freedom of Religion or Belief and the Freedom of Expression." *Religion and Human Rights*, Vol. 4 (2009), 197–235.

Gunn, T. Jeremy. "The Complexity of Religion and the Definition of 'Religion' in International Law." *Harvard Human Rights Journal*, Vol. 16 (2003), 189–214.

Habermas, Jürgen. "The Concept of Human Dignity and the Realistic Utopia of Human Rights." *Metaphilosophy*, Vol. 41, No. 4 (2010), 464–480.

Higgins, Rosalyn. "A Babel of Judicial Voices? Ruminations from the Bench." *International and Comparative Law Quarterly*, Vol. 55, No. 4 (2006), 791–804.

Howard, Erica. "Religious Rights Versus Sexual Orientation Discrimination: A Fair Deal for Everyone." *Religion and Human Rights*, Vol. 10 (2015), 128–159.

Mutua, Makau. "Savages, Victims, and Saviors: The Metaphor of Human Rights." *Harvard International Law Journal*, Vol. 42 (2001), 201–245.

O'Flaherty, Michael. "Freedom of Expression: Article 19 of the International Covenant on Civil and Political Rights and the Human Rights Committee's General Comment No. 34." *Human Rights Law Review*, Vol. 12 (2012), 627–654.

Pierik, Roland, and Wibren van der Burg. "What Is Neutrality?" *Ratio Juris*, Vol. 27 (2014), 496–515.

Puppinck, Grégor. "Conscientious Objection and Human Rights: A Systematic Analysis." *Brill Research Perspectives in Law and Religion*, Vol. 1, No. 1 (2017), 1–75.

Razack, Sherene H. "Imperilled Muslim Women, Dangerous Muslim Men and Civilised Europeans: Legal and Social Responses to Forced Marriages." *Feminist Legal Studies*, Vol. 12 (2004), 129–174.

Rehman, Javaid, and Eleni Polymenopoulou. "Is Green a Part of the Rainbow? Sharia, Homosexuality and LGBT Rights in the Muslim World." *Fordham International Law Journal*, Vol. 37 (2013), 1–52.

Sikkink, Kathryn. "Latin American Countries as Norm Protagonists of the Idea of International Human Rights." *Global Governance*, Vol. 20 (2014), 389–404.

Stuart, Alison. "Freedom of Religion and Gender Equality: Inclusive or Exclusive?" *Human Rights Law Review*, Vol. 10 (2010), 429–459.

Temperman, Jeroen. "Blasphemy, Defamation of Religions and Human Rights Law." *Netherlands Quarterly of Human Rights*, Vol. 26, No. 4 (2008), 485–516.

Wiener, Michael. "Freedom of Religion or Belief and Sexuality: Tracing the Evolution of the Special Rapporteur's Mandate Practice over Thirty Years." *Oxford Journal of Law and Religion*, Vol. 6, No. 2 (2017), 253–267.

Wiener, Michael. "The Mandate of the Special Rapporteur on Freedom of Religion or Belief: Institutional, Procedural and Substantive Legal Issues." *Religion and Human Rights*, Vol. 2, No. 1 (2007), 3–17.

ACKNOWLEDGMENTS

This book is the result of discussions, research, and numerous encounters with human rights defenders, civil society activists, victims of human rights violations, members of religious or belief communities, politicians, journalists, academics, and other people concerned about the right to freedom of religion or belief, both at the international and domestic levels. Any attempt to thank all those who have contributed to shaping our perceptions and conceptual analyses in this field seems futile. The list would be far too long.

However, we would like to extend our special gratitude to those who, within the Office of the High Commissioner for Human Rights, professionally supported from 2010 to 2016 the mandate of the United Nations Special Rapporteur on freedom of religion or belief, including Dolores Infante Cañibano, Nathalie Rondeux, Brenda Vukovic, Sharof Azizov, Eimear Farrell, Jon Izagirre Garcia, and in particular Chian Yew Lim. The views expressed in this book are those of the coauthors and do not necessarily reflect those of the United Nations.

We owe a lot to Bert Lockwood, as series editor of the Pennsylvania Studies in Human Rights, and Peter Agree, as senior social sciences editor at the University of Pennsylvania Press, for their encouraging support of the book project from its early stages. We are also grateful to the two anonymous readers, who provided critical comments that caused us to reconsider some passages of our manuscript.

Last, but not least, we would like to deeply thank our families for their unwavering support and understanding throughout the whole drafting process.